25

Q-SHIPS

Q-SHIPS

by

CARSON I. A. RITCHIE

TERENCE DALTON LIMITED
LAVENHAM . SUFFOLK
1985

Published by
TERENCE DALTON LIMITED

ISBN 0 86138 011 8

Text photoset in 11/12 pt Baskerville

Printed in Great Britain at
The Lavenham Press Limited, Lavenham, Suffolk

Contents

FOR JANET

Index of Illustrations

Acknowledgements

I T IS a pleasure to acknowledge all those who have contributed in some way or another to this book. Miss Pat O'Driscoll was not merely kind enough to read the whole work in manuscript, but made many helpful suggestions about both sources and illustrations which would otherwise never have come to my knowledge.

My warmest thanks are due to Mr Francis, of the Imperial War Museum, for guiding me towards the Q-ship archive in the Public Record Office, Kew, and to the staff of the Public Record Office for their help. Philip Reed, Caroline Reed and George Close, of the Imperial War Museum, and the staff of the Library, the National Maritime Museum, proved valuable allies, while Mr Douglas Matthews, of the London Library, was just as helpful to me as Librarian as he had been in the past as Deputy Librarian.

The Cataloguing Staff of the National Film Archive, and the Staff of the Stills Department, the British Film Institute, helped me in finding illustrations. Mr John Kelly of Movietone Library, Denham, kindly arranged for a showing of the remaining footage of *The Blockade* and supplied me with prints from it. It is to my publishers that I owe the suggestion to use this film, originally issued as *Q-ships, Vampires of the Deep*, as a source of illustrations.

I should particularly like to thank the publishers of the three classic books on the Q-ships campaign for permission to illustrate this book with pictures taken from these works: Barrie and Jenkins, modern representative of Herbert Jenkins, Hodder and Stoughton, and Sidgwick and Jackson.

Finally I should like to express my very warmest thanks to my photographer, Mrs Stella Mayes Reed, for coping so skilfully with the many difficulties imposed by the nature of the illustrations.

Introduction

THE WORLD has forgotten the vessels known as Q-ships, mystery ships, U-boat traps, decoys and Special Service vessels. For many years their existence and the extraordinary part which they played in the First World War have ceased to be a matter either for learned research or for popular interest. Only a few of the older generation remember Captain Gordon Campbell (later Vice-Admiral) coming to their school to give a talk about the work of the mystery ships, or recall being carried up the gang-plank of the *Suffolk Coast* under the brawny arm of a seaman to tour that Q-ship as she went on public exhibition.

The visit of the *Suffolk Coast* and the *Hyderabad*, those last words in up-to-date mystery ships, to certain ports, and the film made by the New Era Film Company some years after the war, *Q-ships, Vampires of the Deep*, may be said to mark the last appearance of the Q-ships in the public eye. Those who watched the extras in *Q-ships*, some of whom were former crew members of Commander Harold Auten's *Stock Force*, and admired the ships and U-boats in it, may have recalled that the existence of the Q-ships was kept secret during the war, and that the information about them which became available after the end of hostilities did not wholly satisfy the curiosity of the public.

Those who read the brochure produced by New Era about the making of the film and noted that the U-boat proved very difficult to sink may have recalled that in reality, in wartime conditions, it was also very difficult to dispose of a U-boat.

Those whose appetite was whetted by the film may well have read one or all of the three books written about Q-ships after the war. Lieutenant-Commander Harold Auten, V.C., R.N.R., had got in first with "*Q*" *Boat Adventures,* published in 1919. Three years later, in 1922, E. Keble Chatterton, late Lieutenant-Commander, R.N.V.R.,* published *Q-Ships and Their Story*, while in 1928 Vice-Admiral Gordon Campbell, V.C., D.S.O., published *My Mystery Ships*. Campbell's book became a best-seller, going into thirteen editions by 1936 and satisfying the demand for information about the Q-ships so completely that no new books on the subject appeared thereafter.

Only those like the present writer who had personal contact with some member of the Special Service, who told him how he had carried a

---

*Royal Naval Volunteer Reserve (R.N.V.R.) which in 1956 was absorbed into the Royal Naval Reserve (R.N.R.). The R.N.R. had originally been volunteers, officers and men, from the Merchant Service prepared to serve with the Royal Navy (R.N.) during war or emergency.

phial of quick-acting poison all his life aboard the Q-ship, ready to swallow if he were ever taken prisoner, may have wondered whether there was some area of the history of the Special Service which the books of the three gallant officers just mentioned had not covered.

Auten, Chatterton and Campbell were all in the position of wanting to tell a story, and yet being forced to become tongue-tied at certain parts of it. The restraints on their narrative powers took various forms. They were restrained by the Official Secrets Act, which until 1969 prevented consultation of the really formidable array of archives from which this book has been written. The Act had swept under the carpet for several decades the most interesting of the episodes of the Q-ship campaign: the fact that the Germans deliberately set out to *strafe* the mystery ships in 1917 and destroyed a third of their 1916 number; the attempt by Jellicoe to disguise a Q-ship as a crashed Zeppelin; the destruction of the British submarine *J.6* by the Q-ship *Cymric*; and lastly the answer to that great mystery of the sea, the *Baralong* affair.

No less inhibiting than an official prohibition on research were the professional reserve of the Royal Navy and personal regard for fellow

Last survivors of the Q-ships, H.M.S. *Chrysanthemum* lies ahead of H.M.S. *President*, formerly the convoy sloop H.M.S. *Saxifrage*, in the Thames. *Chrysanthemum* was one of the *Anchusa*-type sloops which served as decoys in 1917–18.

Royal Naval Reserve, London Division

officers. This was what made the three gallant historians avoid all mention of the *Baralong* if they could help it, as if the whole subject was accursed, which indeed it was in the eyes of the Admiralty and the British Government, because it was the only possible counter charge that the Germans could bring to offset the atrocities committed by the U-boats.

Mutinies or states of near-mutiny aboard Q-ships are never mentioned. Harold Auten never mentions his difficulties with his mercantile second, A. W. Hartley, Temporary Lieutenant, R.N.R.

The gigantic scale of the Q-ship war prevented any of the officers mentioned from being able to review operations as a whole. Neither they, nor anyone else at the end of the First World War, realised that there had been upwards of 221 mystery ships. They may have kept notes on some of the most vital documents, but they did not have them all under their eyes, nor were they able to quote from them. It is not surprising to find Campbell forgetting something he had written in one of his reports, and saying something else in his book. It is because I feel that reports written during the heat of action are superior to later recollections that I have quoted freely from the Q-ship archives that have become available. Where I do not quote directly, I frequently paraphrase. Only a few of the more important documents have been given references—the apparatus of citations would otherwise have become completely unmanageable in a book of this size.

There was one final consideration which was probably much more

The many disguises of a Q-ship. The *Barranca, Q.3*, painted as a Spanish steamer (below); as a cargo liner with black-topped buff funnel (upper right); as a refrigerated fruit ship trading to the West Indies (middle right); and as a P & O freighter (lower right). From *Q-ships and Their Story*.

Shells from the Q-ship's guns strike the U-boat in a still from the film *Q-ships, Vampires of the Deep*, for which Commander Harold Auten was the technical adviser and liaison officer on the British side.   *British Movietone News Film Archive*

inhibiting than anything mentioned so far on the published Q-ship histories. This was the question, put in so many words by Campbell but not answered in a very objective way, as to whether the Q-ship campaign achieved effects in proportion to the heroism of the crews and the effort required to fit out the ships. Was it a successful operation, or was it, like so much else in the First World War, just another ghastly blunder? Campbell and his companions stood too close to the war to be able to take an objective view, while if Campbell had come to a different view than the one he expresses—that the campaign was a reasonably successful one—he might have felt some diffidence in expressing such a view as he was still a serving flag officer.

I shall not anticipate any of my conclusions on this heading here, the reader will find them at the end of the book. I ought, however, to make it clear that it was to arrive at conclusions about the effect of the Q-ships that I wrote the book in the first place. In order to reach these conclusions in the shortest possible time, I have stopped my account of the campaign at the point at which it ceases to have any effect at all, that is at the end of 1917. I have also, perforce, omitted much about which the other Q-ship historians have had a good deal to say. My account of the actions fought between Q-ships and U-boats has been rigorously selective. Only those which disposed of a U-boat or those which for some other reason are particularly significant are dealt with at any length.

These actions are by no means representative of the encounters between Q-ships and U-boats as a whole. Over seventy duels took place, but only thirteen of these resulted in the sinking of a submarine (Campbell's considered score was eleven, but I have added the two fought by Q-ships with the partnership of a British submarine).

Aside from the actual fighting encounters which were productive of a U-boat kill, as opposed to the inconclusive actions—actions which did not seem inconclusive at the time because the submarine was believed to have been sunk—I have concentrated on the development of the Q-ship fleets, and in particular the responsibility borne by individuals in command for their rise and diversification. I have tried to lay down the clear lines of policy and to indicate how one development influenced another. In order to do this I have adopted a chronological approach, with one later chapter forming an exception. Rather than concentrate on the trees—the individual Q-ship fleets which grew up in various naval bases round the country—I have preferred to concentrate on the wood, the story of the mystery ships as a whole. I feel that this was the right choice, as although various local fleets provided many fine actions, not all of them had sufficient influence to determine the success or failure of Special Service operations seen from the point of view of the whole war.

Inevitably this book will read very differently from the published classics of Q-ship adventure. These were either accounts of personal experiences or in the case of Keble Chatterton the amalgamated experiences of the writer and a number of friends who provided the information from which the book was written. Nothing will ever replace the verve and freshness with which these first-hand accounts of the Q-ship campaigns were written, but many of the experiences recounted in them had absolutely no effect on the war as a whole. Yet I should be the first to admit that the published accounts of Q-ships do provide many answers to problems insoluble from the records alone. They should always be kept in view when trying to reach any conclusions about the evidence which the archives can provide.

In conclusion it may well be asked, why dust off the Q-ship file? Why write another book about the subject, thus reopening a chapter of naval history more than sixty years after the events described and more than fifty years after the last of the three classic books on the subject had been written?

This is a question which will admit of more than one answer. One reply would be that it is necessary for the historian to try to differentiate what really happened from the legends which have accumulated around the Q-ships. At the start of their existence they were a closely guarded secret, but as soon as whispers about their real nature began to circulate, they became part of British folklore. *Mr Punch's History of the Great War* emphasised this glamorised view of the Q-ship:

> She can weave a web of magic for the unsuspecting foe
> She can scent the breath of *Kultur* leagues away
> She can hear a U-boat thinking in Atlantic depths below
> And disintegrate it with a Martian ray
>   She can feel her way by night
>   Through the minefield of the Bight
>   She has all the tricks of science, grave and gay

The folklore of the mystery ships merged with the harsh realities of Q-ship life. It made its contribution to the *esprit de corps* which was such a feature of the Special Service. Just before the crucial action of the *Dunraven* Campbell sights "a three-masted schooner, painted white, and looking a perfect picture", which disappears in the fog. The crew have seen it too, and like Campbell they feel that an unescorted ship has no business to be in the Bay of Biscay at this period of the war. They gravely discuss whether the "phantom ship" is going to bring them bad luck or not, but even though some of them are about to be torpedoed for the fifth time they are unmoved by the loom of coming events and the business of the ship goes on as usual.

A four-inch gun and its crew on board the sailing Q-ship *Rentoul*, from E. Keble Chatterton's *Q-Ships and Their Story*.

Even if the Q-ship men had had no effect on the course of the war whatsoever (and I shall try to prove that just the opposite was the case), they would be worth studying because of their status as an elite. They really were a Special Service, in deed as well as in name. Though there were 420,000 officers and men serving in the Royal Navy during the First World War, none perhaps were called on to show more daring than the Q-ship complements. No one but the Special Service was ever ordered to turn into the track of a torpedo so as to ensure destruction, rather than avoid it, in the hope that the stricken Q-ship might be able to keep afloat long enough to dispose of her attacker. Such an order would seem to doom beforehand some, if not all, of the engine-room watch, many of whom were not professional naval men but mercantile seamen who had volunteered to join the Q-ships and had signed Form T.124.* Although the stokers probably formed the most dissident element in a Q-ship's complement, they never showed their militancy by declining to take the post of greatest danger. The fact that, miraculously, so many of the engine room staff escaped from a torpedoing time after time enabled admirals to ask their captains to get themselves torpedoed and captains to give the order to turn in towards a torpedo with a good conscience. It was not then, and is not now, policy in the Royal Navy that anyone should be given an order which entails no possibility of survival.

It was not just the engine-room crew who stood in peculiar risk. The "panic party" of selected non-combatants who had made a mock evacuation of the ship were often literally caught between two fires, those of the submarine and the Q-ship.

Yet it is very difficult to decide whether any of the Q-ship men were at greater risk than others. They all firmly believed that if they were caught by the Germans they would be murdered. In the *Dunraven* action the U-boat actually sprayed the lifeboat crew with Maxim fire once it had been discovered that they had to do with a Q-ship. Elsewhere I shall have to tell how a complete Q-ship's complement was lost without trace.

Like the Special Service personnel, the Special Service vessels offer a unique interest. Mystery ships comprised many types of vessels: armed boarding steamers, tramps, colliers, cargo ships, coasters, commissioned escort ships, convoy sloops, P.C. boats, fleet messengers, salvage vessels, store carriers, tugs, yachts, whalers and trawlers. Not surprisingly, great interest has attached to the sailing ships because although, as will be seen in the first chapter, sailing ships of war had never disappeared from the Royal Navy, it seemed an anachronism to the people who served in the sailing Q-ships that they should be engaged in fighting, under sail, the

*An agreement signed by Merchant Navy officers and men taken into the Royal Navy for temporary service.

most advanced of modern vessels, U-boats with diesel and electric propulsion.

Besides the strangeness of sailing ships fighting the U-boats, there were other strange aspects of the Q-ship story. One is the discovery that the very earliest Q-ships were legally pirates, because they had not been

The purpose of the "panic party" was to persuade the U-boat commander that the ship had been abandoned and so to encourage her to come within range of the Q-ship's guns. This drawing by Lieutenant J. E. Broome is reproduced from Vice-Admiral Gordon Campbell's *My Mystery Ships*.

commissioned as the Hague Convention demanded. I leave it to some other historian to determine when the last occasion had been when pirates fought alongside the Royal Navy.

The other most salient feature of the Q-ship is of course its perpetual masquerade. As night fell on Campbell's *Farnborough* she appeared a British cargo vessel. As dawn broke on her she presented a completely altered appearance with flush deck, a donkey boiler funnel, topmasts housed, derricks topped, ventilator shifted, an awning on the bridge, awning stanchions and jackstaff showing where there had been none before, with a Danish flag flying, Danish national emblem boards on the sides and a new Danish name.

Yet the transformation from a cargo ship into some other kind of craft was by no means so striking as that of an apparently peaceable merchant vessel into a ship of war. It was this sudden "transformation scene", graphically described for us in this book by a neutral observer, which worried the Germans so much. The fury with which they denounced the employment of armed vessels disguised as neutral merchantmen was due not to any high regard for international law but to the perfectly natural anger of the biter bit. The U-boats themselves habitually sought to disguise themselves as fishing boats, steamers and so forth, but the idea that anybody should play them at their own game seems to have roused their wrath as no other tactic ever could.

To read the breezy accounts of Campbell and his contemporaries of the business of disguising ship is almost to imagine we are watching the preparations for wardroom amateur dramatics with which the officers are going to amuse the men at Christmas. Yet there was nothing amusing or entertaining about the deadly drama which the Special Service had to perform daily, with a repeat performance every night. Anyone who forgot his lines, any extra who failed to apply his make-up correctly, might find that he had given a cue for *exeunt omnes*.

Although the need to disguise themselves as merchantmen gave rise to a multitude of devices and contrivances, boats which fell apart to disclose a gun, bulwarks which dropped down to give it a clear field of fire, and ensign staffs wearing the White Ensign which automatically sprang to attention so that the rules of international law might be obeyed, gadgets which must always attract the attention of the reader, it provided another interesting consequence. The ships in which the Special Service sailed had perforce to look like tramps, and they were tramps, built at a time when coal was cheap and the length of a voyage of little moment. To go to sea in ships such as these, to encounter the most technologically advanced of all First World War craft, the German submarine, was rather like a policeman disguising himself as a one-armed, one-legged sailor by tying up one arm and leg, to catch a ferocious burglar of Herculean strength. He might lull the burglar's suspicions sufficiently to make him attack, but what would happen when the struggle began?

More than once on reading about all the manifold defects of the Q-ships I was reminded of Jane Austen's words in *Persuasion*. "The Admiralty entertain themselves now and then, with sending a few hundred men to sea in a ship not fit to be employed. But they have a great many to provide for and among the thousands that may just as well go to the bottom as not, it is impossible for them to distinguish the very set who may be least missed."

CHAPTER ONE

Aboard a Q-ship

THE SUCCESS or failure of a Q-ship depended almost entirely on her captain. Sailors felt more attached to their captains than to the service and when a mystery ship was sunk, her complement usually went into a new ship as a body unless there was some strong reason why it should be otherwise.

Success should not be taken to mean only the ability to sink a U-boat, although it is upon this aspect of success that this book will concentrate most. In a sense a Q-ship captain was rather like a fly fisherman: if he had succeeded in bringing the trout to take the lure, or the submarine to approach within range, he had done all that skill could achieve, and the rest was up to chance. Captains who had learned the art of luring a submarine within range continued to succeed, even though they did not always land their fish.

The commanders of the Special Service were drawn from an astonishingly varied background. Admiral John Marx was a retired R.N. flag officer who did not disdain to return to the Navy as a captain, R.N.R.; Commander F. H. Grenfell was a retired physical instruction lieutenant; and there was a fair sprinkling of lieutenants R.N. as well as many mercantile skippers holding temporary naval reserve commissions. Probably the strangest captaincy was that of Lieutenant Philip J. Mack, who had been invalided out of the Navy after the Dardanelles campaign. He took up an appointment at Lowestoft with the Yacht Patrol, for duty ashore, "owing to Doctor's advice that the East Coast air would be good for him."[1] When his health improved, he volunteered for service at sea and was given command of H.M.S. *Q.23*, the schooner *Result*.

One of the most successful Q-ship commanders, Godfrey Herbert, was a submarine officer with some ten years' experience of underwater craft—surely a case of poacher turned gamekeeper. He took command of one of the first Q-ships, transferred to the *Baralong* and was successful in sinking a U-boat, and eventually returned to submarines, being one of those to escape from the steam submarine *K.13* when it foundered in the Gareloch in 1917.

The Admiralty, and the admirals, often attached an exaggerated importance to qualities very desirable in an officer in the regular Navy,

The Q-ship H.M.S. *Candytuft*, a convoy sloop built in 1917, ashore on the North African coast after having her bows and stern blown off by torpedoes fired by a U-boat. From *Q-Ships and Their Story*.

smartness and attention to discipline, but which were not always those most useful aboard a Q-ship. The Admiral Commanding Orkney and Shetland, Admiral F. E. Brock, complained to the C.-in-C., Grand Fleet about the commander of the sailing Q-ship H.M.S. *Dargle*, Lieutenant J. Martin, saying that Martin was of "an excitable temperament which is most undesirable . . . He is constantly using his motors and does not appear to realise the importance of making his vessel look like a peaceful merchant ship . . . He is constantly making complaints about his ship."[2]

Martin resigned from his command on the grounds of ill health, but Captain James Startin, Senior Naval Officer, Granton, who felt that he was a very capable officer "but certainly difficult as regards naval etiquette and discipline", had him transferred to another vessel. A year later, as commander of *Fresh Hope*, another sailing Q-ship, Martin justified this good opinion by bringing the fore-and-aft schooner into an encounter with a U-boat on which he scored four direct hits.

Next to a good captain, the other great requisite was a good crew. At first the Naval Depots had sent "hard cases" and impossible ratings to the Q-ships, but when their captains insisted that only the best was good enough, much more suitable personnel were provided.

This imposed a big strain on the machinery of naval recruitment because, considering the size of the ship in which they sailed, complements of Q-ships were very large. Two crews were needed, one to "abandon ship" and ostensibly scramble overboard as the panic party took to the lifeboats and one to remain on board and fight the submarine. As the armament came to be more extensive, with more guns and sometimes torpedo tubes as well, more men were required. In a ship which might have to endure hours of shelling until the submarine drew near enough to be tackled, it was necessary to duplicate some appointments so as to allow for casualties. The need for ever-tighter security obtained for the Q-ships specialist appointments such as quartermasters and paymasters who would never have been attached to such small ships in any other branch of the Navy.

In 1916 the following might be taken to be a standard complement for a large Q-ship: "one commander or lieutenant-commander in command, three or four lieutenants or sub-lieutenants (usually R.N.R.), including one for navigating and one for Q duties, five to seven chief petty officers, petty officers and leading seamen (the C.P.O. sometimes being a Torpedo Coxswain), 20–30 seamen, usually Active Service A.B.s or ordinary seamen, gunlayers included, one seaman telegraphist, one or two signal ratings, three wireless-telegraph ratings. *Engineroom:* five or six engineers, usually the mercantile engineers of the ship, six or seven stoker P.O.s or leading stokers (usually R.N. or R.N.R.), about 25 stokers.

The three-masted schooner *Fresh Hope*, one of the wooden sailing vessels fitted out as Q-ships in 1917. From *Q-Ships and Their Story*.

Artisans: one shipwright, one armourer rating, one painter usually, one lineman sometimes. *Medical:* usually surgeon probationer with or without sick berth rating. *Accountant:* one assistant paymaster, R.N.R., one senior stores accountant or third writer, one cook rating, officer's steward and cook, sometimes Active Service and sometimes mercantile ratings. *Marines:* usually a party of ten or twelve. *Total:* about 70–100 or more according to the size of the ship, armament, etc."[3]

Whereas a large ship might carry eighty or more, as has been seen, the complements of smaller ships such as sailing decoys were correspondingly scaled down. Here is the complement of the auxiliary three-masted schooner *Ianthe* in 1917: one lieutenant R.N.R., in command, one lieutenant R.N.R. (C), one lieutenant R.N.R. (N), one petty officer, to include four gun layers 3rd class, three leading seamen, four seaman gunners 3rd class, twelve seamen, one signalman, one armourer's crew, three W/T operators, one officer's steward, one cook, two motor mechanics.

The efficiency imparted by these large numbers was offset by the fact that they must never be revealed to an observing submarine. Captains were warned by their secret orders[4] not "to allow more than the 'merchant ship' number of men to be on deck at a time—on the other hand always have a few men 'lounging about' on the forecastle, etc. Men employed on odd jobs should be the ones whose 'section station' is nearest the job."

Everything aboard a Q-ship had to be done in the mercantile way. This meant that at least half the officers and men would have to forget everything they had ever learned about running a ship. They had to do the work that the Navy would have done with three men with the aid of only one, and that one man had to be dressed like a mercantile seaman in dungarees or something similar. He had to use the correct mercantile terms. "Get into the habit," say the secret *Hints . . . of use to new Commanding Officers of Special Service Vessels*, "of using Merchant Service terms, Chief Officer, Mates, Purser, Saloon, etc.—when anchoring, 'Mr Mate, 60 in the water', instead of talking about shackles, etc.—this will come in useful when using Pilots, etc. in a strange port—so as not to cause suspicion."

The complement of Q-ships tended to grow, and it was able to grow because the early aspiration of having none but naval ratings aboard was abandoned. Commander Godfrey Herbert of the *Baralong* pointed out on 24th April, 1916, when Admiralty orders had specified an entire crew of naval ratings, that there were many good cooks and stewards in merchant vessels, and also boatswains and carpenters who were anxious to serve. Seven months later the attitude to the R.N.R. had softened sufficiently to allow R.N.R. ratings to be employed "if thoroughly reliable," so long as guns' crews were Active Service ratings.

Noncombatants such as the navigating officer, the surgeon probationer, the stewards, cooks and assistant paymasters proved a Godsend when filling up the lifeboat with the panic party. Those who left the ship did not, as has been noticed, escape from danger, but rather went straight into it. The lifeboats had to be launched in a suitably panicky style, and someone had to slide down the falls. During an exercise of this sort aboard *Q.25* in the face of a submarine, the foremost guy parted while the boat was being lowered, the boat was swung against the ship's side and stove in, injuring some men and throwing others into the water. This caused the foremost fall to part and the boat hung by the after fall. Owing to the heavy westerly swell, the rubbing strake and the ship's quarter came down on top of the boat, capsizing her and killing some of the boat's crew.

Out in the boat, the panic party might find themselves either between two fires, or exposed to machine-gun fire from the U-boat. In this case they had orders to jump overboard, but under some weather conditions this was to invite danger rather than to avoid it.

Those noncombatants left aboard ship all had duties to perform—there were no passengers aboard a Q-ship. They photographed the U-boat as it approached, or made a note of the fall of the mystery ship's shells on its hull and conning tower. This was the regular duty of Assistant Paymaster W. R. Ashton aboard *Q.7*, the collier *Penshurst*. Sometimes fighting members of the crew took photographs as well. Lieutenant H. Christopher, first lieutenant and gunnery officer of the famous sailing ship *Record Reign*, asked for permission to take his camera

The ketch barge *Record Reign*, which served as a Q-ship in 1917–18. From *Q-ships and Their Story*.

with him. It was valued at £24, a large sum for a camera in those days, and Lieutenant Christopher had had experience as a photographic officer with the Air Service in the Eastern Mediterranean.

The *esprit de corps* of the Special Service was built partly on the fact that they were all volunteers. Either they had volunteered directly from the Navy, some from big ships so that they became very seasick aboard the tiny sailing Qs, or they had been given form T.124 and had signed as volunteers from the merchant service. None of the old crews of the merchant ships which were converted into decoys were forced to volunteer, and if they did not like life aboard a Q-ship they were allowed to leave. There is, however, just a suspicion that some of those who did sign T.124 did so for personal as well as patriotic reasons. Serving aboard a Q-ship carried a higher rate of pay than did service aboard a regular ship.

On 9th July, 1917, Acting Commander Archibald H. Reed, R.N.R., of *Underwing* asked the Admiral, Northern Division, Coast of Ireland, Buncrana, to give him Active Service stokers in place of his mercantile firemen. "The firemen have no knowledge of naval discipline or training," he wrote, "they are totally lacking in loyalty, patriotism, and honour, and so are a source of danger to the ship, and a hindrance to the work upon which we are engaged."

Cases of drunkenness, insubordination and leave-breaking had taken place, said Reed, and when three out of the seven firemen who went ashore on special leave were arrested by the police, the scene created at Killybegs was described as the most disgraceful ever witnessed there. "Also I have received reports from all over the town that all the secret details of this ship have been divulged—the number of guns carried—size—mark—and make of the guns—the method of dropping the gunports—the amount of wood in the holds—and in fact every detail of importance. Unfortunately I could find no one who could or would identify the men giving the information . . . The seamen ratings are mostly very good men, but in their case it seems that volunteering for Special Service is often made to avoid the routine in Active Service ships, and to also secure the pay allowance. Men who volunteer from these motives are entirely unsatisfactory, as they have no interest in the work and fail when an extra call is made upon them".[5]

Harold Auten tells us that, when first recruited, the Special Service ratings would try to compensate for the grinding monotony of life aboard a Q-ship by the occasional debauch when on shore, but that nothing was more steadying for them than an encounter with a U-boat. After that they never overstayed their leave, they were too eager to get back to their ship and give of their best.

Nothing was rarer than for whole groups of ratings to misbehave, and to be punished *en bloc*, as happened to the crew of the *Lothbury*. Vice-Admiral Sir Reginald Tupper, whose headquarters was at Stornoway, recommended that she should be paid off and recommissioned without any of her serving officers and men, contrary to the usual practice. "In view of the want of firmness on the part of the officers," came the reply on 16th June, 1918, "the fact that the men are merchant service firemen, and the nature of the service on which the vessel is employed, propose that cell punishment would meet the case, also that she be paid off and recommissioned".

Generally speaking, the Special Service ratings were extremely well disciplined and also very much devoted to their captains and other officers, whether the latter treated them with strict naval punctilio or threw lumps of coal at them to enforce orders, as did Commander Leopold A. Bernays. One steward rushed back to his captain's cabin just as the ship was sinking to get his monkey jacket because he knew that his master would have to report the loss of the vessel and wanted him to be properly dressed. Another apologised for having left the captain's cabin in such a state as he abandoned ship.

The Q-ship H.M.S. *Lothbury* as she appeared when first taken up for Special Service. Later a further gun was hidden behind a dummy hatch, as seen in the illustration on page 157. *Imperial War Museum*

Officers and men, R.N., R.N.R. and R.N.V.R., all learned to depend on one another. The R.N. provided leadership, the R.N.R. and R.N.V.R. the style essential to the mercantile disguise and the experience necessary to get the crazy old engines to work. In the eagerness to dispose of a U-boat, all differences were forgotten.

This was just as well, because life aboard a Q-ship took a most severe toll of both officers and crew. Campbell tells us that the life of a commander was so trying that most broke down with health troubles after a year. This is certainly not borne out by the career of the "aces" such as Campbell himself, Marx, Grenfell and Auten, but it may have been true of others.

The Admiralty's official reasons for paying the Special Service on a different scale were that its men were liable to be shot if captured and that they lived in very overcrowded conditions and so had earned "hard lying money" such as was paid to submariners. Vice-Admiral Sir Lewis Bayly, who commanded at Queenstown (modern Cobh), in Ireland, had been the first to request extra pay for the Special Service. "The hardships endured in a ship of this kind on this station are very real, though little advertised." The Admiralty apparently agreed, for on 9th December, 1916, Alexander Hunt wrote "Hard lying money at half rates is authorised where the Vice-Admiral, Queenstown, is satisfied that the living and sleeping conditions warrant such payment . . ." All except the tiny number required to make up the normal mercantile crew had to keep below, except after dark, when they might be allowed on deck. They were not much less confined than their opposite numbers in the U-boats.

7

Some Q-ships had a deck structure which would allow for conversion into training rooms, and there boxing and other exercise could be carried out, but on Harold Auten's *Zylpha*, a flush-decked ship, all physical drill had to be done below decks.

Crews usually slept by their guns, so as to be ready to fight at a moment's notice during the night. Even if this were not the case, the sleeping and living plans of the ships showed intense crowding, as a questionnaire sent out by W. Graham Greene of the Admiralty revealed. The *Penshurst*, of 740 tons, captained by Grenfell, had a complement of forty-five, distributed as follows:

Ranks and Rating	*Mess*	*Sleeping Accommodation*
4 Officers	Saloon	Separate cabins
2 Engine Room Artificers	In original Mates' and Engineers' Mess aft	Separate cabins aft
2 Stoker P.O.s		
2 W/T Operators		In one 2-berth cabin
1 Petty Officer	Mess formed by 2 cabins knocked into one	In bunks in Mess place
2 Leading Seamen		
1 Shipwright		
18 Seamen	In Smoke Room	12 in five 2-berth cabins (2 sleep on settees) 5 in bunks in in Forecastle 3 in hammocks in passage outside cabins
2 Signalmen	Under Bridge Deck	
2 Cooks	Galley	Cook and Steward in one 2-berth cabin
2 Stewards	Pantry	Cook's Mate and Boy Steward in hammocks in passage outside cabins
7 Stokers	In Forecastle	In Forecastle[6]

Though overcrowded, *Penshurst* was a more comfortable ship than many others . One Q-ship at least, the *Mary B. Mitchell*, offered grandeur if not comfort. "Below decks she had few—if any—equals in the home trade. From the poop a companion led to the saloon, the floor of which was laid in terrazo style, with a decorative star in the centre. The panelling was of rich mahogany and maple. On the starboard side of the saloon, from forward, were the master's room, a stateroom, bathroom, and pantry. To port lay the mate's room and two others."[7]

The *Mary B. Mitchell* had once been the yacht of a Welsh peer, though built in 1892 as a sailing coaster, a role she played for most of her long life. Yet even in luxurious conditions such as these, overcrowding would soon aggravate the plagues of the Special Service ships, lice, bugs, and scabies, which afflicted ships such as the *Princess Ena*. In return for these horrors, which were extirpated whenever a masterful commander like Campbell could get to work on them, the higher rates of pay might seem a small reward. Yet, by First World War standards, the "hard lying money" represented marginal comforts for the crew, such as the 750 Capstan cigarettes which the complement of the *Result* bought for 9s. 6d. (47½p).

As part of the endless impersonation of merchant officers and seamen, Special Service men were forbidden to wear naval uniform, except in protected harbours, until towards the close of the campaign, when Vice-Admiral Bayly decided that there was no point in their continuing to wear civilian clothes in port. It was a decision welcomed by officers and men alike, as the constant masquerade in mufti meant that discipline aboard a Q-ship had to be extra strict, seeing that all sartorial boundaries between officers and men were abolished. An exception to the universal use of civilian clothes was the wearing of War Service Badges, intended to be an assertion of the naval status of the Special

A caricature of Gordon Campbell as the commander of a Q-ship drawn by Lieutenant J. E. Broome, reproduced from *My Mystery Ships*.

Service, if they were unlucky enough to be captured.

We are able to reconstitute the wardrobe of the Q-ship officers and men in some detail because of the claims sent in for damages on the occasion of a disaster which involved a sailing Q-ship, the lugger *Bayard*. The *Q.20*, as *Bayard* was also known, was run down in the dark by the s.s. *Tainui* on 29th March, 1917. As the *Tainui* was a civilian vessel and was held to have been responsible by the court of inquiry, claims for compensation were made.

That put forward by the relatives of the commander, Lieutenant W. L. Scott, R.N.R., D.S.C., comprised the following kit:

> 3 suits of private clothes; 4 suits of underclothes; 3 pairs boots; 1 pair thigh boots; 1 pair knee boots; ½ dozen flannel shirts; ½ dozen white shirts; 1 dressing gown; 1 bridge coat; 1 overcoat; 1 oilskin coat; 2 pairs shoes; 3 white sweaters; 1 dozen pairs of socks; 2 pairs stockings; 3 dozen handkerchiefs; 2 dozen collars; 1 wristlet watch; 1 diamond ring; 1 suit case; 1 pair cuff links; 1 sextant; 1 pair binoculars; 1 Masonic apron; 1 silver mounted walking stick (presentation); 1 velours hat.

The value of the late lieutenant's kit amounted to £102 6s. 6d. (£102.32½). Lieutenant Algernon F. Sellers, R.N.R., who survived, claimed for similar articles and in addition for a uniform suit, cap and badge, two tweed suits for shore use, a tweed overcoat, bowler hat, silk scarf, muffler, braces, slippers, hair brushes, and a safety razor (Gillette), total £59 18s. 6d. "Observing," wrote Sellers, "that I was prohibited from wearing uniform on shore as well as afloat (except on going into action) I was obliged to take civilian clothes with me and those articles of mufti mentioned in above list are entirely exclusive of those obtained with money supplied by Government for that purpose."[8]

It is not easy to see how Sellers could have worn uniform when going into action, because Q-ship actions required the maintenance of disguise down to the last minute and might last for only a very short time, certainly not long enough to don anything except perhaps a uniform coat.

Another claimant, K. Norris, pointed out that the amount allowed for disguise kit, three pounds, "was sufficient to supply clothes for sea use only." Yet Q-ship officers and men had to go ashore, and they must not do so in uniform.

The crew, too, claimed for lost kits. They had taken on board blue cloth caps, comforters, serge jumpers, duck and serge trousers, oilskin coats, mackintoshes, overcoats, diagonal suits, flannel vests, cholera belts and check shirts, along with the usual flannel shirts and underwear. Even the special flannel underwear supplied to officers and seamen in the Navy, which Campbell describes as one of the few comforts of the service, could not be worn aboard a Q-ship, for if left hanging on a clothes line on deck its appearance would soon testify that there were naval men aboard. "Do not hang service flannels, etc., on the clothes lines," says *Hints to Commanding Officers*," "a suitable rig for men is dungaree suits."

As well as losing their clothes, some of the crew of *Bayard* had lost tools as well. Archibald Dupree, deck hand, had owned a number of tools, including two roping palms, two seaming palms, a pair of rigging screws, and one mallet, presumably a serving mallet.

On 20th July, 1916, the order was issued that War Service Badges were to be worn by all officers and men serving in decoys. This was a token concession to German ideas that all combatants should wear uniform if they were to be considered as military personnel when taken prisoner. Sometimes fears of the possible results of disguise for the Special Service resulted in definite orders about the use of uniform for crews of individual ships. "Commission in plain clothes," the complement of *Tamarisk* were told, "hoist Red Ensign, wear War Badges, uniform ready on board to wear before opening fire." "Every officer and man," ran a General Order of 1917, "is to have a cap badge or ribbon sewn into his clothes."

Compared with their opponents, the German submariners, the Special Service men were well fed. The stores transferred to the U.S. Navy when H.M.S. *Arvonian* became the U.S.S. *Santee* included: Soft

H.M.S. *Penshurst* cruising in heavy weather, a photograph taken from the wing of the bridge looking aft. The boat on the hatches is a collapsible dummy and hides one of the Q-ship's guns. From Harold Auten's *"Q" Boat Adventures*.

bread, flour, biscuit, fresh meat, fresh vegetables, unsweetened milk, sugar, tea, coffee, chocolate, jams and marmalade, preserved meat, pickles, rabbit, salmon, vinegar, salt pork, split peas, celery seed, refined suet, raisins, rice, oatmeal, lime juice, haricot beans and marrowfat peas.

Information is scanty about what, if anything, Q-ship men got to drink. The ritual of the rum ration, as observed aboard normal ships of the Royal Navy, would certainly have been too much of a giveaway. Bernays, one of the best of the Q-ship commanders, locked up all the drinks once his ship put to sea and would not let even his officers touch a drop. He made up for it by drinking hard in port, and it would seem that many of the Q-ship seamen did the same.

If living, eating, and sleeping were all subordinate to the great purpose of the Q-ship, to sink submarines, so too were her patrols. These were all directed to those areas where she was most likely to be attacked, and these areas in turn were dictated by recent reports of sinkings, and by intelligence estimates of where U-boats were most likely to be found. Very occasionally Q-ships would be sent off in concert for a joint sweep against some U-boat. When in 1917 the German submarine blockade-runner *Deutschland* made her famous voyage to New York, Vice-Admiral Bayly tried to intercept her on her return by sending *Q.1*, *Q.2*, *Q.3*, and *Q.4* to try to cut across her course if she returned from America to the Mediterranean, while *Q.5*, *Q.6*, *Q.7* and *Q.8* tried to cut off a course which would have taken her to the English Channel and North of Ireland.

Few Q-ships were sent off after such a definite quarry. For the most part they cruised in the hope of inviting attack. At Queenstown the Special Service vessels spent ten to twelve days cruising at sea and four days in harbour. Sometimes a cruise would be laid down for a captain, sometimes an area would be designated and he would be ordered to cruise at his discretion. Individual choice for cruises could produce problems, as when a commander took his ship off into an area where he might encounter French naval vessels, ignorant of his true nature. At the end of the cruise the commander would often send in along with his report a chart of his movements, with the daylight and darkness part of the cruise plotted in different colours.

While cruising the most rigid precautions had to be taken both as regards setting lookouts and the steering of a zig-zag course. The court of inquiry which sat to investigate the loss of *Warner*, which was sunk less than a month after her arrival at Queenstown, drew attention to the fact that no proper lookouts had been posted. All the duty of keeping a lookout devolved on the Officer of the Watch alone. The signalman who should have been on the upper bridge keeping a lookout had been diverted to messenger duty instead; he was on the lower bridge. The guns' crews had been kept beside their guns all day, thus diverting men who could otherwise have been used to organise relays of lookouts in three watches. Later captains felt that it was useless for anyone to keep lookout for longer than an hour. *Warner* had zig-zagged at wide angles such as 90 degrees at slow speed and had remained on a constant speed for twenty minutes.

At a subsequent court of inquiry into the loss of *Penshurst*, her captain, Lieutenant Cedric Naylor, R.N., took care to question witnesses so as to establish that a close watch was being kept. At the time of the sinking Naylor, the navigator, a signalman on the bridge, the quarter-master at the wheel, a man on top of the after gunhouse, and the gun's crew in the after gunhouse were all keeping a lookout. As even a moment's lapse in lookout might result in missing the sight of a periscope, or of an oncoming torpedo, both of which were hard enough to see in any case, it is not difficult to see why great attention was attached to keeping a proper lookout. Q-ship seamen and officers never displayed telescopes if they could help it; they became adept at keeping a lookout while pretending to be doing something else.

Great attention was paid to what they were to do at all moments of the cruise by their general orders, as the following selection from these will show.

The vessel must . . . strictly observe the role of a decoy. If an enemy submarine is sighted, every effort is to be made to escape, and if the submarine opens fire, engines are to be stopped, and the ship's company (except the necessary engine-room staff and the guns' crews, who must be kept carefully out of sight behind the bulwarks alongside their guns) commence to abandon ship. The submarine should be allowed to come as close as possible to decoy, and fire then opened by order of the whistle or steam syren, colours [White Ensign] being hoisted at the same time . . . Do not fire unless you are pretty sure of making a hit. Remember it is the strictest attention to small details that ensures success.

Obtain all latest information of submarines reported, minefields, recognition signals, Q messages, sailing instructions, etc.

When you anchor or moor in any port, on no consideration whatever be in the vicinity of any neutral ship. If possible do not lie in the immediate vicinity of any ship . . . Take every precaution against fire on board. Test the pumps continually and have all tubs and available buckets filled with water and placed about the deck. If you come into action, have the decks wetted as early as possible . . .

Whether a submarine is sighted or not, he may be watching you, although you may not see his periscope, and it is possible for one man wearing a uniform jersey or cap to disclose the identity of the vessel . . .

Rifles with ammunition and bombs and depth charges must be kept ready for instant use should the enemy come alongside. Act in all circumstances as the merchant ship you represent would act. Do not use channels you know are prohibited to such vessels. Ships disguised as merchantmen should always turn during the hours of darkness, if they have to change direction or course, without any apparent object in view. *All lights must be out.*

In addition to the officer, skipper, or mate on watch, it is the invariable procedure amongst merchantmen, as laid down in Board of Trade Rules, to have a lookout at the forecastle head, or on the bridge, and ships disguised as merchantmen should follow this procedure.

Keep a good lookout for floating mines. If sighted, do not pass between two mines; they are often connected by a span.

Do not signal or morse unless absolutely necessary . . . Hoist your aerial only during the hours of darkness . . .

After a submarine has been considered to have been sunk, if an opportunity occurs without risk, listen in with the hydrophone. A vessel observing a patch of oil on the surface of the water, which, from its position or the circumstances in which it is found, might be rising from destroyed or damaged submarines, should endeavour to obtain a sample of the oil for analysis. The most suitable method of obtaining such a sample is by scooping it up in a clean zinc bucket and subsequently transferring it to clean quart bottles, which should be kept tightly corked. As large a quantity as it is possible to collect should be obtained. The use of the hydrophone is invaluable. When in the vicinity of channels or likely places for mine laying,* remember that the hours of darkness are the most used, and it has been found that 10 p.m. is a favourite hour, particularly when this time coincides with high water.

You are to have four depth charges on board, in addition to lance bombs, grenades, smoke boxes, rifles and pistols. One box of ammunition, in addition to projectiles, is to be kept alongside each gun, always ready for use.

Should a vessel put into port, report yourself in plain clothes to the S.N.O. Apply for passes for those of the crew to whom you give leave to go ashore. A proper watch must be kept, and never more than half the crew allowed on shore at one time.

Your crew must carry out target practice every other trip, but not less than every fourteen days. Exercise, each trip, all guns' crews at quarters. Test all your appliances for disguise . . . To obviate a breakdown of the steering gear, relieving tackle must be obtained and kept in readiness . . .

"Abandon Ship" Ruse

The whole principle of the "Abandon Ship" ruse is that you should act as a civilian crew would act in similar circumstances, that your mate, and what would correspond with the civilian crew of a vessel of your size, should abandon ship. The C.O., the skipper, the P.O., and the guns' crews will remain *absolutely out of sight* on the ship. One head seen on board would probably mean the frustration of the whole scheme. When a vessel is abandoned, the crew should take bundles of clothing, food, etc., with them. Be careful to see that each boat has a compass, is watertight, and has provisions and water breakers filled with water aboard.

Vessels adopting the "Abandon Ship" ruse should always carry a sail in their small boat, and step mast and hoist sail, if there be any wind. This delays the boat from getting too far from the ship and gives the submarine time to close . . Boats . . . should be instructed to keep fairly close to the ship, and a bell should be rigged from forebridge to over the stern, so that if submarine does not come up in reasonable time, the boats can be recalled to the ship without anyone on board being seen, the ship being reboarded might attract the submarine.

Naval clothing for the crew manning the small boat should be held in readiness in rough bundles and taken into the boat when abandoning ship. When a vessel is

*This refers to mine-laying submarines.

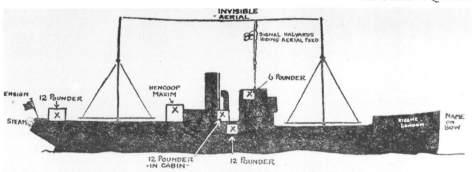

"FARNBOROUGH," SHOWING POSITION OF GUNS AND AS SHE NORMALLY WAS.

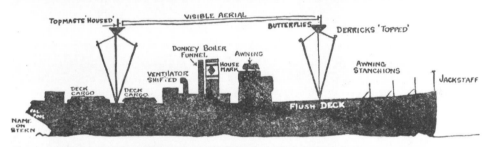

SHOWING THE VARIOUS DISGUISES WHICH MIGHT BE USED.

Two drawings from *My Mystery Ships* showing the way in which a Q-ship, in this case the *Farnborough*, might be disguised. The position of the guns, five twelve-pounders and two six-pounders and a Maxim, can be seen in the upper drawing.

abandoned, it is usual for the boiler to blow off steam. This should not be prevented. On no account must the fires be touched whilst the ship is abandoned. When a ship is abandoned, the engines should not be moved, if the crew have left, as all submarines are fitted with hydrophones. Even a shovel dropped in the engine room, or any other noise, would cause suspicion.

The boat will pull away, either towards the land or towards the submarine, as circumstances dictate. The invariable procedure up to date has been that the submarine at once closes the vessel.[9] The boat should not be allowed to close the submarine nearer than 200 to 300 yards. When this occurs, the ship should open fire, whatever distance the submarine is off. If the lie of the land, and other circumstances permit, the best procedure would be for the boat to row away, so that the ship is between the submarine and the boat . . .

Careful organisation is required to get your men at "action stations" quickly but without raising suspicion—in addition to the men at their guns a few stokers should be watching the submarine from the "well deck" or "forecastle". Cooks and stewards outside the saloon and galley, possibly a woman or two about . . .[10]

Arrange an "alarm" for port and starboard sides, so that officers and men know which side the submarine is, and can act accordingly, i.e. those who require to go on the bridge to go up *(Walking)* the side away from the submarine etc".[11]

15

If the conduct of the C.O. of a Q-ship was very much dictated by his orders, there was one area of operations where he did have a certain amount of scope for individuality. This was in his choice of a disguise. Q-ships always sailed in some disguise or other. They frequently had to alter that disguise, either because they had worn it so long that it had become stale, or because they had been spotted by a U-boat which would remember them on a subsequent occasion, and probably circulate the description of the vessel to other U-boats. *Hints . . . of use to new Commanding Officers* reminds its readers that they must assume a "*definite* name and ship of suitable tonnage and one that can reasonably be in your position, as the Germans probably know whom to expect." They are urged to consult *Lloyd's Weekly Index* and *Lloyd's Register*, and to obtain the name of the owners and to paint the funnel in keeping with house colours. Details such as whether the ship possessed wireless or not should be closely studied. "It will be gathered," *Hints* says, "that the same neutral ship will not be suitable for more than a few days at a time. Neutrals vary their methods of painting their flags, etc., and this should be looked out for. They seldom have Plimsoll marks. Names and port of registry invariably painted on . . . the appearance should be altered frequently, especially after an unsuccessful engagement and after a refit or long stay in one port."

J. A. Powlett of the Royal Naval Depot, Immingham Dock, suggested on 8th December, 1916, that ready-to-display name boards and flag boards should be kept, with other distinguishing markings where suitable. He was having prepared a collection of suitable funnel marks, with routes of neutral ships, so that the markings might match the probable approximate position of the neutral vessel.

The captain of a Q-ship which altered her appearance must always have had the uncomfortable feeling that if anything went wrong, his next part would be Yorick in *Hamlet*. If there was anything which the U-boats disliked more than a Q-ship, it was a Q-ship in neutral disguise.

On 12th April, 1916, Lieutenant Commander John Macleod, R.N., of *Zylpha* sighted a periscope, but the submarine disappeared after an attempt to torpedo his ship. As he had undergone a close inspection he proceeded to Bantry Bay and anchored south of Whiddly Island. "I altered the appearance of the ship from truck to waterline," he wrote.

Captains took immense pains with disguise. The Admiralty was seriously concerned to receive a telegram from the C.O. of the convoy sloop H.M.S. *Aubrietia* on 9th June, 1917: "Request information whether Chile, Argentine, Peru and Uruguay have declared war against Germany, so that I shall know how to act during my next cruise." When asked to explain, he wrote: " Having observed that enemy's submarines

Contrivances and devices: a view of the *Penshurst* looking forward showing the dummy boat which hides a twelve-pounder gun. The voice pipe from the bridge to the two after guns is lashed to the derrick. From *Q-ships and Their Story*.

mostly reserve their torpedoes for enemy's ships, it has been my custom to take on the role of an unarmed neutral, this I have been fortunate enough to do with fair success, only getting a few shells instead of a torpedo fired at me for my pains. From having been at sea and not having read the papers, and not being able to get reliable information at either Milford or Pembroke, I ventured to ask that the wire be sent, as the result of my making a mistake would have upset my plans, and I should have been torpedoed at sight, instead of being shelled at 10,000 yards."[12]

The best disguisers adopted appearances which deceived the U-boats completely, but others were less skilful or less fortunate. When the trawler *Linnet* (GY 999) was spoken to by a trawler disguised as one belonging to Messrs. Kelsall Brothers & Beeching of Hull, he reported: "Though she had her gear about, skipper was of opinion she had not been fishing." A U-boat commander would probably have penetrated the disguise as well.

Paradoxically, the very devices and disguises which were intended to allow the Special Service vessels to pass muster as innocent merchantmen sometimes betrayed them. Thus a large deck house on a sailing vessel, meant to hide a gun, might look out of place. "The 'disguised' aerial fitted" to *Q.24*, wrote Sir Lewis Bayly, "is of such bad design as to betray the character of the ship at a considerable distance."

One of the features of the Q-ships which will always fascinate were the numerous devices intended to conceal their armament and to simulate damage to the ship. Guns were concealed by small companion houses, dummy hatches, canvas boats, real boats cut in half, bunker saddlebacks, and by many other contrivances. "If a ship has a gun concealed in a house aft," said *Hints*, "a small steam pipe from exhaust, led aft and over the stern may help to distract from the house, as with steam issuing from the stern it will become the steering engine house."

Too much need not be said about the way in which Q-ship guns suddenly appeared on a rising pedestal or were unmasked in a *coup de théâtre* by falling bulwarks and disappearing screens, because the illustrations show an authentic concealed gun contrived for the cinema by Q-ship captain Harold Auten. Yet there was one very necessary adjunct for a gun which it was apparently well-nigh impossible to conceal, a rangefinder; all but a few vessels had to do without them, which made accurate shooting very much more difficult.

No disguise however ingenious could succeed if it were leaked to the enemy, either through careless talk in a pub or through discovery owing to some other means. Alexander Hunt of the Admiralty stressed on 13th April, 1916: "It should be impressed on every member of the crew that he is to be very reticent, that correspondence (private or otherwise) is to be reduced to a minimum and that all correspondence must be censored and that letters should not be written on shore."

What is supposedly the greatest breach of security in connection with the Q-ships occurred because of a letter. Jules Crawford Silber, a self-confessed German spy who had fought with the British against the Boers and who spoke perfect English, succeeded in penetrating the postal censorship, first at Mount Pleasant and then at Salisbury House in London and later in Liverpool. In his capacity as censor he opened a letter addressed by a girl to her sister in Canada. The writer said their brother had just been decorated for bravery and was at that moment at home on leave. He was serving on a special kind of ship, the first of its kind, which would soon put an end to all the German U-boats, the girl wrote.

Silber returned the letter to the girl, delivering a stern lecture on the danger of such careless correspondence. He then called in person, warning the girl of the enormity of her blunder and its possible consequences, not just for herself but for her brother and his career. In her own interests he urged her to make a clean breast to him of all she knew. Silber thus learned enough to make him realise that he was on the trail of a very important piece of information. He discreetly inspected the brother's ship, which was in harbour, through field glasses, and began to make a tour of ports which housed Q-ships, compiling a mass of information about them which he later transmitted to German naval intelligence in Kiel.

Was Silber's story true, or did he after serving blamelessly as a censor during the war simply decide to impersonate a spy and write not one but two best-sellers about the intelligence war?

Postal breaches of security did occur. On 17th July, 1918, Willie Hutchinson, sub-manager of Messrs. J. & P. Coats' thread mills in Oporto, Portugal, wrote to his mother and sisters in Scotland.

> On Thursday last I was aboard one of Britain's mystery ships, her outward appearance is all that can be desired, but when the captain gave permission for us to get through her under a promise of secrecy not to reveal anything that we saw, I was amazed at what I saw. By simply pressing a button all the sides rattled down and revealed a pure fortress and besides there were four of these mysterious innocent creatures here. They don't allow anyone on board, and if it had not been that I was a Mason, I should never had seen anything. I am sorry not being able to give you an idea of her armaments, but one thing I can say, she is a holy terror.

The C.O. of *Fresh Hope*, the only Q-ship in Oporto at this time, Lieutenant J. Martin, hastened to deny the truth of everything in the letter. No permission had been given for visitors, no strangers had been aboard, and during his absence from the ship Lieutenant Parker had been left in charge with orders to allow no one on board.

It was no doubt fortunate for Willie Hutchinson that the following month, August, 1918, the Q-ships ceased to be even an official secret. Sir Eric Geddes, First Lord of the Admiralty, described their activities in a speech, though he was still mindful enough of security when referring to the adventures of a Special Service vessel to give it a fictitious number, "Q.50", which no ship had ever borne. As reported by *The Fishing News* of August 10th, he concluded: "While the enemy knew this old ruse, and while there was no need for further secrecy, he and Admiral Sims" (the commander of the U.S. Naval forces in British waters) "had more than one way of trapping submarines."

Even before Geddes had officially torn away the veil from the mystery ships they had ceased to be a mystery to the Germans. "We have been operating in these waters for nearly eight months," wrote the captain of the *Wyandra* (ex *Baralong*) from the Mediterranean on 15th July, 1916, "and everybody out here seems to know who and what we are. It is the same with our similar vessels."

As the first wireless distress signals began to stream from a pursued or torpedoed vessel, various three-island tramps in the vicinity of the call would make an abrupt change of course, and hasten across the ocean to the stricken ship. Sometimes the Q-ships would arrive too late to find anything except a sea strewn with the appalling wreckage of the U-boat war. On other occasions the Special Service might be lucky enough to find a torpedoed ship still afloat. *Q.10*, the convoy sloop H.M.S. *Begonia*, took the torpedoed *Tritonia* in tow. Another convoy sloop, H.M.S. *Tamarisk*, saved the destroyer U.S.S. *Cassin* in a similar way when the American vessel was torpedoed south of Mine Head in County Waterford, though weather and sea were bad and getting worse, and the *Cassin* was on a lee shore.

If there was no ship to be saved, there were often survivors, most of whom would not have survived long had it not been for the arrival of the Q-ships. On March 26th, 1916, *Q.4* sighted a derelict steamer down by the stern and with a heavy list to port. The C.O. reported:

> On approaching the vessel, someone was observed to be waving from the bridge. I lowered a lifeboat, giving the officer in charge orders to bring off any survivors and to see if it was possible to take her in tow. The officer returned with one survivor, and reported that as she was starting to settle, he only waited long enough to get her chart from the bridge. As the boat came alongside *Q.4* the ship suddenly stood on end and sank stern first. The survivor, Emile Caulier, aged 17, of 5 Rue de la Vieille Côte, Blosseville, Bensecours, near Rouen, stated on being questioned that the ship was the *Montreal* of Havre. He further stated that the ship must have been torpedoed on the night of Saturday, but he did not know at what time, as the first thing he knew about it was when he awoke next morning, and found himself alone on board.

A much more typical rescue was that of survivors trying to make for land in a boat, or struggling in the water. Commander Adrian Keyes of H.M.S. *Mavis* reported how the Greek steamer *Hadziaka* had two torpedoes fired at her by a submarine, the second of which blew her open, so that she sank in twenty minutes.

> Boats were lowered, but owing to heavy sea one boat was broken up and the other swamped. Captain and 22 men were clinging to wrecked boats when submarine came to surface and approached them, but made no attempt to render assistance and steamed away on surface. They were in water for 48 hours and dropped off one by one, till only three men remained. They managed to patch one boat up and upright her—eventually bailed her out and made sail, and had been sailing for 10 hours when picked up, having been 58 hours without food or water they were in a very exhausted condition.[13]

Saving life was all part of the day's work for the Special Service. It was a break in the monotony of the long hunt for U-boats. This was almost the only subject talked about on board, and inevitably it was

The hatch covers burst up, the gun on its special mounting is uncovered and the bulwarks drop down to allow it a clear field of fire: a still from *Q-ships, Vampires of the Deep*.
British Movietone News Film Archive

coupled with a discussion of the amount of prize money the crew were likely to receive for a sinking, or even for an action in which the U-boat was felt to have been badly damaged.

When the *Farnborough* sank *U.68* on 22nd March, 1916, £1,000 was paid out in prize money to the ship. This sum was divided into shares of £1 18s. 1d. (£1.90) and every man was allotted a different number of shares. The number varied with his rank and with the part he had played in the sinking of the U-boat. Thus A. Kay received the six shares due to a leading seaman plus an additional share because he was the first to sight the submarine. Second Lieutenant Beswick got twenty shares worth £38 1s. 8d., while as Bayly noted: "James Duncan, Mercantile Cook, deserted at Plymouth on 23rd May. His share (£11 8s. 6d.) will therefore not be paid." Other reasons for failure to draw a share aboard *Q.8* and *Q.14* could be the serving of a prison sentence. In the case of *Q.14*, the convoy sloop *Viola*, two of the crew were doing ninety days' hard labour in County Cork Gaol for refusal of duty, and two others had run and been recaptured.

From the moment that a submarine was sighted, down to that in which she submerged or sank, or until the mystery ship herself went down, everyone had his duty to do. He might be a messenger carrying the orders to the guns' crews, or in charge of the magazine, passing up the rounds of ammunition on deck; he might be one of the guns' crews, or have the duty of raising the White Ensign when fire was opened. Every post was one of extreme danger, from that of the panic party in the lifeboat to the engine-room watch, ready to get steam up at any moment

21

while knowing that they were in the front line so far as torpedo attack was concerned.

If the worst happened and the Q-ship was torpedoed without any hope of retaliation, the captain would dispose of the confidential books, codes and log by throwing them over the side in the metal box in which they were kept. The paymaster would rush to his cabin and get his ledgers, which were every bit as important a piece of equipment to take with him to the lifeboat as his swimming waistcoat and oilskins. Everybody knew his lifeboat and his place in it for a real as opposed to a pretended abandon ship. When the Q-ship H.M.S. *Warner*, *Q.27*, was attacked Lieutenant R. Roberts reported:

> Ship was struck by torpedoes right aft on port side, lifting after gunhouse and killing two men and wounding two others, ship settling down aft till counter was awash. She remained in this position for about fifteen minutes, in the meantime waist guns were manned, remainder of crew to 'abandon ship' stations, lowering lifeboat, cutter, and dinghy starboard side. Torpedo was then seen approaching ship, which was stationary, striking vessel in engine room port side. Vessel seemed to break in two and sank immediately. All boats on starboard side except cutter were capsized by force of explosion, throwing all occupants into water.
>
> I left ship as she was sinking, by jumping off forecastle, swimming to overturned lifeboat, which after about ten minutes we righted, and about 10.30 took in twenty-four men, including myself, from raft and floating wreckage.

Some of the torpedoed *Warner's* crew, about ten mercantile ratings, "grumbled among themselves and refused to take their turn at the oars, also as regards bailing of the boats." This was a very unusual occurrence in the Special Service, and these ratings were dealt with summarily by the Commander-in-Chief, Devonport.

The story of the survivors of H.M.S. *Paxton* helps to fill in the gaps in our knowledge about those Q-ships which were lost without trace. After an action earlier in the day with a U-boat which had ruined some of the lifeboats aboard, *Paxton* was torpedoed twice by another U-boat on 20th May, 1917.

> The vessel immediately began to turn over and break up. The crew took to boats and rafts . . . some of the crew had to walk over the vessel's broadside to get rescued.
>
> The submarine came up and turned a machine-gun upon the survivors and threatened to destroy all unless captain and engineer were delivered up. The captain surrendered, not as captain, but as navigating officer, stating the captain was killed. The second engineer was taken, the chief having been previously killed in the earlier action.
>
> The survivors got upon a raft with eleven others, but a boat took four off, leaving eleven, promising to come back at daylight and shift them on to another better raft, the one they occupied being staved in and the barrel containing provisions and water destroyed. No boat returned, although it was seen next morning sailing to the eastward, and the men had nothing to eat or drink until rescued by the *Dundrennan*, in bitter cold weather and seas breaking over constantly.
>
> One man died after getting on the raft. The others first went mad, and then died, the last one to go being a Marconi operator.[14]

With some omissions, such as an account of the regular gun drills and the accidents that sometimes arose from them, the weekly lectures on first aid which took place aboard some ships, and the accidents which overtook some ships, such as *Brown Mouse*, which was destroyed by fire, life aboard a Q-ship not engaged in an action has now been sketched in. What happened once the order to drop the disguise and open fire "Stand by! Let go!" had been given will be described in subsequent chapters.

Right: The crew of Harold Auten's *Suffolk Coast* dressed as merchant seamen.

Opposite: The same crew in naval uniform. Both picutres are from *"Q" boat Adventures*.

CHAPTER TWO

The Beginning

THE ORIGINS of the Q-ships are obscure. Though the Germans, in the controversy over the *Baralong* incident, professed to be able to see their origins in Britain's war with France in the 1770s, and although Gordon Campbell drew the same conclusions, it is not necessary to push them back quite so far.

Already by the beginning of the twentieth century, Q-ships were in regular use. They had not yet received that name, and it might be said in passing that when the mystery ships were given "Q" numbers, the choice of this particular letter of the alphabet was almost certainly dictated by the fact that so many of the Q-ships sailed from Queenstown. The Q-ships in question were called decoys, a word which continued to be used throughout the war. In the language of peace a decoy meant live bait that was intended to attract large game animals to their destruction, such as the goat tethered beneath a tree in which a big game hunter watched with his rifle for the tiger to approach the bait.

During anti-slavery campaigns against the Arab slave traders the Royal Navy found itself seriously hampered by the lack of suitable sailing ships. The sailing whalers which operated in the light winds and tricky waters of the Red Sea and Indian Ocean found themselves consistently outsailed by the Arab dhows, so the Admiralty purchased two dhows and fitted them out at Malta in the summer of 1902. They had a covered three-pounder in the bows and a movable Maxim gun amidships. Their complement showed the same kind of division that we shall see in the Q-ships, with their mixture of R.N. and reserve officers and men. The dhows were commanded by an R.N. lieutenant, with a naval crew consisting of a leading seaman and ten able seamen, together with an Arab crew made up of a dhow captain and twelve hands. All the ship's complement wore native dress, and the dhow simulated the activity of a peaceful merchantman, sailing along the usual shipping lanes, inviting attack.

The dhows proved an irresistible temptation to pirates and slave raiders. One lieutenant captured no fewer than four pirate ships, and later rose in the service to become Vice-Admiral Earl Granville, K.G., K.C.V.O., C.B., D.S.O. So when war broke out, Granville was merely one of a number of serving officers with Q-ship experience.[15]

Though the Royal Navy certainly invented Q-ships as they were used in the First World War, the idea was not completely foreign to the minds of the navies of the Central Powers, even in the early stages of the conflict. Admiral Scheer mentions that the orders issued to the German Navy cautioned U-boat commanders against attacking in surface trim, owing to "the danger of possible attacks by enemy ships." Gayer, the German historian of the U-boat war, said that when the 1915 campaign began, the U-boat commanders were warned against "submarine traps," yet at that time Q-ships were only being used in penny numbers.[16]

Later, probably without direct inspiration from the British Q-ships, the Germans fitted out a fleet of their own decoy vessels, of which there were eight, the first being the *Marie*, commissioned in December, 1915. Long before the first British Q-ship sank a U-boat, a Turkish mystery ship attacked the British submarine *E.12* in the Sea of Marmora.[17]

The inspiration to use Q-ships in British waters came from one of the Sea Lords, Harold Auten says. So far as the Admiralty was concerned, the first moves in the campaign had been as follows. *Report On Disguised Steamers*, submitted in compliance with a minute by the First Lord of the Admiralty dated 3rd April, 1915[18], states:

> The vessels so far fitted out have been (1) A steamer, name unknown, from Portsmouth, (2) s.s. *Lyons*, late salvage tug, (3) Great Eastern Railway Company's steamer *Vienna*, (4) s.s. *Baralong*.
>
> When submarines first appeared off Havre a telegram was sent to the Commander-in-Chief, Portsmouth, November 26th [1914] to fit out a vessel with concealed guns and send her to cruise as a merchant ship in the neighbourhood of Havre. A ship was sent, but she was reported to be unserviceable, and Commander-in-Chief Portsmouth wrote on December 9th that she had been paid off.
>
> On February 4th, [1915] the *Lyons* was ordered to be prepared for this service; guns and ammunition were sent to Blackwall for embarkation, labelled as pump, gear, and metal fittings, and the *Lyons* proceeded to Poole to fit out in an unfrequented harbour there.

The report went on to detail *Lyons'* search for a supposed U-boat base near Portland, her cruise to the Scillies, Waterford, Scillies again, Lundy Island and Land's End. *Lyons* was next sent to the Isle of Man, where submarines were reported, and after steaming there she cruised between Liverpool and the Tuskar on the trade routes.

U-boat attacks on the Great Eastern Railway's North Sea packet *Colchester* on 11th December, 1914, and 17th February, 1915, made the Admiralty decide that although *Lyons* had had no success so far they would nonetheless take up another Q-ship. Their choice fell on the G.E.R. passenger packet *Vienna*, then being used as an accommodation ship for submarine officers at Harwich. The *Vienna*, which is usually referred to in the same breath by her assumed name of *Antwerp*, was used to impersonate a G.E.R. Company boat running between Harwich and Rotterdam. She was armed with two twelve-pounders.

Vienna/Antwerp's usefulness ceased when early in March, 1915, information was received that the Dutch knew all about her true purpose, and consequently the Germans must do so too. So she was transferred to the Irish Sea to work in company with *Lyons*. The captains of the two ships, of whom more anon, arranged to cruise on specific routes in the Irish Sea. *Lyons* had gone to work in the approaches to Liverpool, as the *Lusitania* was expected there. She next moved south (10th March), returning along the Channel, where there were reports of submarines, to coal secretly at Poole.

Meanwhile the first encounter, albeit a bloodless one, between a Q-ship and a U-boat had taken place in the Western Approaches. On 12th March, 1915, two merchant ships, the *Headlands* and the *Indian City*, were sunk just a few miles south of the Isles of Scilly. The *Vienna* was then sixty miles to the north, but on intercepting radio messages she proceeded at full speed towards the spot where the two vessels had been attacked. She was able to pick up the crew of a third vessel, the *Andalusian*, which had been captured by a U-boat and scuttled twenty-five miles west-north-west from the Bishop Rock. Lookouts in the *Vienna* sighted *U.29* about four miles off and the Q-ship held to her course as though she was an ordinary vessel, "but *U.29* refused her," says the official report of the incident.

"Her commanding officer asked that he might have a tramp steamer instead, and this was approved," stated the report. "The *Baralong* has been fitted out with *Vienna's* guns and is now on her way to cruise to the Eastward on a special mission. The *Vienna* has been allocated to transport service."

This, then, was the beginning of what was later to become almost a navy within a navy; two ships, the *Lyons,* commanded by Lieutenant-Commander A. P. Gardiner, R.N.R., and the *Vienna/Antwerp,* commanded by the much more famous Lieutenant-Commander Godfrey Herbert, R.N., a submarine officer who was to win glory, and execration, as captain of the *Baralong*. The Portsmouth ship was apparently the coasting steamer *Victoria*, commissioned on 29th November, 1914. She plied the Channel armed with guns concealed beneath crates of vegetables on her deck, but she never even sighted a U-boat.

Why had such a good idea as the Q-ships been employed so sparingly at the outset? There were not wanting men of vision who had urged it should be otherwise. On 19th August, 1915, Admiral Sir Stanley Colville had written to the Admiralty of the need that "a large number of merchant ships of all sorts and sizes be immediately commissioned,

The *Antwerp*, formerly the Great Eastern Railway steamer *Vienna*, entering Harwich Harbour, from *Q-Ships and Their Story*.

armed, and sent on the trade routes around England, especially moving in waters particularly infested with submarines. These ships should be officered by very specially selected officers on the active list (not R.N.R.) and the guns' crew specially selected active service men. The armament (four twelve-pounders) should be *most carefully* hidden and the work of disguising and fitting out these vessels should be carried out away from a dockyard."

Admiral Sir John Jellicoe, the Commander-in-Chief, Grand Fleet, had put the need for Q-ships even more strongly in a minute, written at the same time to the Admiralty. He had already ordered that the armed trawlers, though commissioned, should not be painted battleship grey, but given fishing numbers and funnel markings as in peacetime. Writing to second Colville's proposal, he said that he was in the fullest agreement with the Admiral, who had been indefatigable in fitting out vessels at Scapa Flow on the lines he suggested. The officers and men under him had worked very hard and successfully.

"It is certain," wrote Jellicoe, "that the decoy system offers by far the best chance of overcoming the growing menace from enemy submarines when once they are away from their own waters, and I submit that it is far better to utilise thirty or forty merchant ships in this way, with every chance of their destroying submarines, than to lose the same vessels and their cargoes tamely with no corresponding reduction in the enemy's forces. The undoubted result will be that enemy submarines will be forced to work under water against merchant ships and to abandon the use of guns. This will certainly reduce their power of damaging our trade."

There was no single reason why the Admiralty determined not to follow this advice. Ships, men and guns were all in very short supply, yet these were not the main reasons for their refusal, the real factor behind their reluctance to launch a whole Q-ship fleet being the poor performance of the mystery ships to date.

Poor Lieutenant-Commander Gardiner had been ordered to carry out two apparently incompatible tasks, run a salvage service with a salvage ship which was not readily disguisable as anything else, and operate as a Q-ship as well. His orders bear a strong resemblance to those subsequently issued to all other Q-ship captains. He had to cruise in such a way that he was likely to meet an enemy, get all the information he could from patrol vessels or other ships, yet take care not to disclose the service upon which he was bound. Special passes were to be produced and shown, along with Gardiner's commission, to any R.N. or French naval vessels which showed a persistent interest in *Lyons*. These passes simply stated that the ship was operating under the instructions of the Admiralty and was not to be examined or interfered with.

Mention of Gardiner's commission suggests that *Lyons* herself did not have one. Like a number of early Q-ships, she had not been regularly commissioned as a fighting vessel and in consequence, according to a subsequent Admiralty decision, she was under the Hague Convention a pirate.

The status of *Lyons* was an academic point, of much less interest than

the question of whether she would ever find a submarine, and how she would tackle it if she did. She had been armed with a number of concealed guns, but she was also equipped with a Maxim and ammunition, thirty-six rifles and ammunition, and revolvers and ammunition. The small arms were probably intended as a help in rounding up prisoners, though at this early date in the Q-ship campaign even the Admiralty still believed that a few Mills bombs and some picked marksmen would dispose of a U-boat. *Lyons* was ordered to hurry to an attacked ship so as to help the stricken ship or her survivors. "A ship chased by a submarine," he was told, "will hoist her largest flag half-mast at foremast head or on triatic stay, and make calls with her syren; if fitted with wireless she will make 'S.O.S.' followed by a series of 'S's". This was the order which had brought *Vienna/Antwerp* charging towards the sinking *Andalusian*. On this occasion, *U.29*, rightly suspicious of a merchant ship which appeared to be sailing straight to disaster, submerged. On a subsequent encounter with a submarine, however, this policy was to have good results for Godfrey Herbert, then in command of *Baralong*.

Lyons had had such bad success with the U-boats that the Admiralty first decided to send her to the Mediterranean with salvage plant, then cancelled the order and sent her to the naval base at Kingstown (modern Dun Laoghaire) in Ireland. The southern approaches to Ireland were to be the scene of the most determined activities of the U-boats; here, if anywhere, Gardiner ought to be able to encounter his first submarine. The Rear-Admiral, Kingstown, was ordered to employ her in cruising in the approaches to Liverpool, outside the local Liverpool areas, but he might also employ her on other services, particularly salvage. "*Lyons* has salvage plant aboard," he was told, "and may at any time be required for

Opposite: The *Antwerp's* after deckhouse, showing the dummy liferaft which concealed two twelve-pounder guns.

Right: The sides of the dummy raft have collapsed to reveal the gun and its crew ready for action. Both pictures are from *Q-Ships and Their Story*.

salvage work in other parts; nothing is to be done to prevent her from being able to proceed upon short notice to any place at home or abroad."

Lyons in fact had become a complete maid of all work. Now disguised as the *Elva* of Rotterdam, she was acting as an escort for important ships such as the White Star liner *Georgic*. Gardiner only succeeded in making contact with the *Georgic* nine miles off Ushant, which did nothing to avert the wrath of his superiors that was about to descend on his head. Now, having abandoned important ships for the time being, *Lyons* was busy looking for mines in a minefield which was apparently purely mythical. Doggedly, Gardiner began firing with a rifle at all the casks and wreckage on the scene of the "minefield", just in case they should contain mines.

Two of the great obsessions of the Admiralty were that there was a U-boat base somewhere in the British Isles, and that the U-boats were being supplied at sea by a service vessel sent out from Germany. Gardiner was involved in looking for the mythical supply vessel on at least two occasions. In March, 1915, he was sent to investigate the suspected vessel *Flora*. When later in the year he encountered another suspect vessel he was reprimanded by the Admiralty and told that his action was very unsatisfactory. During the same month, July, 1915, he was co-operating with the military in Yorkshire, trying to catch a German agent who supposedly signalled messages to U-boats from Flamborough Head. This assignment brought Gardiner his first sight of a submarine. He sighted the U-boat two miles away in poor light, pursued her, but had the chagrin to observe her submerging when he was over a mile away.

It was not merely Gardiner's bad luck with the U-boats which had irritated his superiors; he was the kind of officer who was always submitting proposals. Not that these proposals were frivolous or impractical; one of them at least appears very well founded. It was for a net barrier across the Channel with "a line of wire nets of, say, four feet mesh, using cement blocks for anchors and the ordinary wreck marking buoys as used in salvage for the floats . . . If necessary another net could be laid from Goodwin Sands to Calais, leaving a clear run between England and France for everything, and keeping submarines from coming south of the Goodwin Sands." A Channel net barrier similar to what Gardiner proposed had in fact already been laid, and it had thus far proved its effectiveness. The lieutenant-commander also outlined suggestions for buoying the positions of sunken ships and purchasing an icebreaker.

More unwelcome to his superiors than this stream of submissions was Gardiner's reaction to orders. In March, 1915, he wrote at length explaining the difficulty there would be in carrying out his orders to fit *Lyons* as a salvage ship. Why, he said, she even lacked a tender, without which no salvage ship would move. The *Lyons* was in splendid shape for Q-ship work, but to refit her for salvage would take at least six weeks, whereas any ordinary vessel could be equipped with the ship's gear in less time than a refit would take. Then Gardiner wrote complaining about his new chief engineer and asking for his old one back.

Irritation at Gardiner reached boiling point and the career of *Lyons* as a Q-ship came to an abrupt end. She was transferred to Kirkwall for salvage work, with all her guns removed except one and all her R.N.R. crew transferred. As she paid off as a Q-ship and re-commissioned with a mercantile crew, Gardiner sent in a characteristic protest.

At the Admiralty, Hugh Sinclair, Director, Mobilisation Division, Admiralty War Staff, wrote: "The action of Lieutenant-Commander Gardiner, in continually questioning Admiralty orders, especially with regard to the crew of *Lyons*, savours of ill-discipline. As a matter of fact he has no business at all to have all these naval ratings on board *Lyons*, but it is understood he obtained them at the outbreak of war by 'bouncing' the Drafting Authorities at Chatham. He now appears to desire to repeat the process on the Admiralty!" "Concur with D.N.D." noted another Admiralty official. "Lieutenant-Commander Gardiner has given trouble before and appears to be unable to accept an order without questioning it." "Concur with D.N.D." wrote a second. "This vessel is unsuitable for the special service in which she has recently been employed and it has been decided that she is to resume salvage duties. No reason is seen why this decision should be reconsidered."

Rear-Admiral Henry Oliver, Chief of the War Staff, wrote: "The Captain of *Lyons* had a very free hand to catch submarines for over six months, he has been well tried at the work and has not made good, and has been a source of trouble owing to his disinclination to do as he is told and to always make excuses to refit and stay in harbour."

Although Lieutenant-Commander Godfrey Herbert of *Vienna/Antwerp* had not caught any U-boats either, nobody felt disposed to sack him because he was known to be a good commander, a veteran submariner who understood the psychology of the U-boat commander, and a man so dedicated to the disguise of his ship that he even appeared on board her wearing the kind of wig that would disguise him as a Dutch pilot. They felt that, with luck, Herbert would bring in his submarine. On 3rd February, 1915, the Fourth Sea Lord had submitted to the First that he attached great importance to the use of a merchant ship with concealed guns to entrap submarines. "Ships of this sort," he wrote, "should cruise in the area of the raiding submarines, stop ship when they are challenged, allow a boat to come alongside from the submarine and then sink the submarine by gunfire, taking the boat's crew prisoners or firing on them, as convenient." In other words, the Q-ship experiment was still a secret to some of the Lords of the Admiralty, if to no one else.

Oliver explained in a minute of the following day the progress that had been made to date: "One steamer [*Vienna*] is already operating on the Harwich, Hook of Holland route: she was finished fitting out about a week ago. A second steamer [*Baralong*] is being fitted out with guns now to commence duty in the Irish or English Channel. About two months ago a steamer [*Lyons*] was fitted out at Portsmouth and worked off Havre but it was evident she was not being run on the proper lines and she was paid off. There should be little difficulty in getting four more small steamers, the greatest difficulty is to get the right sort of Commanding

Commander Godfrey Herbert disguised as a Dutch pilot, even to an unkempt wig, on the bridge of the *Antwerp*. From *Q-Ships and Their Story*.

Officer for an enterprise of this kind. The Commanding Officer in the steamer fitting now has been engaged in mine laying and blockade running, and is an enterprising man who will probably be a success."

If my identification of Herbert as the enterprising man is correct, this was high praise. Yet, in spite of Herbert's many good qualities, he had evidently lacked in his first command what time was to show as one of the vital qualities of a Q-ship captain, a tight hand on security. "The use of the G.E.R. steamer *Vienna* is well known in Rotterdam," reported Mr Burke, Continental Manager of the Great Eastern in Rotterdam, "and therefore in Germany. This is because she is working from Harwich, where her men meet those of other boats and yarn with them, and they repeat the news to all their friends and others in the cafes on the other side. Also all the G.E.R. boats have had their appearance altered, so that *Vienna* stands alone in the original appearance of a Great Eastern steamer."[19]

Unwittingly Herbert had committed the two deadliest sins that a Q-ship captain could encompass. He had allowed his men to talk, a fault that later captains like Gordon Campbell were to cure with a dose of the cells, and he had adopted an unsuitable disguise. It shows that Herbert was a man who could learn from his mistakes; the cover of his next ship, *Baralong*, was to be immaculate. He was also the first captain to appreciate to the full the need to suit the kind of fly to the condition of the stream, if the trout were to rise.

The first intimation that *Vienna/Antwerp* was not tempting bait had been borne in on him as he hurried to the scene of the *Andalusian* sinking. As he took the crew of the Ellerman liner aboard his vessel and listened to Captain Malley as the latter told him that he thought from the sound of the submarine's engines that she was "out of gear" he kept watching the *U.29*. As she submerged he reluctantly concluded that *Vienna/Antwerp's* cover was an unsuitable one. "I came across *U.29* ten miles west of Scilly," he wrote in a letter of 23rd August, "but he refused to be tempted, notwithstanding he was busy holding up cargo steamers. This incident led to me getting the *Baralong*." "This class of ship," he added on another occasion, meaning *Vienna/Antwerp*, "is too fast to tackle *or* she is known to the enemy, although in the latter case he would simply have tried to attack me, diving on sighting me."

The *Baralong*, which was to make Herbert famous, was the classic Q-ship, a converted tramp of 4,192 tons, built in 1901, with a speed of ten knots and an armament of three twelve-pounders. Apart from her speed and armament, which were not much with which to tackle a U-boat, the *Baralong* was a very suitable ship. Save for the *Victoria*, about which not much is known, all the Q-ships hitherto had been rather unsuitable. The *Lyons*, as Herbert had said, was "not a decoy vessel unless in the role of a tug." The *Vienna/Antwerp* had also been unsuitable, except for her speed. A railway steamer could not be disguised as any other kind of ship; because she used so much coal she had to enter harbour frequently, and it was at those moments that her cover was likely to be blown. What was more, a railway steamer had no business to be anywhere save on her proper route. This was not ten miles west of Scilly, which may have been what made *U.29* shy off; U-boat commanders knew as much about British merchant shipping as did Royal Navy captains. They had with them seamen who had sailed in British merchant ships in peacetime, a large proportion of all mercantile British crews having been Germans or Scandinavians. They also had current copies of *Lloyd's Register of Shipping*.

Jules Silber, self-confessed German spy, prided himself on having smuggled a copy to the German Admiralty.

A consultation of *Lloyd's* and a study of *Baralong*, as seen through a periscope, was unlikely to alarm any U-boat commander. She looked so very nondescript. "Suitable for this special duty," said someone who knew her, "being a cargo boat of ordinary type she does not excite suspicion." The first tramp decoy offered at least the possibility of another advantage, temporary unsinkability. It might be possible to make her so buoyant that, even though torpedoed, she could float long enough to dispose of her attacker.

Next to their surprise value, it was the slow sinking factor which was to be the dominant characteristic of Q-ships down to the end of their useful life, so it is not surprising that Herbert was particularly concerned with buoyancy as he supervised the fitting out of *Baralong* in Barry Dock. On 31st March he wrote announcing his intention of cruising in the Channel, as his orders laid down, and sailing first for Devonport, where he had requisitioned 2,680 empty casks to fill the *Baralong's* holds. Submitting a sketch which showed two of the holds full of empty barrels, he said: "I regret that I am not a better artist, but you will see that if she is holed anywhere in No. 2 hold, or as far aft as No. 3 her trim will not be altered very much, and if hit anywhere else, she should still be quite all right on account of having so many empty casks in Nos. 1 and 4 holds."

Herbert's enthusiasm, rather than solid results, must have convinced the Admiralty that there was a future for Q-ships. In February, 1915, they ordered the taking up of *Nigel* and *Peveril* "for special service similar to H.M.S. *Antwerp*." *Eildon* was also selected. The new vessels were to be armed with two guns forward, and manned with a mercantile crew with

The *Baralong* in Malta during her service in the Mediterranean, after her name had been changed to *Wyandra*. From *Q-Ships and Their Story*.

R.N. gunners. As so often happened with Q-ships, the requisition was dropped hurriedly. It was not merely that Lieutenant F. M. Simon had declared *Peveril* to be unsuitable—the Fourth Sea Lord pointed out that German submarine policy had changed. Slow, unhandy vessels such as *Peveril* and *Nigel* had become easy targets for the submerged U-boat, so the Admiralty dropped the *Eildon* and *Nigel*, retained *Peveril* and took up s.s. *Princess Ena*, which in the light of Herbert's advice seems a poor choice. The *Princess Ena* had been built to run between the Channel Islands and Southampton as a fruit boat for the London and South Western Railway Company. She had a gross tonnage of 1,198, and an armament of three twelve-pounder guns. "Not suitable for decoy work except on the routes of railway company steamers," was the predictable comment about her. "She is unlike an ordinary tramp." The only possible argument on behalf of *Princess Ena* was that she was speedy, with a speed of 15 knots. It is not surprising that within nineteen weeks of being commissioned, this vessel, nominally rated a fleet messenger, was paid off from Special Service work.

With *Baralong* as his flagship and *Lyons* and *Princess Ena* as his command, Herbert cruised continually in search of U-boats. *Princess Ena* plied regularly to Ushant, so he left the Channel to her and cruised in St George's Channel, keeping between the Scillies, the Smalls, Queenstown and the Fastnet. In a letter of 31st May, 1915, Herbert explains why it was not possible for a Q-ship to be sure of catching U-boats. Sinkings were considerable, and of course he hurried to the spot, ready to take on one of the duties which the mystery ships performed so successfully, succouring the survivors, yet the total percentage of British and Allied shipping compared to those ships sunk was enormous.

"I am very sorry not to be able to report any success," he said on 12th June, "but if they *will* persist in sinking things like Plymouth schooners, with 150 tons of coal aboard, when the ocean is thick with large steamers, I can't help it . . . I can only hope that by continuing at it, I shall one day meet with success." By June, 1915, he reckoned he had steamed 10,000 miles without any success. "It seems I am destined to bad luck." To relieve the monotony of his chase in search of the elusive enemy, Herbert wrote letters asking for promotion, and for a motor boat. "I don't know whether I am aspiring too high," he wrote to Captain Henry Grant, Assistant Director of the Operations Division, Admiralty War Staff, "but do you think it would be possible to rate me Acting Commander in view of the fact that I have got two ships beside my own? Of course I shouldn't expect to keep the rank as soon as I go back to submarines, but just while I have command of this show I thought possibly the extra 'guns', so to speak, would be an advantage."

Herbert's constant requests for a motor boat seem strange in view of the fact that *Baralong* was impersonating a three island tramp, the kind of vessel that relied strictly on manpower at the oars for her contact with the shore. Yet the instinct that prompted the request was a good one.

Ere we come to the end of this era of complete non-success, it is necessary to glance briefly at a ship which has remained something of a mystery among mystery ships. The *Meg*, or *Z.1* to give her the original nomenclature, had been called into being by the Admiralty obsession that somewhere in British or neutral waters there was a secret U-boat base from which the commerce-raiding submarines were supplied. On 23rd February, 1915, the Admiralty were first told of the existence of a Dr Jean Charcot, a French expert on the Faeroe Islands. He had been collecting information about their possible use as a U-boat base, and Captain Hodges, British Naval Attaché in Paris, said he was worried by the growing pro-German sympathies of the Islanders. The original hatred for Prussia which had been fostered in the Faeroes by the settlers who had been driven from their native Schleswig and Holstein to the islands had ebbed due to friendly visits by the German Fleet, who offered free repairs of fishing boat motors. So as to frustrate any plans Germany had to use the islands as a secret base for submarines, Charcot offered his services as a freelance Q-ship commander. Hodges told the Admiralty that the doctor was a good practical seaman who had commanded his vessel for many years, a man who spoke English with absolute fluency, someone interested in dealing with the U-boats and with his own ideas as to how this could be done. "For example," wrote Hodges, "he feels that an excellent type of vessel to employ in this connection would be the steam whalers built of late years in Norway, vessels steaming 15 knots, extremely handy, splendid sea boats and carrying a gun in the bows. He knows all the people in this trade and feels he could purchase some of them without anything being known."

Hodges must have known, but did not tell, of the fact that Jean Charcot was the son of the famous physician and hypnotist Dr Jean Martin Charcot, of whom there is such a striking portrait in Axel Munthe's *Story of San Michele*. Jean Charcot (1867–1937) had already made a more than respectable career as an explorer, carrying out surveys of the west coast of Graham Land in his ship the *Français*. Evidently Charcot had inherited some of his father's talent for hypnotism, and could practice it at a distance, because the Admiralty took to him wonderfully. "I think we may expect much from Charcot," wrote the First Sea Lord. It was then debated whether it would be preferable to purchase the best steam whaler available and to place Dr Charcot in charge of it "to watch the Faeroe Islands and discourage submarines,"[20] or to procure a whole squadron of whalers and use them to chase submarines. If the scheme turned out satisfactorily, then the whalers' uses need not be limited to the Faeroes; they could for example be sent to the Scillies, now very much in need of attention.

The First Lord felt that, after all, it would be better to try the original plan with just one whaler. Dr Charcot would use this ship to search the Faeroes, and if the search revealed nothing then the vessel would revert to ordinary anti-submarine work round our coasts. But by the time *Z.1* had been completed by the Smith's Dock Company, Middlesbrough, Yorkshire, under the supervision of the Captain Superintendent of Contract Built Ships, and had completed her sea trials, the original plan of the Admiralty had been completely altered. Not merely had no evidence come to light that the Faeroese were actively sympathetic to Germany and would consequently afford the U-boats a base, but a Danish fishery gun boat was patrolling the Faeroe Islands in order to ensure neutrality. It would be highly inadvisable for Charcot to poke his nose in there at a time when everything was being done to ensure co-operation from the neutrals.

"He is of the freelance type," minuted the Chief of Staff in August, 1915, "is only an artificial naval officer, and is unaccustomed to discipline. From conversation with him I gather that his one ambition is to do harm to the foe and his one aspiration is to be given a free hand, within of course, reasonable limits. He is nevertheless anxious to do what he is told. I don't think it would answer to make him one of the Orkney and Shetland auxiliary patrol. Complications would, I imagine, ensue as he would have to work in conjunction with and under the orders of all sorts of different people, and generally he would be Senior Officer on the spot, which would be awkward. He expresses a desire to work from Stornoway, which seems more suitable, as the Rear-Admiral there lends himself to having to deal with this would-be Corsair."

From every point of view the command of *Meg* by Charcot was an anomaly. He had been promoted by the French Navy from *Médecin de première classe de Réserve* to *Lieutenant de Vaisseau Auxiliaire*. He had a French second in command, *Enseigne de Vaisseau de Réserve* Fleuriais, while apart from two trained gunners, a signalman and a wireless operator, all the members of *Meg's* complement of twenty-eight were French. *Meg* flew the tricolour, but was under the orders of the British Admiralty.

There was also much that was anomalous about the ship herself. Though intended to be a U-boat chaser, she had a small radius of action, and a large complement for the accommodation available, like every other Q-ship. She could steam for six days at 10 knots (1,440 miles) or for five days at her full speed, 13½ knots (800 miles). She was not disguisable as anything other than what she was, a steam whaler. "This boat," said Charcot, "can never be made to look like anything else than a little naughty warship." Most serious of all, the *Meg* was unseaworthy, like so many Q-ships. Charcot nearly went down in her off North Rona Island, and considered her "to be quite unfit to be at sea in Atlantic winter weather, and only fit for service inside the Minch in small seas."

Charcot's opinion about *Meg's* unseaworthiness gave the Admiralty an excuse to propose her transfer to the Western Mediterranean. What had begun as an attempt to use a foreign expert's services against the U-boats had now changed, as the Charcot influence wore off, into a public relations operation designed to flatter the French. When Charcot was transferred to the command of Rear-Admiral Tupper, S.N.O. Stornoway, the First Sea Lord had written "the case is somewhat peculiar and one that will require delicate handling . . . It should be understood that a compliment is being paid to this officer and through him to French enterprise, and it is important that nothing should occur to mar the impression created in his country by the British Admiralty having asked for his services."

The transfer of *Meg* to the Mediterranean, which had been intended to remove the thorn in the Admiralty's flesh, never took place. Charcot suggested, via the French naval attaché, that he should surrender *Meg* to the Royal Navy, and instead resume command of his old exploring sailing vessel, *Pourquoi Pas*.

"*Pourquoi Pas?*" the Admiralty must have exclaimed. "Why not indeed?" H. F. Oliver, the Secretary to the Admiralty, submitted on 6th December, 1915, that there was no objection to *Meg* being returned; she could be manned by a British crew. "As regards *Pourquoi Pas* we have no objection to Dr Charcot cruising up north in her if the French like to commission her for the White Sea. Dr Charcot requiring more attention than the War Staff can afford to a single individual in wartime and his services having not proved of more value than those of any other Captain of a Patrol Vessel, it will be a very good thing to be quit of him."

On 13th January, 1916, *Meg* paid off. Renamed *Zedwhale*, she recommissioned at Granton with a British crew and joined the Dover Patrol.

A reading of the unpublished sources for the history of the Q-ship war certainly throws light on Keble Chatterton's otherwise cryptic comment that success depended on the right kind of commanding officer. "Slackers," "grousers," and "King's-hard-bargains," he says, "were useless."

CHAPTER THREE

"Stand by! Let go!"

THE SUMMER of 1915 was to be the crux of the whole Q-ship war. It gave the mystery ships their first successes, so that their future was assured for the rest of the conflict. There were so few methods by which a U-boat could be tackled successfully that, long after the Q-ships had ceased to be successful, they were to be continued in use. Yet, curiously enough, in the very success of the Q-ships lay the causes of their failure. Because the decoys had, single-handed, managed to sink U-boats, the most promising device used against submarines hitherto, the submarine/Q-ship partnership, was to be abandoned after only a short trial, to be resurrected, too late, in the closing years of the war.

The effectiveness of the Q-ship/submarine partnership can be seen from the fact that it accounted for two U-boats, *U.40*, torpedoed on 18th June, 1915, in the Forth by *C.24*, and *U.23*, torpedoed on 11th July, 1915, on the West Coast by *C.27*, more than were sunk by surface Q-ships working alone during the whole of the following year. The partnership scheme originated with Paymaster Commander Frank Spickernell, secretary to Vice-Admiral David Beatty, who commanded the First Battle Cruiser Squadron. As will be seen, the Q-ship campaign was not directed by the Admiralty alone but by individual admirals, who tended to be a law unto themselves in their own commands.

Once Beatty had adopted the idea, for which he gave his secretary full credit in a letter to the Admiralty of 25th June, he placed the British submarine *C.24* under the orders of Admiral Sir Stanley Colville and ordered her to work in unison with the armed trawler *Taranaki* (A 445). The latter, an Aberdeen trawler which had been taken over for minesweeping duties soon after the outbreak of war, was a real Q-ship in that she carried a crew disguised as civilians and acted as though she were a peaceful fishing vessel.

On 24th June, 1915, the *Taranaki* sailed out on her maiden trip and sighted the *U.40*. The German ship began to shell the *Taranaki* but she had had time to fire only one shot when the *C.24* cast off the tow by which she was attached to the trawler, surfaced, and sank the German submarine. Three of the German submariners, the captain, an officer and a seaman, were saved and promptly despatched by rail to Edinburgh with an escort. For the whole of the morning of the sinking the U-boat captain had kept watch on the trawler, inspecting her minutely through his glasses, ready to sink her as soon as she was out of sight of other vessels so that the sinking would go unreported.

This was the first success in the Q-ship war, obtained largely because of the careful planning and detailed instructions of Admiral Sir Stanley Colville, who was flying his flag in the Grand Fleet repair ship *Cyclops* as Admiral Commanding Orkney and Shetland, and was fitting out Q-ships at Longhope. The submarine had been taken in tow by the *Taranaki* as if she were a trawl down. A telephone line had been attached to the cable, so that trawler and submarine were in communication until the tow line was slipped. The *Taranaki* had been most carefully disguised as a fishing trawler, with a dark green top, red bottom, black funnel with a white "H" above and red markings below. The crew had done nothing to give the game away, but what was most important of all, the *C.24* had *torpedoed* her adversary. The U-boat was almost invulnerable to gunfire, except at very close range. She had a pressure hull, designed to help her withstand the pressure as she submerged, she was frequently armoured, and she very often attacked in semi-diving trim, with little but the conning tower showing above the water. The conning tower appeared to be a vulnerable part of the U-boat, but it was merely an excrescence, like the horn of the rhinoceros. U-boats could, and did, return to base with their conning tower completely shot away, and with all those on the bridge who had not got down the hatch in time blown into the sea. They could, and did, survive severe shelling. But there is no record of any U-boat surviving a successful torpedo attack.

During the summer the submarines *C.26* and *C.27* worked with the torpedo boat destroyer *Express* and with *Taranaki*, while the two submarines were also towed by the trawlers *Princess Louise*, formerly the Ostend trawler *Princess Marie José*, and *Wolsey*. Other trawlers were teamed up with C-class submarines, including *Ben Hur*, commanded by Lieutenant Raikes, R.N., and *Vina*, commanded by Lieutenant Alexander Tarver. Both of these were working from Baltasound in the Shetlands.

Combined attacks of this sort posed the greatest dangers for Special Service men and submariners alike. When one of the submarines grounded, the report went round that there was a U-boat ashore and urgent telegrams directed all kinds of craft, including a motor boat carrying explosives, to effect her destruction. Fortunately the submarine was able to get away and enter Aberdeen. So as to minimise this danger to the submarine while she was at sea the trawler towing her had to hoist a large red burgee on the approach of British vessels. Nothing could be done, however, to lessen the physical demands on her crew. During their long voyages under tow the submarine commanders, Lieutenant C. Cantlie and Lieutenant-Commander C. Dobson, noted that "in some

A C-class submarine of the kind which co-operated successfully with a number of Q-ships in 1915.

cases it was found that the slightest physical effort was difficult, and it was necessary to take advantage of a clear horizon to come to the surface for a few minutes to ventilate the boats."

Once the submarine was nearly rammed and sunk by a U-boat. The submarine officer carried aboard the trawler *Taranaki* had telephoned to report the whereabouts of the U-boat. "I slipped," reported the submarine commander, "and proceeded to cut her off. I brought the periscope above the water shortly after slipping and after some difficulty, located the submarine." Lieutenant Marrack, the submarine officer on the trawler, reported that the weather at the time was very hazy, and the morning rather dark. "I dipped the periscope and expected to be in a position to bring off an attack in about ten minutes. After about seven minutes I raised the periscope and found the submarine was very close to me, coming straight at me at high speed, about 15 knots. She had turned so as to come up to the *Taranaki* from astern. She was so close to me that it was useless to fire, so I dived as quickly as possible, and heard her go over me."

On another occasion, 26th July, 1915, the attack failed for another reason. *C.24* having slipped and surfaced found herself too far away to take part in the action, so Lieutenant F. E. Peterson had to tackle a U-boat "excellently disguised, on the starboard resembling a steamer with yellow funnel and black top, so that if she had had her masts up it would have been almost impossible to take her for anything but a steamer."

On 20th July the partnership had its second success. *Princess Louise* left harbour towing submarine *C.27*, commanded by Lieutenant-Commander C. C. Dobson, R.N. Lieutenant C. Cantlie, R.N., from *C.26*, was the submarine officer aboard the trawler, which was commanded by Lieutenant L. Morton, R.N.R. At 7.55 a.m. the trawler sighted a U-boat at 2,500 yards range. The news was telephoned to *C.27* with orders not to slip yet as the German submarine steered at right angles across the *Princess Louise's* bows and began to shell her. Seven shells fell round *Princess Louise*, without any hits being made. By that time the telephone line attached to the towing cable had broken, as it often did during these combined operations. Without any guidance save the sound of the shells hitting the waves above him, Dobson decided to surface. The trawler's crew meanwhile were engaged in hoisting out a boat and simulating panic. On coming to the surface *C.27* fired two torpedoes, the second of which hit and destroyed the U-boat, *U.23*, which sank almost immediately. Three German submariners were picked up by the trawler and seven by the submarine.

For the first time, a classic Q-ship ploy, the simulated panic, had been put into action successfully. There had not been time for this to be

H.M. Drifter *Principal*, one of a number of fishing vessels employed as decoys, with her six-pounder gun ready for action. When not in use the gun was ingeniously disguised as part of the foremast, which is here seen to be merely a dummy.   *Imperial War Museum*

carried out when *Taranaki* and *C.24* had sunk *U.40*. Credit for this device must go to Sir Stanley Colville, who outlined his considered thoughts about it in orders issued just a week before the sinking of *U.23* by *Princess Louise* and *C.27*. He also stressed another of the great principles of Q-ship warfare, keeping up the disguise down to the very last moment. He wrote on 12th July, 1915, less than a week before *Princess Louise* left port: "If the enemy is sighted and a shot fired to make the trawler heave to, she must comply as soon as possible with the order, but she is never to stop until she has slipped the submarine. The trawler must then endeavour to allay suspicions as long as possible by such means as commencing to get their boat out and generally appearing to be hurriedly preparing to abandon ship, etc. On no account is the trawler to lay herself open to suspicion by uncovering the gun or manoeuvring for position. It may even happen that a portion of the crew will have to leave the trawler in the boat, leaving hands for wheel, engines and two for the gun on board, who must remain out of sight. The White Ensign is ready to hoist if the trawler has to open fire. This will only be done if the [British] submarine has failed ... It is very important for the trawler to have every appearance of a fishing craft and great care must be taken to ensure this—otter boards* must be in place, no ensign staff, etc. etc."[21]

The combination of Q-ship and submarine had been an irresistible one. Within a month two submarines had been sunk. Why had such a brilliant idea been shelved so quickly? As David Beatty pointed out, it had only been with the greatest difficulty that he had been able to force through the idea at all against the enormous prejudice which existed against the scheme in the first place. There were other problems about the double attack. Its secret had become known to the Germans, because of the U-boat which had steamed over *Taranaki's* escort. It required very capable officers to carry it out successfully. Beatty himself, when warmly recommending it on 25th June, and proposing its extension "with a number of vessels," had added "in every case they should be craft with specially reliable and competent crews who can be relied upon not to bungle their attack and thus give away the plan to the enemy."

Some of the most strenuous objections to the mystery ship and submarine combination were only stressed when it was revived in 1917, but their effects must have been felt even more forcefully two years before. In 1915 Colville had noted that *C.26* and *C.27* could not be taken in tow or work in anything but fine weather. On 2nd January, 1917, the Commander-in-Chief, Grand Fleet, noted: "In selecting the area of operations consideration has had to be given to the unseaworthiness of these vessels, inasmuch as they are unable to remain on the surface with a

---

*Boards used to keep open the mouth of a trawl net.

bumpy sea running, owing to the damage which they quickly sustain to their hydroplanes."

In the same year, Captain James Startin, the Senior Naval Officer at Granton, in the Firth of Forth, noted: "with reference to trawler towing submarine, it is not found practicable to fish and tow at the same time, experience having shown that bogus fishing now does not in the least deceive the enemy, cases having occurred in which trawlers have been watched for some time (in one case half the night) to see if they were really fishing, i.e. shooting and hauling the trawls, which generally takes place every two hours, or two and a half hours, according to the nature of

Vice-Admiral Sir Lewis Bayly.

the bottom, with which the submarines are acquainted, having our Fisherman's Chart, and these operations cannot be simulated." For these reasons and for others, such as the urgent need for submarines in other theatres of war, the partnership was dissolved. The Q-ship would now have to struggle alone with the U-boat, with a success which, to say the least, was to be very varied.

There seems little doubt that if the conduct of the Q-ship war, and of anti-submarine operations in general, had been confined to some single individual to direct, then the results obtained would have been more satisfactory. Admiral Sir Lewis Bayly, about whom more will be said in the future, had been proposed as the very man to direct operations as a whole because of his experience in fleet co-ordination. This proposal was not accepted, however, possibly because of the intense jealousy that would have been aroused in the breasts of admirals entrusted with local commands. Instead the task of raising and equipping Q-ships took a different turn according to which admiral was in charge of a local command. If much was lost through lack of co-ordination, something was gained because of the enthusiasm and drive of the individual officers concerned.

No-one could have been more go-ahead than Captain James Startin. After the destruction of a neutral schooner carrying a cargo of pit props to Granton on 10th June, Startin proposed taking up a steamer and disguising her to look like a neutral timber carrier by means of a small deck cargo of pit props. The ship might be manned with six volunteers and armed with an "available three-pounder gun on board and some available bombs." Though apparently plying between Granton and the continent, the Q-ship would in reality stay within the range of the Armed Trawler Unit in whose area she operated. These armed trawlers, disguised as fishing boats, would be able to join in if it came to a fight with a U-boat. Startin ended by volunteering to pay for the whole cost of the scheme out of his own pocket. He forwarded his submission, warmly backed by his superior, Admiral Sir Robert Lowry at Rosyth, Admiral Commanding on the Coast of Scotland, to the Admiralty.

Rear-Admiral Henry Oliver, Chief of the War Staff, accepted the idea straight away. "Concur as the expenses will not be large," he wrote, "but I am not very sanguine of results. We have had three disguised steamers working for six months, and the greatest trouble was taken to fit them out secretly and their cruising ground has been frequently altered. If this schooner is fitted out in the Forth it will soon be known about, as there are always agents there."

Startin's idea now ran up against one of the snags which kept interrupting Q-ship proposals—there was no suitable ship available. Lowry scoured several ports without finding a schooner with auxiliary engine which could be hired. Determined not to be baulked by this circumstance, Startin proposed instead of hiring a vessel to buy a suitable Swedish schooner for £800, put in a good motor which, fitted in place, would cost £200, and purchase a cargo of pit props for about £100.

Rear-Admiral Oliver conveyed the Admiralty's agreement to Startin. Lowry could purchase the vessel secretly through brokers. The new ship might be used with or without a British submarine escort, for "the present means by which submarines have been sunk will become known and there is some advantage in having another expedient ready." On receipt of this agreement the brigantine *Sailer Thyrza* was purchased for £800 for the hull and £450 for the engines from James Livingstone and Sons, shipbrokers, of Grangemouth. This first sailing Q-ship was renamed *Ready*, armed with two twelve-pounders and commissioned on 30th August. She was to serve till the Armistice under the names of *Ready* and *Probus*, and have more than one close encounter with a U-boat.

Startin, determined not to be held up in his search for submarines by the delay in fitting out *Ready*, had already taken to sea in search of submarines in the armed trawler *Quickly*, which had been specially disguised as a small neutral trading steamer. She was intended to cruise from Granton to Aberdeen and Holy Island alternately. As it happened, Startin himself was to command her in her first encounter with a submarine on her maiden voyage.

In company with another disguised armed trawler, the *Gunner*, *Quickly* left St Andrew's Bay, where Startin had joined her, and sailed to the Bell Rock, carrying out target practice as she went until the S.N.O. was satisfied the guns' crews of both vessels had shaken down. At 12.30 p.m. on 19th June, Startin sailed for Latitude 57° N Longitude 3° E, an area lately visited by U-boats, *Gunner* being ordered to follow an hour behind. During the afternoon Startin disguised *Quickly* as a Norwegian cargo boat, Norwegian colours being hoisted at the mizzen masthead and painted on prepared slips of canvas placed on each side amidships. Two derricks were also placed on the foremast, one before and the other abaft the mast.

By 10 a.m. on Tuesday, 20th June, Startin sighted a large U-boat on the surface. She had two masts and two guns. The submarine shaped a parallel course with *Quickly*, at about four miles' distance, and continued to steam on this course for ten minutes, evidently scrutinising the Q-ship. At last she decided to attack, altered course to cut *Quickly* off, lowered her masts, and closed to about 1,500 yards. Meanwhile Startin had ordered the crew to prepare for action quietly and under cover.

At 10.25 the U-boat had closed to 1,000 yards. She hoisted the German ensign and displayed the International code flags ML meaning "Stop her." As the U-boat fired the first shot, Startin had the Norwegian flag hauled down, the White Ensign run up and the strip of canvas with painted Norwegian colours on the side taken off. Then at 10.32 *Quickly* opened fire with her twelve-pounder, "a splendid lucky shot striking the hull abaft the conning tower. Much smoke was seen coming from her." Next the six-pounder opened fire and apparently put the foremost gun of the U-boat out of action. "The third shot from the twelve-pounder struck the submarine right forward, and flames were seen by myself and everybody coming from her bows," Startin said in his report of the action.

At 10.50 the U-boat submerged till only her conning tower was awash, then she surfaced once more and tried to steam away on the surface. By this time *Gunner* had arrived and joined in shelling the U-boat. Both trawlers moved in on the submarine, which was steaming very slowly, was enveloped in smoke, and had the conning tower shattered by another hit from *Quickly's* twelve-pounder. By 11.15, just as the two trawlers closed her, the U-boat had sunk in an eruption of oil and bubbles. The depth was checked to 42 fathoms and the trawlers dropped a depth charge timed to explode at about 16 fathoms. Nothing came to the surface, but Startin was convinced that he had sunk the U-boat. So was the Admiralty, which entered the operation in a special file called: "Operations. I. Enemy submarines destroyed, etc."[22]

Nonetheless the submarine was able to return to base. Her loss does not appear in the definitive list of kills established long after the war by Gordon Campbell, in consultation with German naval records.

Even a fallacious success can have a tonic effect, however, and Lowry wrote to Admiral Sir Stanley Colville: "The scheme has met with immediate success, a submarine being sunk. I should like to try the plan up North as already discussed; a disguised trawler, or small collier, would seem to be suited for the purpose. I understand you have already sent out the collier *Prince Charlie*." Colville had indeed been hard at work fitting up the collier *Prince Charles*, a Mercantile Fleet Auxiliary, to act the part of a Q-ship. There need be no surprise that this mystery ship had a rather ambiguous name, either *Prince Charlie* or *Prince Charles* according to which document is consulted, but it was under the name of *Prince Charles* that the new Q-ship was to win fame as the first Special Service ship to sink a U-boat unaided.

On 20th July, 1915, Admiral Colville had ordered Lieutenant W. P. Mark-Wardlaw, R.N., to proceed aboard *Prince Charles*, taking with him Lieutenant J. G. Spencer, R.N.R., one petty officer, two leading seamen and seven able seamen, all of them volunteers from the repair ship *Cyclops*, the flagship of Rear-Admiral Francis Miller. The naval crew had orders to protect the vessel as she sailed to Baltasound and Stornoway with a part cargo of coal. They had a three-pounder and a six-pounder as armament. As we might expect, Colville's orders to Mark-Wardlaw had been meticulously drafted. They appeared to envisage the error which had caused Startin to lose his submarine, opening fire at too long range. "The object of the cruise," wrote Colville, "is to use the *Prince Charles* as a decoy, so that an enemy submarine should attack her with gunfire. It is not considered probable, owing to her small size [373 tons] that a torpedo would be wasted on her. In view of this I wish to impress upon you to strictly observe the role of decoy. If an enemy submarine is sighted, make every effort to escape. If she closes and fires, immediately stop your engines and with the ship's company (except the guns' crews who should most carefully be kept out of sight behind the bulwarks alongside their gun, and one engineer at the engines) commence to abandon ship. It is very important if you can do so to try and place your ship so that the enemy approaches you from the beam. Allow the submarine to come as close as possible, and then open fire by order on whistle, hoisting your colours (Red Ensign). It is quite probable that a submarine may be observing you through her periscope unseen by you and therefore on no account should the guns' crews on watch be standing about their guns."

Lieutenant Mark-Wardlaw left Longhope in Hoy, Orkney, at 8 p.m. on Wednesday, 21st July, and steamed for the whole of the next day without sighting anything except Dutch luggers and armed patrols. At evening he was ten miles East South East of North Rona Island when he sighted a three-masted vessel with one funnel, stopped about three points on the port bow.* Fifteen minutes after this sighting, at 6.35 p.m. he observed a submarine lying close to the vessel. *Prince Charles* continued on her course, steaming as if nothing had been seen. The guns' crews were closed up behind the screens and the merchant crew standing by to get out the boats. At the sight of *Prince Charles* apparently sailing out of reach, the U-boat started her engines and steamed towards the collier at full speed. Mark-Wardlaw hoisted the Red Ensign, and at 7.05 p.m. the submarine, from about three miles away, five points on the port bow, fired a shot which pitched 1,000 yards over the Q-ship.

Mark-Wardlaw then stopped the engines, put the ship's head to the swell from North North West, blew three blasts on his whistle and ordered the crew to get the boats out. The submarine continued to close *Prince Charles* at high speed, and at 7.10 p.m. fired another shot which passed between funnel and foremast, landing in the sea fifty yards away. The U-boat then turned so as to bring her broadside to *Prince Charles* at a range of 600 yards, and as the submarine kept on firing Mark-Wardlaw decided there was no point in waiting further. He opened fire with both guns.

"Directly I opened fire," he reported, "the guns' crews of the submarine deserted their guns and entered conning tower, and she apparently attempted to dive. Whilst doing this, she was struck 20 feet abaft conning tower, she then turned round, showing the opposite broadside, and commenced to rise again, her bow coming very high out of the water. *Prince Charles* then closed range to about 300 yards and fire was continued rapidly, frequent hits being scored, the men were then observed to be coming out of the conning tower, and the submarine settled by the stern, her bow lifting gradually out of the water.

"Fire was still continued, as no external damage was seen, several shots going through fore part. The submarine's bow then continued to lift until nearly vertical, and when projecting about 30 feet from the water, she took a sudden plunge and disappeared. No oil was seen. A

*Three points = 33° 45′ since the circumference of the magnetic compass card is divided into thirty-two points, each of 11° 15′.

A German submarine of the same class as the *U.36*, destroyed by the *Prince Charles*

large number of men were observed swimming in the water and every attempt was made to pick them up."[23]

All in all, Mark-Wardlaw succeeded in saving fifteen of the *U.36's* crew, all of whom had lifebelts on. So sudden had been the demise of the submarine that one of the survivors still had in his possession her official diary—he had not had time to sink it.

"Great skill was shown by Lieutenant Mark-Wardlaw," commented Admiral Colville, "in handling the situation, and in spite of being fired on he withheld fire until exactly the psychological moment, when such an extraordinary and rapid fire was poured on to *U.36* that it even drew forth expressions of admiration from the prisoners after they were rescued from the water ... I would here mention the fact that the German prisoners remarked to the merchant seamen that, being civilians, had the action gone the other way, they would have been treated as *Francs Tireurs* and shot."

The steamer which had been lying stopped when *Prince Charles* came up closed the Q-ship after the action, and Mark-Wardlaw signalled her to stop instantly, firing two shots across her bows. She was the Danish s.s. *Louise*. "I considered," wrote Mark-Wardlaw, "that she might possibly be a submarine supply ship, and as she had witnessed the whole action, I considered it advisable to try to do something to prevent her spreading the information." The Admiralty had something of an obsession about neutral steamers acting as U-boat supply vessels. Nor was the suspicion that a steamer seen near a submarine might be working in conjunction with her wholly unfounded, as it was known that German submariners had boarded steamers and used them to attract the company of other vessels, so as to add to their kill. Mark-Wardlaw evidently felt that the *Louise* might be intending to ram *Prince Charles*.

In the event, the captain of the *Louise* turned out to be very co-operative. There was no reason why he should not have been because the timely arrival of the Q-ship had saved half his crew from a watery grave, as one of their lifeboats had been swamped on launching it. He agreed to be escorted into harbour, and he told Mark-Wardlaw that he was very friendly towards England and would not report the sinking of the *U.36* when he returned to Denmark; but some of his crew might not have been equally discreet, so right at the outset of the Q-ship campaign, the mask of secrecy was torn from the mystery ships.

The fifteen prisoners, one senior lieutenant, two lieutenants, a chief engineer, an engine room artificer, a coxswain, four petty officers, three stokers, a seaman and a wireless operator, represented exactly half the complement of the U-boat. They did not seem promising intelligence material, and Assistant Paymaster G. S. Childs, who interrogated them, felt that they had been warned by their C.O. to be reticent, as they avoided even ordinary topics of conversation. Yet though Childs felt that "Officers and men lied freely," the crew of *U.36* had obviously been shaken at having been bested by a ship so much smaller than their own, and they gave quite a lot of information, most of it accurate.

The *U.36*, they told Childs, had one 88-millimetre gun, a fourteen-pounder, and seven torpedoes. They had an allowance of four torpedoes per trip, as they were getting very scarce. Those they had used had all been made in 1896. The submarine could steam at 15 knots submerged and over 20 knots on the surface, they said. She had a turning circle of 300 metres, and could dive in one and a half minutes "but later ones in considerably less than this." She had no armour "and only in the very newest boats was armour employed." The U-boat kept in touch with her base, usually Kiel as she belonged to the Kiel Submarine Division, though on this occasion she had sailed from Heligoland, by means of a Telefunken-type wireless installation, a six kilowatt set run off a dynamo. One operator was carried to work this set, which had a transmitting range of 90 to 100 miles, and a receiving range of 120 miles. "One officer said they always read Poldhu and Nordeich[24] at night when on the surface." They had received Thursday night's message from Poldhu. The survivors threw out other snippets of information such as the fact that German submarines found difficulty in diving during bad weather. The officers were most emphatic that *Prince Charles* was too small a ship on which to waste a torpedo.

All this was very much grist to the mill of Room 40 of Naval Intelligence in London, but there was more to come. On 24th July Lieutenant Mark-Wardlaw had reported that he had obtained "the official diary of *U.36*" from one of the prisoners. On 31st July a second diary turned up and Rear-Admiral Francis Miller forwarded it to Colville, along with a translation. It had been found in some clothes lent by the crew of *Prince Charles* to the prisoners. This later diary was really the Observation Book of Navigating Petty Officer H. Standt of *U.36*. Navigating petty officers were a standing institution in the German Navy and were responsible for practically the whole of the navigation in small craft. Standt had kept a meticulous record of the voyage of *U.36* down to 5.20 a.m. when the submarine started off in pursuit of the s.s. *Louise*.

After checking the sights which Standt had taken and verifying their working out from other observations in the diary, Naval Intelligence was able to discover that *U.36* was at 36 feet depth when her periscope was just above the surface, that the depth for cruising submerged was 66–72 feet, that the surface dead slow speed of the U-boat was four knots, her slow speed five to seven, and her full speed fifteen to sixteen knots. The speed of twenty knots mentioned by Mark-Wardlaw in his report and by one of the prisoners was purely a notional one.

In many ways the later career of the *Prince Charles* is just as informative to the historian of Q-ships as her unique success against *U.36*. By 16th November, 1915, a lull in the U-boat war against merchant shipping, combined with a shortage of steamers and suitable commanders, made Vice-Admiral Sir David Beatty urge the putting down of *Prince Charles* as an "Armed Merchant Cruiser (Special Type)." German submarines had temporarily abandoned the North Sea, and there could be no doubt about the unseaworthiness of *Prince Charles*. A survey of the ship, made by her new commanding officer, Lieutenant-Commander James Bayley, R.N., and the engineer lieutenant and the carpenter of the battle cruiser *Princess Royal*, a unit of the 1st Battle Cruiser Squadron, revealed a number of telling facts. The Q-ship had been built in 1905 as a trader to go up the Scheldt to Brussels. While she would probably weather any gale, she rolled and pitched so heavily in even moderate winds as to cause her engine to race unduly and thus injure the bearings. During the winter there were few occasions on which her guns could be used efficiently owing to her excessive rolling on very slight provocation. Her coal supply of seven days was insufficient for her patrolling duties, especially since head winds reduced her speed so much and "seven knots does not appear to be a high enough speed for her present purposes." The combustion chamber of the boiler was distorted, the condenser needed re-tubing, the pumps were incapable of dealing with large quantities of water, and in general the engine had suffered from serious neglect.

Captain Startin, in a letter written on 15th November, 1915, suggested that in view of her unseaworthiness her work would be more efficiently performed by one of the Auxiliary Patrol trawlers, which could acquire her guns and be easily disguised. The Commander-in-Chief would have none of this, and in a handwritten letter pointed out that *Prince Charles* was the only ship, as opposed to trawlers, manned for Special Service by the Fleet in Rosyth. The other Special Service vessels were the small craft *Quickly* and *Gunner*, both trawlers, and the *Ready*, a sailing ship. Rosyth ought to be able to send out one reliable steamer manned by the First Battle Cruiser Squadron, if not *Prince Charles*, which was obviously unseaworthy, then another ship. "German submarines," he wrote, "may at any time resume their attacks on the Mercantile Marine, and we should be ready to counter them by the means which has proved to be most effective." There was no need to have a commander aboard; a lieutenant should be able to carry out the duties, which were less exacting than those of commanding a destroyer. There was no point in trying to substitute a trawler Q-ship for a steamer—a trawler could only work in fishing areas.

Taking up the *Prince Charles* had revealed what might be termed the Q-ship paradox. In order to be appealing bait for a submarine, yet not attract a torpedo, a Q-ship had to be a small merchant craft. Yet the average tramp was, or so it would appear, badly maintained, unseaworthy and unable to maintain the speed and agility required for naval manoeuvres, and a hell on earth to sail in. This latter aspect is borne out by a report by Lieutenant-Commander Bayley of a cruise made in the ship in October, 1915. By this time she had been regularly commissioned (hitherto she had been, legally speaking, a pirate) and assigned to Rosyth, in the Coast of Scotland Command, and fitted with wireless.

> Condition of ship not good. Men badly bitten. Employed hands clearing out messes and cabins. Disinfected bedding and fumigated ship. Exercised hands at rifle and gun drill. Examined all gear, cleaned, refitted and lubricated ship generally. Repaired boats which leaked badly. Took down and lubricated all steering gear sheaves, hand steering being hardly workable. Cleaned up ammunition and made covers for guns, ammunition and rails. Repaired windlass and leaky scuttles. Ran all engines and steering gear . . . Reported at Granton and proceeded at 12.30 p.m. on Wednesday along trade routes as ordered, having carried out firing in St Andrews Bay first.
>
> S.E. gale commenced to rise during the night, and ship rolling and pitching very heavily. Part of the deck cargo carried away, and two practice ammunition boxes. Seas coming right over ship and flooding stokehold down ventilators, engines racing badly. Reduced speed. As the wind speed was increasing and it would be impossible with the limits of our coal supply to wait for calm enough weather to be able to work the guns, course was altered 16 points. When 96 miles out from May Island on Friday morning, steam was only kept with difficulty, and steam steering having given out, ship was steered by hand, which in the gale took a complete watch. Screens for the guns were knocked away in places by the heavy sea. This has been remedied and will not occur again.

Refitted ship, rebricked boilers, took in coal and water, and proceeded again on Wednesday morning, returning to Granton in the afternoon of the following Tuesday. Proceeded along trade routes as ordered, having disguised ship as a Norwegian. Moderate westerly wind behind us, which, however, was sufficient to render ship a very doubtful and latterly impossible gun platform. Made from 4–6 knots according to relative direction of wind, dropping to 3 knots when wind rose. Saw no signs of enemy on either trip.

Steering gear broken down. Engines knocking badly, and condensers leaking so much that boiler was scaling and burst tubes were expected. At this time of the year the occasions on which guns from this ship could hit anything are extremely rare indeed. Most of the men (coming from large ships) are incapacitated from sea-sickness, and bearing in mind the great reduction of speed in a head wind, the coal supply puts a limit to her efficiency and compels too early a return to harbour.

Lieutenant-Commander Bayley's report certainly reveals some of the weaknesses of the early Q-ships. They were mechanically very imperfect, and their imperfections were emphasised by manning with an all R.N. crew. The mercantile crew of the *Prince Charles* had been offered the chance of serving aboard her out of Rosyth and had declined. Later Q-ships were to be very much better equipped for their task because they had a large proportion of R.N.R. or R.N.V.R. crews, merchant seamen signed as volunteers under Form T.124. These men could show R.N. ratings the knack of handling a merchant ship, while the T.124 engineers, who had never been used to mechanical perfection, unlike their R.N. equivalents, could coax very much more out of the tired old engines.

On 4th December the weary odyssey of *Prince Charles* ended. The Admiralty decided to pay her off as a commissioned ship and not replace her, because mercantile tonnage was so short. If she had done nothing else, the first successful single-handed Special Service submarine-hunter had publicised just how bad conditions were aboard the mystery ships. Captain Henry B. Pelly, who commanded the battle cruiser H.M.S. *Tiger*, from which Bayley, the last C.O. of *Prince Charles*, had been drafted, wrote to the Admiralty on 27th November, 1915, urging that the men aboard her should have hard lying money, a special allowance paid to submariners, and that her C.O. should be paid "the established sea-going command money of his rank." Admiral Sir Robert Lowry backed this up by a letter to the Commander-in-Chief in which he said "to my personal knowledge the crew of the *Prince Charles* had a particularly hard time, and the crew of the schooner *Ready* had a worse experience."

The special allowance, which was eventually to be paid to all Q-ship personnel, became the distinguishing mark of their elite nature, and it may have helped to bring in volunteers when eventually they were called for.

It was to some extent irrelevant that the *Prince Charles* was an unseaworthy old tub. She had sunk a U-boat, and how many capital ships could say as much? It is not surprising, therefore, that admirals in various parts of the British Isles now strove to emulate the work of Startin and Colville. Indeed in some cases their efforts had begun before the first success.

Vice-Admiral Sir Charles Coke, who preceded Vice-Admiral Sir Lewis Bayly in command at Queenstown (Cobh), had written as early as 19th July, 1915, that "having received information from various sources that enemy submarines occasionally appeared alongside Irish fishing vessels and obtained fish from them, it occurred to me some time ago that if I were to take up one of the two lobster boats belonging to Mr F. H. Keane, of Ardmore, and place on board a crew of young officers disguised and a supply of lance bombs, automatic pistols, etc., there would be a very good chance of attacking successfully an enemy submarine." Hitherto, added Coke, he had been unable to find suitable young officers, but quite recently Commander Bircham, R.N.V.R., who had cruised a good deal on the South Irish Coast in the drifter *Golden Effort*, had offered his services. He could use his ratings from Boom Defence Construction as a crew.

Coke added that he had accepted the offer and Commander Bircham had taken up a vessel called *Smelt*. He now felt the time had come to mention this project so that it could be communicated to the Director of Transport, as the owner would have to be paid for the hire of the vessel.

The poop of the *Baralong*, with one of her twelve-pounder guns revealed. Normally this was hidden by a dummy life raft cover, as seen on page 57.   From *Q-Ships and Their Story*

Coke's letter has been worth quoting on two counts. First it shows the light-hearted attitude which was taken at this early date towards the problem of sinking U-boats. Lance bombs, which Vice-Admiral Coke proposed as being suitable for the task, were bombs with impact fuses attached to wooden staves. They were intended for use at close quarters, but on the only recorded instance when one was thrown at a U-boat it simply bounced off the casing. The other notable feature raised by Vice-Admiral Coke's letter is the status of Q-ships as regards the law of nations. Accepting Coke's proposal to take up *Smelt*, Rear-Admiral Henry Oliver, Chief of the War Staff, commented on 24th August, "The ship will require to be taken up and commissioned as a tender, or she will be a pirate. (Act I. Hague Convention VII)." So *Smelt* and later *Flower of the Fleet*, both motor drifters, were taken up and commissioned as tenders to H.M.S. *Colleen*, the former light cruiser *Royalist*, serving as base ship at Queenstown.

Did this decision mean that the early Q-ships such as *Prince Charles* and *Baralong*, which had not yet been commissioned, had been pirates? Apparently it did, because on 15th September, the Admiralty decided that Q-ships must be commissioned. This explains the anomaly of some ships being taken up by the Navy long before they were commissioned.

Coke's successor, Vice-Admiral Sir Lewis Bayly, was to have a great deal to do with the development of the mystery ship. On 7th August, 1915, only sixteen days after taking up his new command, Bayly sent to the Admiralty a submission containing more than one idea which was to be put into practical effect in the coming campaigns.

The submarines appear to be operating further at sea, are probably larger and faster, and therefore less easy to find and attack. I therefore request that a tramp steamer, to be called the *Chestnut* (two would be better), may be fitted out at a British port, with hidden guns, manned by a sufficient crew to man the guns and work the engines, with few officers, but these most carefully chosen. The following appear to be some of the necessities:-

(1) She should approach the submarine area 49°–51°N., 9°–11°W., from the seaward, representing a homeward bound ship.

(2) She should be ballasted down to her Plimsoll mark to represent a heavily laden ship.

(3) She should proceed outwards, passing about 80° from Ushant, thereby standing a chance of being attacked on the way.

(4) Her funnels, masts, and boats should be painted similar to some line of steamers trading from South America.

(5) Salt water should be sprayed on the fore part of her funnel and her side should be rather rusty so as to have the appearance of returning from a long voyage.

(6) Until attacked or before attacking she should fly an old Red Ensign, the officers and men should be dressed as in some line of the Merchant Navy.

(7) An old jib and staysail hoisted with a beam wind should help.

(8) She should have one 4-inch gun on each quarter, and one on each bow and be fitted with an automatic sweep. The gunlayers must be picked men, they will have to hit in the first three rounds. She should be fitted with bilge keels, and the ballast so stowed as to make her a steady platform.

(9) The guns should be on the main deck, and hidden behind the ship's sides; the berthing should be capable of being thrown down suddenly (the hinges being on the lower side) so as to open fire at once. This will necessitate the gun muzzle being inboard, but if the plates thrown down cover enough space, the gun will have a good arc of fire. It is of no use to put the gun high up, and then to hide it by some additional erection. The submarines are very cute, they have splendid glasses and watch for any sign of a trap and will sheer off. The best way is to photograph the ship when taken up; and when fitted, to compare her appearance with the photograph, to see that there is no difference when viewed from ahead, astern, or on the beam.

(10) The vessel should, if possible, be twin screw, so as to be able to manoeuvre as quickly as a submarine, and of at least sixteen knots speed.

(11) It would be an advantage to fill the hold with cork, as merchant vessels are not as a rule sufficiently strongly built to be able to ram, without serious injury.

(12) Coal would be suitable as ballast to enable the ship to keep at sea for a long time.

One or two merchant captains of sea experience could say at once if there were anything in the appearance of the ship to give her away. Promotion should follow on success.[25]

In this submission Bayly had anticipated the points which would be developed in later Q-ship warfare. They are the use of coal ballast (a bad idea, as it turned out, because coal is prone to spontaneous combustion), the need for a buoyant cargo to keep the Q-ship afloat if she becomes a casualty, impeccable disguise and guns which can be unmasked by some mechanical device.

Rear-Admiral Oliver's comment on the letter shows that the whole decoy idea was still very much in the balance as far as the Admiralty was concerned.

Submit to reply that this idea has been tried before, and has only met with success once, though four steamers in all have been fitted out, and the scheme has been worked for eight months. Tramp steamers of at least 16 knots speed do not exist, they are like the mythological 15 knot trawlers officers frequently ask for. There is no objection to the V.A. trying the plan again, with 12 pdr. guns, as there are no 4-inch guns to spare.

Bayly replied on 22nd August, 1915, that he was aware the idea was not a new one, "and I was of opinion that experience had shown the value of the plan." He wanted a cargo steamer fitted out with four twelve-pounders a side, seeing those were the only guns available, together with one ahead and two astern.

The Admiralty decided that Bayly could have two steamers to replace *Lyons* and *Princess Ena*, and that they would be fitted out under

A twelve-pounder gun on the *Baralong's* poop concealed by a dummy life raft cover which was hinged at the lower edge.

his orders at Queenstown. Oliver commented acidly:

> The V.A., appears to have got away from the decoy steamer idea and is contemplating a tramp line of battleships. Thirteen twelve-pounder guns would destroy the innocent reputation of any steamer, especially when the number of men carried to man them is considered. The guns cannot be spared, and it is proposed to transfer the armament of *Princess Ena* to the new vessel.

While Bayly had probably been asking for more than he expected to get, his instinct, that the latest breed of Q-ships must be provided with a much heavier armament than *Prince Charles* or the other existing decoys had been given, was a sound one.

Hitherto the employment of Q-ships had not provoked any comment from Germany or the neutral powers, but in August, 1915, two international incidents developed which gave the whole matter of Q-ships such wide publicity that they could no longer be considered a secret. On 12th August the Danish ambassador to the Court of St James, Mr H. Grevenkop Castenskiold, called the attention of Sir Edward Grey, the English Foreign Secretary, to a communication which he had had from the German Government. At 11 a.m. that day a U-boat had stopped a steamer of about 800 tons flying the Danish flag about twenty miles east of the Firth of Forth. Suddenly the ship had opened fire on the submarine, lowering the Danish flag after the first round and hoisting the British Naval ensign after the fifth or sixth round.

Admiralty investigations established that the White Ensign had been run up at the right time, before the first shot had been fired, and false colours struck at the same moment. The Danish flag had not been flown during the action. Either the personnel of the U-boat had been badly flurried by the incident or the Germans were trying to make propaganda capital out of the incident, as they certainly did out of another incident just afterwards, an encounter between *Baralong* and *U.27*.

The indefatigable Herbert had steamed 12,000 miles in his ship since 1st April, 1915, and his lack of success hitherto may have made him all the more determined to act quickly, perhaps too quickly, once his opportunity came. At 3 p.m. on 19th August, 1915, he was steering East (Magnetic) in Latitude 50°22′ North, Longitude 8°7′ West, in the hope that he would fall in with an enemy submarine (actually *U.24*) which had that morning sunk the 15,801-ton White Star passenger liner *Arabic* off the south-west coast of Ireland with the loss of forty-five lives. It was a sinking that inflamed public opinion in America as well as in Britain, and angered the men of the *Baralong* as much as it did others. His ship was flying the Stars and Stripes of the neutral U.S.A. What followed became the subject of one of the most intense controversies of the war, so it is worth quoting his official report, which like all the Q-ship material remained an official secret until a few years ago.

> My attention was called to a large steamer about nine miles off, bearing S.W., making a large alteration of course. Almost immediately I received by W/T "S.O.S. being chased by enemy submarine, Lat. 50.22 N. Long. 8.12 W.," and altered course accordingly to S.W. ½ S., flying neutral colours. Between now and 3.25 p.m. the signals attached were exchanged.
>
> After steering S.W. ½ S. for two miles the submarine hove in sight about a point and a half on my port bow, approximately 7 miles distant, heading towards the *Nicosian* [the steamer stopped by the U-boat], both appeared to be stopped. When within 3 miles of the submarine I hoisted the International Signal VIC-QRA, meaning "Save life."
>
> The submarine now commenced to shell the *Nicosian* at a range of about 1,000 yards, approaching her victim all the time at slow speed, until at position 2 on attached diagram, when she called in her gun's crew, "Trimmed Down" a few feet, altered course towards me at a high speed for a few hundred yards. I then turned towards the *Nicosian's* boats which were four points on the starboard bow and stopped my engines.
>
> The submarine now gave herself a little more buoyancy, manned her gun again, and altered course, apparently with the idea of preventing me effecting a rescue. The moment she was out of sight behind *Nicosian*, I struck the neutral colours and hoisted the White Ensign, and trained two guns just in front of that

vessel's bow, ready for the next appearance of the submarine, which I knew would be at close range.

In a few seconds she appeared 600 yards off, and Sub-Lieutenant G. C. Steele, R.N.R., in charge of the guns and their disguise, carried out his duties admirably; and I consider it largely due to his smartness that we received no shot from the enemy . . .

The Marines kept up an incessant rifle fire from the start and accounted for several of the gun's crew before it was possible for them to retaliate. Thirty-four twelve-pounder shells were fired, mostly taking effect, the second and third being hits on the water line under the conning tower. She heeled over about twenty degrees towards us, and the crew could be seen making every effort to save themselves by jumping overboard. She disappeared in a little over a minute, and shortly afterwards, two large volumes of air escaped to the surface, indicating that she had submerged for the last time.

The *Nicosian's* boats were now called alongside and whilst clearing the boats, I observed about a dozen Germans who had swum from their boat swarming up ropes' ends and the pilot ladder which had been left hanging down from *Nicosian.*

The action of 19th August, 1915.

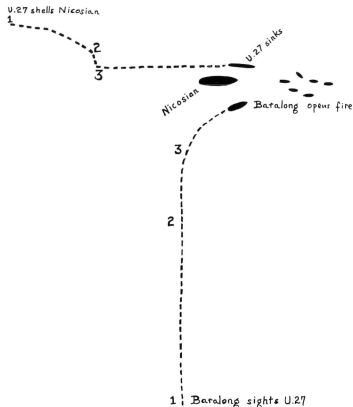

Fearing they might scuttle or set fire to the ship with her valuable cargo of mules and fodder, I ordered them to be shot away; the majority were prevented from getting on board, but six succeeded.

As soon as possible I placed my ship alongside and put a party of Marines on board under Corporal F. G. Collins, R.M.L.I.*, warning him to be careful of snipers in case they had found the rifles which I was informed by *Nicosian's* captain had been left in the charthouse.

A thorough search was made, which resulted in six of the enemy being found, but they succumbed to the injuries they had received from lyddite shell shortly afterwards and were buried at once.

The *Nicosian* had at least two shot holes in No. 1 hold below water line, and several above water line further aft, also one boiler damaged. I took her in tow at 6.20 p.m., and as she made no more water, though No. 1 hold was flooded, headed for Avonmouth, for which port she was bound, reporting same to Admiralty, via Land's End . . .

Lieutenant G. Swinney, R.N.R., the Master of this ship, has been invaluable, and with his careful navigation, coupled with the use of W/T, I have been able to destroy an enemy's submarine and save a valuable ship. In addition to the names mentioned in this despatch, I beg to submit for Their Lordships' consideration the conduct of Corporal Frederick G. Collins, R.M.L.I., No. 17036, in charge of the Marine Detachment, for his good leading and the expeditious manner in which he cleared the ship of the Germans with his men, an awkward job in an unknown ship.

The marksmanship of his Detachment was most telling and accurate when first engaging the submarine, as mentioned in my paragraph 1.

The enclosed cap ribbon is all that I could pick up. Note the submarine had no number but was apparently similar to *U.29*.[26]

This hurried despatch, in which Collins is mentioned twice, does not give any details about the deaths of the German submariners aboard *Nicosian*. The German authorities were to accuse Herbert of having had them killed in cold blood. The whole *Nicosian* affair was to be blown up into a Q-ship atrocity, as a counterpoise to the U-boat atrocities which had begun to accumulate since the beginning of the war.

The German accusations, made formally to Sir Edward Grey, the British Foreign Secretary, fell under two heads, one concerning the misuse of a neutral disguise, the other alleging a violation of the laws of humanity by the slaughter of surrendered prisoners.[27]

The *Nicosian*, a British ship belonging to the Leyland Line, was loaded with mules being shipped from America for use on the supply lines in Flanders, and with the mules were a number of American muleteers. After the *Nicosian's* return to America a number of these muleteers, together with a passenger and a seaman who claimed to have sailed in the *Baralong*, made sworn statements before the German ambassador to the United States and others about what they said they had seen during the *Baralong's* rescue of the *Nicosian*.[28]

The accounts given by these various people do not entirely agree one

*Royal Marine Light Infantry.

with another, and there is certainly serious cause to doubt the veracity of some of their statements, but their story of the death of Kapitän-Leutnant Wegener, the U-boat commander, and the survivors of his crew may be summarised as follows.

When the *Baralong*, flying the Stars and Stripes at the stern and with the same flag on large shields on her sides, had borne down on the *Nicosian* there was nothing about the Q-ship to indicate that she was a warship. However, she soon belied her peaceful appearance and the signal she was flying by opening fire, the American flag still flying from her ensign staff; it kept flying, the witnesses said, until the rifle fire had ceased.

As the submarine was hit by shells from the *Baralong* and began to sink the commander and some of the crew sprang overboard, "the seamen having first removed their clothes." Some reached the *Nicosian* and clambered aboard, but others could do no more than seize the ropes left hanging down when the steamer's boats were lowered, and those men were killed by rifle fire from the crew of the *Baralong* and by shellfire, according to the sworn statements made by those who had escaped in the *Nicosian*'s boats. Then, they said, the *Baralong* steamed alongside the *Nicosian*, made fast to her, and sent a search party aboard to find those Germans who had clambered aboard. Two of the witnesses said they heard Herbert give a definite order to his men to "take no prisoners."

One of the witnesses, Larimore Holland, the man who claimed to have served in the *Baralong*, gave a graphic account of how the U-boat commander was killed. "After our crew boarded the *Nicosian*," he said, "we found the only one of the crew who had escaped on the deck, and as stated found him to be the commander of the submarine. Our captain and others of our crew asked him for information concerning other German submarines. He refused to give such information. He was also asked if his submarine had sunk the *Arabic*. I do not remember certainly his reply.

"He was commanded to stand back and hold up his hands," Holland went on. "He asked . . . 'What for you shoot?' One of our marines, known as our engineer, fired one shot from his pistol into the body of the German commander."

Others of the witnesses told a different story, saying that Wegener escaped to the bows of the *Nicosian*, dived into the water and swam round the bows. Though he raised his hands in the water as a sign of surrender he was shot at least twice, once in the mouth and once in the neck, by English seamen aboard the *Nicosian*.

Holland's story of how he came to join the *Baralong* is a curious one. He said that on arriving at Liverpool from America he had been persuaded to join the Royal Navy, giving a false name and a Canadian address. After serving aboard Jellicoe's flagship H.M.S. *Iron Duke* and in the *Victory* he was shifted to a ship the name of which he did not know. It seemed to be an old merchant ship, disguised and carrying guns, and he was later told it was called the *Baralong*.

Accounts of how the shooting of the German submariners was carried out varied wildly between the witnesses. One of them, James J. Curran, whose Irish name may explain his picturesque use of detail, and perhaps a political bias as well, says the massacre was headed by the ship's carpenter of the *Nicosian*, who levelled his revolver at the cringing German sailor before him and shot him in cold blood. The *Nicosian's* engineer was said to have accounted for another German.

One of the witnesses, Charles D. Hightower, claimed to have seen one of the British Marines wearing a wrist watch and shoes taken from one of the dead Germans; other witnesses spoke of the Germans, apart from Wegener himself, having been naked when they reached the *Nicosian*.

What happened aboard the *Nicosian* that August day seems likely to remain for ever one of the great mysteries of the sea. In the eyes of a fellow officer, Herbert appeared little better than the perpetrator of a massacre. "Griff," to give this officer his pseudonym, had been first lieutenant aboard the Majestic-class battleship H.M.S. *Mars*. He wrote:

> It would be difficult to give a correct account of what followed. One account depicts a terrible scene when the British Marines rushed at the Germans with iron bars, and in more than one case strangled the murderous Germans who had so wantonly fired on a defenceless passenger steamer. The ghastly fight continued in the tunnel leading from the engine room to the stoke-hold, where the furnace doors were thrown open, and the Germans pitched headlong into the flames. Another account describes the British Marines discovering the German sailors in the *Nicosian's* engine room drying their wet clothes over the hot steam pipes, and before they could escape, fired into them at close range, until every German had paid the penalty for their murderous crime.[29]

The official Royal Navy account is even more damning in its absence of exoneration.

> A number of Germans got on board. The danger of losing the ship therefore continued and as soon as possible Lieutenant-Commander Herbert placed his ship alongside the *Nicosian*, and ordered a party of Marines to board her and recover possession . . . The Germans were nowhere to be seen. They had made no signs of surrender, and in the chart-house rifles and ammunition had been left readily accessible. He therefore warned the men to be on their guard against surprise and to be careful to get in the first shot. Over what happened next he had no control. It would seem that after a short search the Germans were found in the engine room, and the Marines in hot blood, and believing that they had to do with the men who had so wantonly sunk the *Arabic* in the morning, shot them all at sight.[30]

A sketch made by Commander G. C. Steele, V.C., then a sub-lieutenant and First Lieutenant of the *Baralong*, showing the *U.27* clearing the bows of the *Nicosian* and being struck by shells from the *Baralong's* guns, one of which is visible in the left foreground.

As the varying nature of these accounts would suggest, the story of the *Baralong* had lost nothing in the telling. By the time "Griff" and Sir Julian Corbett wrote it had become part of the folklore of the First World War.

Yet the incident of 19th August, 1915, can only be understood in the context of the Q-ship war and of the feelings engendered by the war as a whole. The sinking of the Cunard liner *Lusitania* by *U.20* with the loss of no fewer than 1,198 men, women and children ten miles south of the Old Head of Kinsale on 7th May, 1915, caused enormous and world-wide revulsion and anger.

> This unspeakable outrage inflamed the minds of the *Baralong's* crew [says Commander G. C. Steele, R.N., who as a young R.N.R. officer was First Lieutenant of the *Baralong*]. It was just the culminating point of a long series of minor violations of war, and inhuman practices . . . it just required the sight of those silent figures of drowned children from the *Lusitania*, as they were laid out on the front at Queenstown in a temporary mortuary to rouse the deepest hatred in the *Baralong's* crew, composed as they were of a mixed collection—naval, mercantile, and marine ratings—who had never so hated before. A meeting was held . . . and it was agreed to avenge the *Lusitania* by giving no quarter to German submarine crews.[31]

That mood of brooding anger had not subsided when on 19th August a wireless operator ran to the bridge of the *Baralong* and handed to Godfrey Herbert a distress message from the *Arabic* saying she had been torpedoed about eighty miles from Queenstown and required immediate assistance. News of the sinking of another passenger vessel caused that anger to boil up, and when the Marines boarded the *Nicosian* there can be little doubt that they believed they were engaged in an act of revenge against an enemy who had "sunk an unarmed, outward bound steamer" and "taken no part in rescue work, but had steamed callously among the survivors," to quote Commander Steele's account.

> They spread out, took occasional cover and, seeing here and there some German figures crouching behind hatches, winches, or anything else, opened fire. The Germans scattered and fled. The captain of the submarine locked himself in a deck cabin; the corporal pursuing him battered down the door with the butt of his rifle. But the captain escaped through the port and slid down to fall into the sea, whereupon the corporal shot him through the head whilst the fugitive was swimming off. Our boarding party, with cries of "*Lusitania!*" shot four remaining Germans at fairly long range. The ship was unlit down below and it was not possible to ascertain whether these men were armed or not at the time, for they were discovered in dark passages and the engine room.

Twenty years after the incident when tempers had cooled sufficiently Commander Herbert also gave an account of what happened that day, describing the action which resulted in the *U.27* being sunk.

> The range had been about 600 yards, and of those Germans who did not go down in the submarine, most were killed by gun or rifle. The *Nicosian's* boats were now called alongside. Captain C. H. Manning, master of the *Nicosian,* joined me on the bridge and told me he had a cargo of 700 or 800 mules for the British Government. Whilst we were talking, my signalman called attention to the fact that several of the sunken submarine's crew were trying to climb aboard *Nicosian* by means of ropes and the pilot ladder which had been left hanging down. Fearing that, if these men succeeded in getting aboard, they might set the large amount of fodder alight, I ordered them to be shot away. In spite of this, six reached the *Nicosian's* deck, but the rest flopped back.
>
> Instead of going to a prominent place on the upper deck and holding up their hands in surrender, these six darted down below and left me no option but to assume they were about to destroy the steamer; so I turned the *Baralong* round and went up alongside her (You can imagine from this how calm it was!). Sending for Corporal F. G. Collins, in charge of my Marines, I told him to take his men on board and clear the ship of the enemy; warning him that the latter would be desperate men, that he was to take no chances but shoot first. Captain Manning had just informed me that in the latter's charthouse were some rifles and ammunition, so I told Collins these might already be in the six men's hands.
>
> A few minutes later, the *Nicosian's* chief engineer and carpenter came and asked me if they could go down and ascertain what damage had been done by German shells, and possibly the dynamo (which had been shut off before abandoning ship) might be restarted. I advised them that if they went aboard, they

must be careful to keep out of the Marines' way, who undoubtedly would shoot them unless properly recognised. Assuring me they would go down the engine room escape, and get the lights on first, they made straight below and found that the door of the propeller shaft alley had been shut. On opening it, they observed two or three hiding Germans huddled up at the end. Without further ado, these were shot. Meanwhile the Marines continued their search and found the remainder, who, in default of surrender, were put to death likewise, and buried at once.

Later on, both in Germany and America, much criticism was made concerning this shooting; but it should be remembered that the shots were made in what one might call the heat of battle. I was influenced by the knowledge that if we were to save the *Nicosian*, we must do so with all speed. Further, during this period when we lay stopped and alongside, I was expecting any moment to have the *Baralong* torpedoed; for I still kept in mind Captain Manning's signal "Captured by *two* submarines." Evidently he was wrong. Only U.27 was there.[32]

"This is the plain and unvarnished story of the *Baralong*, which in spite of having taken place years ago is still very vivid in my mind," said Commander Herbert, who had good cause to remember the events of that day. To judge from his own account, there was a certain amount of disquiet at the Admiralty over those events, and over the political consequences.

The action between *Baralong* and *U.27* was a turning point in the Q-ship war. Its success convinced the Admiralty that Q-ships could dispose of submarines, and perhaps prevented the resumption of the old British submarine and Q-ship partnership until it was too late to be effective. The publicity attached to the *Baralong* affair made the Q-ship anything but a secret weapon. It increased the difficulties of the Special Service by making it a hundred times more difficult to tempt a U-boat into range than it had been before.

U-boat commanders received orders which set out exactly how they should act in their campaign against shipping in the War Zone, which Germany had declared to be all waters around Great Britain and Ireland, including the whole English Channel.

The first consideration is the safety of the U-boat. Consequently, rising to the surface in order to examine a ship must be avoided for the sake of the boat's safety, because, apart from the danger of a possible surprise attack by enemy ships, there is no guarantee that one is not dealing with an enemy ship even if it bears the distinguishing marks of a neutral. The fact that a steamer flies a neutral flag, and even carries the distinguishing marks of a neutral, is no guarantee that it is actually a neutral vessel. Its destruction will therefore be justifiable unless other attendant circumstances indicate its neutrality.[33]

The principal effect of the *Baralong's* sinking of the *U.27* was not a strategic but a psychological one. Though not an atrocity, it looked like one, the principal British "atrocity" of the First World War. The average

U-boat commander, as Admiral Sims was later to point out, was neither a murderer nor a sadist. In this imperfect world, most German submarine commanders were very good fellows, men whom their opposite numbers in the Royal Navy said they would like to meet, and shake hands with, after the war.[34] Yet the *Baralong* business seemed a ready-made justification to the type of U-boat commander who was not chivalrous, kindly, and considerate for any attack on civilian or neutral shipping, any bad treatment of the crew of a torpedoed ship, and any reprisal on the Special Service men, if they were ever so unfortunate as to fall into enemy hands.

One of the *Baralong's* concealed guns, and in the foreground two of the ship's complement of Marines, dressed in civilian clothes. From *Q-Ships and Their Story*.

CHAPTER FOUR

The Gathering of the Fleets

PAINFULLY AWARE that his name had become so associated with British "atrocities" that one high-ranking German officer had stopped talking about "the English" and instead always said "the Baralonglanders," Lieutenant-Commander Herbert addressed a submission to the Admiralty. His *Remarks on the Anti-Submarine Campaign* of 23rd August, 1915, stressed the necessity of having more ships armed on similar lines to the *Baralong*.

> Since April she has frequently been lying at anchor in Falmouth, close to foreign merchantmen, mostly Dutch, but there is nothing about her which under the closest scrutiny, will discover any guns. Tramp steamers are most suitable for this work . . . In the case of *Lyons* or *Princess Ena* anyone alongside can see what they are. Decoy ships should have a single aerial and at least two call signs each too prevent to much repetition in one day of the same call sign. A single aerial because it is unnoticeable and although not so efficient, will receive quite far enough any "S.O.S." which a 10 knot ship will be able to cope with. The guns should all be aft for the following reasons.
>
> (a) They will be expected forward in a Government Armed Vessel. (b) The poop is more suitable for concealing. (c) If forward there is a great temptation to open fire at an outside range, also in bad weather they will be most likely covered in spray and circuits made defective. (d) Being together they come under one officer. (e) Guns' crews living under poop are always handy and have not got to run about the ship, possibly giving rise to suspicion.
>
> Decoy vessels must be able to prevent any Patrol Boat or Man-of-War from proceeding to the same "S.O.S." as himself, as if this happens the submarine will dive on sighting the latter. About 10 Marines, good rifle shots, should form part of the crew.
>
> A motor boat is essential for each ship for these reasons.
>
> (1) Communication with the shore without resorting to use of Service boats.
>
> (2) To enable the Commanding Officers to proceed direct to the Senior Naval Officer on arrival, often a laborious proceeding in a ship's lifeboat when anchored 2 or 3 miles from a landing place, against strong tide, such as Milford Haven, Falmouth, Queenstown.
>
> (3) Salving gear at sea. Had *Baralong* had a motor boat she could have brought in quite a lot of valuable wreckage.
>
> (4) Had two submarines, as reputed, been attacking *Nicosian* a motor boat armed with a depth boat bomb would probably have been the means of saving both ships . . . The foregoing remarks are submitted for consideration. They are based on my experience after being in two classes of Decoy Vessels and steaming 15,000 miles almost entirely in the area between Long. 6° and 12° between the latitudes of Fastnet and Ushant.

Herbert also stressed the unsuitability of both *Lyons* and *Princess Ena*, particularly the latter: "She having already fired on a German Submarine, it is probable when the latter dived he came fairly close and got a description of the vessel which is now circulated to all their submarines."

The Admiralty obviously did listen to such suggestions. They had already promoted Herbert, following a suggestion of Sir Lewis Bayly's that promotion should follow success. Herbert had also been decorated and those members of the crew of the *Baralong* who were not commissioned R.N. personnel had in addition to any decorations they received been awarded a grant of £1,000 to be divided among them. This was the "full grant," while a "special grant" of £300 was paid when the sinking had been a doubtful one. *Baralong* had been placed under Bayly's orders the week after she had sunk *U.27*. Herbert felt he had done all he could in her, and was given a new ship, but *Baralong* was kept in commission as she was felt to be good bait.

Not surprisingly the success of *Baralong* brought more demands for Q-ships from the admirals. The Q-ship fleet began to expand rapidly, and only contracted in the first months of 1918. On the very day of the action with *U.27*, Admiral Sir Stanley Colville had asked the Admiralty for "a large number of merchant ships, of all sorts and sizes" to be sent to the trade routes, particularly those infested with submarines. The officers should be carefully selected from the active list, not R.N.R., and the guns' crews should be specially selected active service men. The armament of the ships should be four twelve-pounders, carefully hidden, and all the work of disguising the ships should be carried out away from a dockyard or a commercial port so as to ensure secrecy. The ships could be used for carrying coal, stores, etc., to the fleet, but before entering any commercial port the guns would have to be dismounted and stowed away. "It is imperative," concluded Colville, "that something be done, and done quickly, to stop the immunity with which submarines are now sinking vessels and cargoes worth millions."

Rear-Admiral Oliver's reaction to this submission was that it was impossible to take so many vessels out of trade, but he picked up Colville's suggestion, almost a new idea, that the work of a decoy could be combined with that of an ordinary carrier. Decoys could carry cargoes, but carry them through areas of maximum danger. The scheme might be begun with Grand Fleet colliers, oilers, and store ships, as well as with the mechanical transport ships running between Avonmouth and Rouen. "A limited number of 'free lances'," Oliver wrote, "can be arranged. The 'free lances' could be small cheap ships of coasting steamer type, and a few timber ships in North Sea."

Admiral Sir Arthur "Tug" Wilson voiced the pessimism that many still felt about Q-ships. "I do not know how many decoys Admiral Colville has equipped," he commented, "but they have only found one submarine so far, and *Baralong* steamed 12,000 miles before meeting her." He added that transport ships would have to be commanded by naval officers to have any effect.

The discussion over Colville's submission led to the Director of Transport being approached to obtain two tramp steamers. They were to be bought through shipbrokers and armed secretly, not in an Irish port. Only one confidential book was to be allowed them, M.V.3, the kind of code book a mercantile vessel ought to have. Oliver's next words show he had been impressed by Herbert's advice. "These two vessels can be given two call signs each . . . and should be fitted with Wireless Transmitter (single aerial). They should have a motor boat and a depth bomb."

Colville was told it was not possible to supply all the ships he had asked for, owing to the great shortage of tonnage for other purposes, but that four small coasting steamers and four lumber steamers of the Scandinavian type should be taken up in Northern ports, secretly armed and manned from Grand Fleet resources. These should be used solely as decoys, but Grand Fleet colliers might act the decoy on passage to and from the fleet. "Judging by the number of Fleet Colliers which have been already lost, this arrangement should prove productive of success."[35] The guns and mountings should be unshipped and concealed before the colliers entered a commercial port, such as Cardiff. The two mechanical transport ships would require a naval officer, not in command, in addition to the master, "and the same ratings, guns, etc. as *Baralong*, in fact be exactly on the same lines except that they will continue to carry out their transport duties and be commissioned. *Baralong* is only M.F.A.,[36] but should have been commissioned."

Considerable discussion went into these proposals for new types of decoys. Would it be possible to conceal the status of the mechanical transports as they plied out of Avonmouth, Gloucestershire? Should colliers be used as decoys when they were so urgently required? A collier spent only one-seventh of her life at sea; if thirty colliers were taken up their aggregate time at sea would only be equivalent to that spent by five vessels used exclusively on this service. The Director of Stores, M. M. Walker, pointed to the difficulty of preserving secrecy at commercial ports, and said that it would be much better to have from five to ten vessels which were exclusively decoys than have a number of part-time decoys. There would thus be far greater efficiency as an outcome of the constant training. New types of mystery ships were also proposed such as victualling carriers like the *Leicester*[37]. The only point on which there was unanimous agreement was that there must be more Q-ships.

By 5th September it had been decided to put down *Princess Ena* and

Lyons, another of Herbert's suggestions, and transfer their armaments to two suitable vessels under the command of the Admiral, Queenstown; and to take up four small coasting steamers and four small timber ships and to turn them over to the Commander-in-Chief, Grand Fleet, to man and arm solely as decoys. Two mechanical transports, *Chevington* and *Glendevon*, were also to be taken up, as had been already proposed.

The victory of the *Baralong* opened the floodgates to a mass of suggestions for new types of Special Service vessels. Jellicoe had already considered the use of a small oil tanker, but felt that it would be impossible to obtain or to spare such a ship. Lieutenant-Commander George Hartford, commanding H.M.S. *Acorn*, a destroyer serving in the 2nd Destroyer Flotilla, Grand Fleet, put forward a much more ambitious project for a large oil tanker, painted in U.S. colours and made unsinkable so far as possible, to be armed with concealed guns and to be deployed off the west coast of Ireland. An oiler was particularly well suited as a decoy, argued Hartford, as the vital part of the ship, the engine room, was well aft, and so she was less likely to be put out of action with a torpedo fired without warning.

Hartford followed this proposal with a more daring one for a Q-ship to be disguised as a derelict. She should lie with engines stopped in the submarine track in a position where the least shipping was likely to be found, should be trimmed down by the bows and should look like an abandoned ship, with no one on deck. A submarine which approached her would take her for a half-sunk vessel left by another U-boat and, rather than waste a torpedo, would try to sink her with a bomb.

These proposals were considered to be inappropriate, partly because they called for a neutral disguise; yet it was under an American flag that *Baralong* had scored her first resounding success. That same vessel, under her new name of *Wyandra* and with a new commander, Lieutenant-Commander A. Wilmot-Smith, R.N., was very soon to score a second victory no less significant.

Between 9.45 a.m. and 7.20 p.m. on 23rd September, 1915, the *U.41* under Kapitän-Leutnant Claus Hansen sank three steamers south-east of the Fastnet, and Vice-Admiral Sir Lewis Bayly ordered Wilmot-Smith in the *Wyandra* to proceed to the area. Sixty-seven miles south-west by west of the Bishop Rock Wilmot-Smith sighted a steamer lying stopped and blowing off steam. It was the Wilson Line steamer *Urbino*, under attack by *U.41*.

Endeavouring to tempt the U-boat within range, Wilmot-Smith altered course to the southward after seeing her submerge when the *Wyandra* was still five miles away. Hansen in *U.41* took the bait, and after steaming towards the Q-ship submerged, rose to the surface and

Portsmouth, asking for large sailing Q-ships to be used at the entrance to the Channel, off the south-west coast of Ireland, along the Spanish coast, in the Mediterranean, and in the North Sea. He pointed out that sailing ships could keep at sea in all weathers, were fast in a moderate breeze and very seaworthy. They would also appear easier prey than a steamer to a U-boat, which would approach a sailing vessel with less caution than it would a tramp. Another advantage of the sailing ship lay in the fact that she could not be detected by a submarine's hydrophones.

The kind of sailing vessels that Hammond wanted were wooden ships of the kind built in Nova Scotia and North America. He suggested pairs of ships, one a schooner, the other square rigged, and nothing less than 1,000 tons register. "These large schooners," he wrote, "are very handy craft and very fast on a wind, and carry a very small crew for their size. They should be ballasted to a good sailing trim, the remaining holds stowed tightly with a very light kind of lumber, or preferably bales of cork. This would make them practically unsinkable, even if torpedoed." As armament Hammond suggested "a twelve-pounder underneath the forecastle, with ports easily manipulated and capable of firing on each bow, a similar gun aft under the poop, firing astern and on each quarter, another on the boat deck abaft the mainmast, screened on either side by dummy boats, and capable of firing on either side. A few depth charges might be added. They should be fitted with wireless, which, with their tall masts, could easily be so constructed that it could not be seen. They should also be fitted with two powerful acetylene searchlights for use in case a submarine was sighted at night on the surface."

So much was the sailing decoy in the air at this time, and so little of a mystery was the mystery ship, that a private shipowner even wrote to the Admiralty suggesting that they should take up one of his ships. Mr E. O. Roberts, of Jones, Roberts & Co., Liverpool, wrote in September, 1915, to explain the good points of his three-masted schooner *Tecwyn* as a decoy. He had as good an eye for these points as any admiral, as his enumeration of them shows.

> It is not so much from the presence of the motor on board where I think that the utility of the vessel would come in, but from the fact that a very powerful gun could in my opinion be placed in the wheelhouse aft, which wheelhouse could be considerably enlarged and whilst not allowing the gun to be seen, the top portion could be made collapsible and to fall down in the matter of a few seconds.

Obviously this enumeration of the good points of *Tecwyn* was not merely intuitive; Roberts must have heard someone talking about what was needed in a sailing Q-ship. He even went so far as to assure the Admiralty that the schooner would stand up to the recoil of a gun, because she was stronger in her plates and scantlings than Lloyd's

The barquentine *Rentoul*, otherwise known as *Pamela* or *Resolute*, a vessel which was nearly half a century old when taken over for use as a Q-ship in 1918. From *Q-Ships and Their Story*.

requirements. She had been built by his father-in-law and he had supervised her building.

> I feel sure that if this vessel were to cruise about around the Fastnet, or on the fringe of the Bay of Biscay, with a hidden gun in her wheelhouse and appearing ostensibly as an ordinary trader, she would give a good account of herself, particularly so if the submarine, learning that she was a motor vessel, would be very likely inclined to stop her with a view of replenishing his fuel supply.

Offered *Tecwyn* and another sailing vessel, the *Gleniffer*, Vice-Admiral Bayly chose *Tecwyn*, because *Gleniffer* had too deep a draught for small harbours on the south coast of Ireland. The *Tecwyn* was taken up and a captain and crew were arranged. She was to be fitted out at Portmadoc, an old slate-shipping port in North Wales, and armed at Haulbowline, the island dockyard in Queenstown harbour. In the midst of all this preparation it was discovered that *Tecwyn* was too small to take two twelve-pounder guns, while if two six-pounders were used as an alternative they would have to be concealed in an enormous deckhouse. "This would be a large and unusual type of deck erection for a vessel of this size, and . . . as a disguise, it would not be effective." So the plan to convert *Tecwyn* was dropped.

The proposals to fit out the new vessels had certainly helped to clarify the Admiralty's ideas about sailing decoys. They looked at a proposal to use Dungeness pilot boats, and noted that "Three Fishing Smacks are now being used for much the same purpose elsewhere."[38] They were doubtful about wireless "as it is so apparent through a pair of good glasses. I would suggest pigeons if considered necessary, or else W/T with the aerial always down during daylight hours."

"This suggestion is worth considering", commented Rear-Admiral Oliver. "Schooners or brigantines would probably be best for the purpose. We have a sailing vessel working in the North Sea, and also one off S. W. Ireland, both with motors also, but so far they have not had a chance."

Vice-Admiral Bayly wrote on 19th October, 1915: "I entirely agree with the principle of disguised armed ships as the best means of sinking submarines. The armed yachts, sloops and trawlers are excellent for protection of trade, rescuing crews and passengers, escorting, etc., but except in thick weather or at night, their chance of getting close to a submarine is small. What at first is not apparent, though very real, is that the appearance of our sloops, armed yachts, and trawlers very often frighten the submarines away from the area in which they are working, and save the ships which are in, or approaching, that area, though none except the submarine knows or will know that such a thing has happened."

One final point about this interchange of views regarding sailing vessels must be noted. Referring to *Tecwyn*, Oliver wrote: "If he desires the vessel she will be shown as a yacht attached to Q[ueenstown] commissioned in order to satisfy international requirements." This comment shows that the Admiralty now felt that the earlier, uncommissioned Q-ships had been illegal under international law, while the mention of the letter "Q" may be the origin of the famous Q-ship nomenclature adopted subsequently.

With the sailing ships temporarily out of view, interest centred on the conversion of the mechanical transports *Glendevon* and *Chevington*. Though listed by Dittmar and Colledge in their *British Warships 1914–1919* as colliers, these ships had undoubtedly been used for trooping, as the modifications made to them show. On the poop, under which "troops, not cargo, are carried," a steel gun platform four feet square was built. On the platform a gun was mounted, concealed by a deckhouse 7 foot 6 inches high.

> Deckhouse will be made of 1″ deals, tongued and grooved, stiffened by 3″ and 3½″ grounds, it will be hinged at half the height (3′ 9″ above deck) and will therefore leave a 9″ coaming above working platform of gun. The two sides and after end will hinge down ... The hinged portions of deckhouse can be secured together inside by wire and released by a slip.

In the proposed position, the poop gun had an arc of training of 70° forward of the beam on each side and right around the stern. The poop was supported from beneath by four pillars of six-inch channel bar at the four corners of the box, bracketed to beams. The gun crew, and a small lock-up magazine, were accommodated under the poop "without cutting out any trooping accommodation now in use". Like so many converted Q-ships, the two mechanical transports were a masterpiece of ingenious craftsmanship. Unfortunately, as with so many Q-ships, this ingenuity never bore any results, and one is left wondering whether the effort might not have been better spent in other directions.

The two transports were each to have a mercantile crew and navigating captain, enlisted under form T.124, who were to serve alongside naval ratings. The latter included one gunlayer 3rd. class, three seaman ratings, trained in gunnery, and one R.N.R. W/T operator. Lieutenant-Commander Horace W. Tatham was to command *Glendevon* and Lieutenant Colin S. Thomson, *Chevington*. The two commanders were ordered to take over command if a submarine was sighted, or a signal received indicating one was in the vicinity of the ship, "but it is to be distinctly understood that on the passage *from* England to France with mechanical transport, or other military requirements on board, the *Glendevon/Chevington* is not to be diverted from her course solely with the view of engaging an enemy submarine. On her passage from France to England, the *Glendevon/Chevington* will also act as a decoy ship for enemy submarines."

Tatham and Thomson were given the usual Q-ship orders. They were to hoist the White Ensign before firing, and to withhold their fire till the U-boat was so close that it was a sure target. "You will understand that it is very important that any engagement should be successful, and that an engagement that is likely to be unsuccessful—unless in an extreme emergency it is undertaken for self defence against an enemy submarine—is to be avoided.[39] . . . You are to impress on the crew the vital necessity of absolute secrecy on the subject of the engagement and point out the disciplinary consequences of any infraction of your instructions on this subject." Obviously the Admiralty had become aware that a strict injunction to secrecy was not enough. Cell punishment had to be held over the heads of those who might talk and thus imperil the safety of the whole ship.

The decision to run two Q-ships on a fixed route smacked of a return to the old blunder of the *Vienna/Antwerp*. Tatham and Thomson could not hurry to the scene of a sinking, yet that was exactly what the *Baralong* had done twice, with complete success. The route on which they sailed was sure to be well guarded by the destroyers, dropping their

76

Wasserbomben, which the men of the U-boats disliked so much.

Whether from selection of the wrong ships, or simply from bad luck, neither *Chevington* nor *Glendevon* ever sank a submarine or even came in sight of one. Perhaps they did not have a long enough trial, for when Tatham asked for an increase of armament in June, 1916, his request merely resulted in an Admiralty decision to pay off the two vessels as Q-ships, leaving the existing gun in place and treating them as armed transports. Yet another expensive experiment had come to an abortive end.

Meanwhile Herbert's advice to use tramps had been followed by the Admiralty. Those fitting out included some of the most famous of all Q-ships such as *Farnborough*, fitted out at Devonport. Originally called *Lodorer*, her name had to be changed when a telegram arrived from the Admiralty on 5th November, 1915: "Urgent. Anonymous letters have been received indicating that fact of *Lodorer* being armed and prepared for special service is known. I therefore submit that ship should leave here as *Lodorer* and change her name on passage to Queenstown." So *Lodorer* took the new name of *Farnborough*.

Other decoys fitted out at this time included the *Penshurst, Zylpha, Vala* and *Glen Isla*. Unfortunately these steamers had the sort of defects which one would expect to find in tramps. The *Glen Isla*, whose

The *Penshurst* at anchor. The bridge screen on the port side has been dropped, revealing one of the guns fitted on the bridge wings. From *Q-Ships and Their Story*.

A four-inch gun on the *Baron Rose*, formerly the American schooner *Samuel S. Thorp.*
Imperial War Museum

dimensions were only 250 feet by 32½ feet, 786 tons net, had a speed of only eight knots, very much less than that of a submerged submarine. The *Vala's* dimensions were 215 feet by 32 feet, 609 tons. When built as a collier more than twenty years earlier, *Vala* had had no great need of speed, but now that she was a Q-ship matters were different. When inspected early in 1916 the *Zylpha* displayed the usual deficiencies caused by a lifetime of neglect. The centre furnaces of the boilers were cracked through in several places, on the line of the fire bars.

In the fitting-out process the new decoys were given a much heavier armament than anything which had been contemplated thus far. *Zylpha* and *Lodorer* were armed with three and four twelve-pounders respectively, in addition to a Maxim. They were manned with a crew that was partly merchant, signed under T.124, and partly naval. Merchant officers were given a "step down" commission in the R.N.R. Thus a master became a lieutenant. "The Master should as a rule work the ship, the Naval Officer taking charge when an engagement is probable." Usually this arrangement worked well, though there were exceptions, such as Harold Auten and his mercantile second. All officers and men were forbidden to wear uniform, and in harbour had to endeavour to appear *bona fide* merchant service officers.

The dockyards exerted the greatest ingenuity to disguise the new mystery ships effectively and to fit their masked guns so that they could be brought into action within seconds of the order "Stand By. Let Go!" The dockyards felt that it was better to have a gun mounted aft rather than forward,

> as an excrescence on the forecastle is suspicious. A wheel house on the poop is good cover for a gun ... A form of concealment which has proved suitable, is a deckhouse with hinged sides. A coaming about two feet high is fixed permanently to the deck and the sides hinge to it, being kept in a vertical position by stays and slips which are let go when it is necessary to unmask the gun, the sides falling outwards on the deck. Shell and cartridge bags hang inside the coaming. Berthon boats[40] have been used to conceal guns and vegetable crates have also been used, but whatever device is used the guns must be effectively concealed from strangers in harbour as well as concealed from outside the ships at sea.

On 19th December, 1915, Colville wrote to the Admiralty from his flagship H.M.S. *Cyclops* announcing the completion of the latest merchant ship to be fitted out as a Special Service decoy ship, and sending profile sketches of each ship to show where the armament was placed. He warmly praised the work of Captain A. Farrington and Mr J. Legg, carpenter of the *Cyclops*, "in arranging suitable positions for the guns and accommodation for the guns' crews close to the guns, and also for the great ingenuity displayed in devising methods of hiding the gun, so that although absolutely invisible from the outside of the ship when close to, yet these guns can actually be in action in seven seconds."

Along with concealed guns and disguise went disguised wireless transmitters and one, perhaps two, wireless operators who could monitor S.O.S. calls continuously. Somewhat later *Penshurst* had an aerial made from 96 feet of copper wire, painted with anti-sulphuric paint, stretched to represent a triatic stay between the foremast and mainmast. The set had a range of 150 miles. A collier with engines aft like the *Penshurst* did not normally have a triatic stay.

Even at that stage the usefulness of Q-ships on some coasts and in bad weather was still doubted. On 5th October, 1915, Sir Robert Lowry, Admiral Commanding Coast of Scotland, Vice-Admiral E. E. Bradford, Vice-Admiral Sir David Beatty and Captain James Startin met in conference at Rosyth. They reported that they had concluded that it was much less possible to use decoys effectively at that time than in the previous two months, in that area which could be worked from the Firth of Forth. It was almost impossible to keep the fitting out of Q-ships secret in the Firth of Forth because neutral shipping was always passing through it.

In any case there were already two steamers, *Quickly* and *Gunner*, and one sailing vessel, the schooner *Ready*, fitted and armed as decoys and working from Granton. These were as many as the area could support, so they did not recommend the taking up of the three ships authorised by the Admiralty, the *T. G. Hutton*, *Webburn* and *Santa Cruz*.

This was a good example of the tail wagging the dog, as far as admirals and Admiralty were concerned. "Whilst concurring," wrote Jellicoe in reply, "in the view that the opportunities for the use of these vessels effectively from the Firth of Forth is less than in the summer months, I am of opinion that unless the enemy entirely abandon the submarine attack on commerce, it still affords one of the best ways of attacking submarines. As the trade route St Abb's Head—the Naze has been one on which enemy submarines have worked very freely, I consider that it is very desirable to carry out the original proposal to work more decoy ships from the Rosyth base, but in view of your objections, I have suggested to the Admiralty that only two should be added." Unfortunately the two that Jellicoe proposed to add were *Prince Charles*, which was unseaworthy, and *T. G. Hutton*, which proved to have no suitable positions for mounting guns.

How did unsuitable vessels such as *T. G. Hutton* ever get taken up in the first place? Graeme Thomson, the Director of Transport, explained how these ships got on the recommended list. "To preserve secrecy as far as possible the ships which were selected by this Department as being apparently suitable for the service were only inspected by this Department for general condition of hull and engines. The desirability of this procedure was shewn when the officer inspecting the *Santa Cruz* turned his attention to the deck houses, etc., and the master at once asked him whether the ship was to be a 'decoy duck'."

In an endeavour to increase the numbers of Q-ships in Scottish waters Jellicoe said that the Admiralty would provide a substitute for *Prince Charles*, or failing this, one of the Scapa ships would be sent from Orkney to Rosyth. "Unnecessary", he wrote, "to keep fully manned when no enemy submarines are operating. Practice here is to keep care and maintenance party on board and man fully when required for sea. Submarines may become active on the Naze route at any time."

A sparetime Q-ship did not seem a good idea, any more than another contemporary plan, later scouted by Oliver, of having Q-ships doubling as target practice ships. This, said Oliver, would merely reveal their real purpose to everyone.

Why was the Admiralty so keen to increase the number of Q-ships? The principal reason was that no one had as yet succeeded in thinking of any other plan for dealing with the U-boats. Results might be slender so far, but a slender reed to grasp at was better than none at all. So the Admiralty did its best to build Q-ship numbers, convinced as it was that this was Britain's only hope of survival in the face of the U-boats.

CHAPTER FIVE

The Year of Trial

THOSE WHO had wavered at the prospect of tying up so much strategic capital in the growing Q-ship fleets found their doubts diminished in the early months of 1916, as the mystery ships went into action on a number of occasions and on 22nd March sank another U-boat.

The successful Q-ship was *Farnborough*, commanded by the most famous of all the Special Service captains, Lieutenant-Commander Gordon Campbell. During a long life of broadcasting and writing about his experiences, Campbell might have been supposed to have told all he knew in print or on the air, but, like everyone else in the Special Service, his hands were tied by the Official Secrets Act and he could not quote from his own reports. Here is his own account of the sinking of *U.68*.

When in Lat. 51° 54′ N, Longitude 10° 53′ W., steering N. 27° W. (Mag.) 8 knots, a submarine's wash was observed about five miles distant on the port bow—it remained in view a few minutes and then dived. I maintained my course and speed. About 7 a.m. a torpedo was fired at the ship from the starboard quarter, and the bubbles rose under the forecastle, the torpedo evidently passing just ahead of the ship. I maintained my course and a few minutes later the submarine broke surface about 1,000 yards astern of the ship, passing from starboard to port. When on the port quarter, he fired a shot across our bows and partly submerged. I stopped, blew off steam, and ordered the stokers and spare men to abandon ship and panic under Engineer Temporary Sub-Lieutenant J. S. Smith, R.N.R.

The submarine closed to about 800 yards and a few minutes later fired a shell, which fell about 50 yards short. I ordered "Open fire" and hoisted the White Ensign, 21 rounds were fired from the three twelve-pounder guns, one gun under Temporary Sub-Lieutenant F. G. Russell, R.N.R, firing 13 rounds. About 200 rounds from the Maxim and rifles were also fired. The shooting was good, especially observing the range and bad light, several hits were observed before the submarine slowly disappeared. I then steamed full speed over the spot, and dropped a depth charge: the submarine came up about 10 yards off the ship in a nearly perpendicular position, being out of the water from the bow to abaft the conning tower.

No number was visible, but there was a large rent in her bow, and one periscope had apparently been hit. I opened fire again with the after gun, which put five rounds into the base of the conning tower at nearly point blank range, when she sank. I again went over the spot and let go two more depth charges. A very great quantity of oil, etc., and bits of wood came to the surface and covered the sea for some distance around.

"During the whole winter," commented Sir Lewis Bayly, "the *Farnborough* has faced the gales and has stuck to it, and never for a moment has Lieutenant-Commander Campbell wavered in the faith that he would get a chance. I have had a good deal to do with the ship and have found the same spirit throughout, being largely fostered by Lieutenant-Commander Campbell and his first Lieutenant, L. W. Beswick, R.N.R. . . . The ships here go on from day to day in all weather, always hoping, always trying."

Within a month, on 15th April, Campbell was in action again. While losing his U-boat, through no fault of his own, he managed to save the

Rear-Admiral Gordon Campbell, V.C., who as a captain was the most successful of all the Q-ship commanders. From *My Mystery Ships*.

ship she was attacking, the Dutch s.s. *Soerakarta*, whose Second Officer, R. F. F. Jeneson, gives us a good account of what a Q-ship looked like to an outsider, and particularly the impression made by her sudden transformation from tramp steamer into warship.

When near the South West Coast of Ireland, Lat. 52° 2' N., Long. 10° 53' W., suddenly a German submarine marked on his bow with a white "U" hoisted the German Navy flag and the signal "T.A.F." ("bring me your papers").

We stopped, lowered lifeboat Port No. 1, and would just advance slowly to tow the lifeboat near the submarine, when suddenly a shot was heard from a steamer who was already on the same course at a distance from us about two miles. The steamer was a tramp steamer with a white band on the funnel. More shots were heard and lightings seen coming from the starboard side in the midships. Also a machine gun was seen standing on the lower bridge, at first hidden by a lifeboat, which boat was now lowered.

Then I saw the submarine turn towards that steamer and shoot too, about five shots and I saw a Navy flag [White Ensign] hoisted at the steamer's fore masthead. Then suddenly a shell reached the turret of the submarine, the flags and sailors who were there disappeared, the sailors who stood near the guns tried to reach the turret. The submarine turned over, I saw his screws and A-frame, and then in 30 seconds the submarine disappeared, and the surface of the water was covered with a large patch of oil.

The U-boat, which had not been destroyed, owed her escape to a piece of incredibly bad luck for Campbell, as he related in his report.

As the submarine broke surface between us I took no notice until she hoisted a signal, which I could not read—I then stopped and blew off steam, but kept jogging ahead to edge in and avoid falling into the trough of the heavy swell. At this time the submarine was laying full length on the surface, with no one visible but two guns on deck. In addition to having my answering pendant at the dip, I hoisted the signal: "Cannot understand your signal." She then closed towards me and manned

A crude sketch of a Q-ship made by a neutral observer, redrawn from ADM 137/1933. With the sketch was this explanation: "I Behind this lifeboat was a machine gun, aft was also a gun. III Opening in the bunker in which was a black gun…"

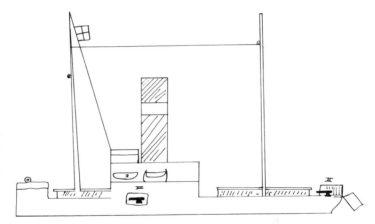

the foremost gun. In the meantime I turned out the bridge boat and gave my "papers" to Engineer Sub-Lieutenant Smith, R.N.R., to take over to the submarine. At this time—6.40—he fired a shot which passed over the ship. Unfortunately one of my guns, thinking that we had fired, opened fire. This forced my hand and I had at once to give the general order to open fire, the range being about 900 to 1,000 yards. At the same time I proceeded full speed ahead to bring the after gun to bear. Altogether, 20 rounds were fired from the twelve-pounders, six from the six-pounders and about 250 from Maxim and rifles. Of these I consider that there were three good hits ... The *Farnborough* was rolling between 5° and 10° which made the firing rather slow.

Bayly decided that in view of the report, the U-boat was a ninety per cent possible, and arranged for the reward of the usual £1,000 to the vessel and for "six days' leave to be given to each watch of *Farnborough* at Plymouth, commencing about 16th May. It is undesirable to allow Special Service vessels to give short leave in the ports near which they operate, as it is not possible to prevent the men's conversation giving away the nature of their employment."

With this action, one of those lulls which punctuated the Q-ship campaigns set in. It was caused by the German High Command's decision to return to warning before sinking steamers, and it was to last till 6th October, 1916. Good use was made of the lull to recondition the existing Q-ships and to intensify the training of their crews. New decoys were also taken up, because nobody knew how long the struggle was going to last. Nor had anyone as yet devised a counter to the U-boat more efficient than the Q-ship.

Constant patrolling throughout the winter had not improved the condition of the Queenstown fleet. On *Vala* the steering frame was defective and the engines generally needed an overhaul. The high pressure slide valves in *Penshurst's* main engine, together with her reducing valves, were so defective that she found great difficulty in going astern. Her boilers required scaling and cleaning, and the engines cried aloud for attention. Her bottom was so covered with weeds that her speed had been reduced to a mere five knots, three knots less than that of a submerged submarine. *Zylpha's* furnace needed replacing.

> These Special Service vessels [Bayley wrote on 12th April] should have an excellent chance of success on the Coast of Ireland station; but it is necessary that they shall be in a highly efficient condition, both as regards material and personnel. The delay necessary to refit them is therefore time well spent. Unless the machinery and guns are in easy working condition and the crew thoroughly drilled they are much more likely to be sunk by a submarine than to sink one.

While pressing on with minor improvements, such as fitting a half-kilowatt Marconi wireless set with silent receiving cabinet, powered from a Robey dynamo set, to *Vala*, Bayly also proceeded to tackle his main problem, that there were too many unsuitable ships in the Queenstown fleet. He put down *Glen Isla*, which had been built as long ago as 1878 and, like many another mystery ship, was not up to her work, as she had shown since she had been allocated to Bayly on 28th December, 1915. On a passage between Rathlin Island and Queenstown in strong westerlies and moderate gales she had only made five and a half knots, so that her cruising speed was probably six or seven knots, not enough to follow a submerged submarine. Bayly suggested that she should be returned to trade as a collier, in view of her many defects, due to old age, and the damage to her rudder. She was old-fashioned in appearance and unlikely to attract the attention of enemy vessels. "Being slow and unhandy," he wrote, "she is more likely to be sunk by them than to sink any enemy ship which came near her."

Permission was given to put down *Glen Isla*, and her armament was transferred to *Farnborough*. Campbell's command now had five twelve-pounders, two six-pounders, and a Maxim. "The value of a vessel of this type," wrote Bayly, "is entirely dependent on the promptness of bringing the guns to bear and the accuracy of aim; there are no second chances."

The replacement for *Glen Isla*, which Bayly had wished might be a faster and a newer ship, of ten knots at least, turned out to be *Vala*. Built twenty years before the outbreak of the First World War, she had a length of 215 feet, a beam of 32 feet and a net tonnage of 609. So she was smaller than *Glen Isla*, but no faster, as she had a speed of only eight knots. The Admiralty was aware of all her defects, but nonetheless proposed to give her "another chance in the South."

The idea of a buoyant Q-ship which would sink very slowly if torpedoed had been raised more than once. It was now pressed forward by Rear-Admiral Henry Oliver, Chief of the War Staff, in the spring and autumn of 1916. "If approved to have more decoy ships," he wrote, "I think some trouble should be taken to make them unsinkable, and they should be loaded with empty barrels and timber."

The call for more Q-ships had arisen partly in connection with a submission of Captain Richard Webb, Acting Director of the Trade

The *Penshurst* at sea, from *Q-Ships and Their Story*. It will be seen that her appearance differs from that seen on page 77; here the mizzen mast and topmasts have been removed and a white band has been painted on the funnel. The bridge screens conceal guns, and so does the boat on the main hatch, which is a dummy.

Division, Admiralty War Staff, on 9th March, 1916, on *The protection of British Seaborne Trade*. During the previous weeks, he said, trade had come to a complete halt due to the detention of about seventy British and Allied merchant vessels and forty transports in port owing to the presence of U-boats off the mouth of the Channel. This meant that practically all west-going trade was removed, and only homecoming vessels and neutrals were passing through the area. As this sector had practically been swept clean of shipping, Webb thought that the chances of a decoy being able to attack a submarine were very much greater.[41] He therefore suggested the taking up of four decoys which should be kept available to send into the mouth of the Channel when U-boats were known to be coming down south from the Irish coast. They should closely resemble ships which did not carry defensive armament, such as those belonging to lines running to U.S. ports, or smaller lines running across the Atlantic for which no armament had yet been found. They should steam along the trade routes, taking full advantage of "the fact that, at the present juncture, enemy submarines will not attack, without previous warning, vessels which may carry American passengers."

To demonstrate to Webb that the Admiralty had by no means neglected the possibilities of decoys, Director of the Mobilisation Division, Admiralty War Staff, in reply to his letter produced a list of those Q-ships which were operating at the time. Of the ships in operation, *Remembrance*, *Bradford City*, *Thornhill* and *Penhallow* had been allocated to the Senior Naval Officer, Gibraltar; *Baralong* and *Redbreast* were at Malta; *Penshurst* and *Vala*, both of which had once been operating from Scapa under the C.-in-C., Home Fleets, had been placed at the disposal of Bayly at Queenstown; the two trawlers *Gunner* and *Quickly* were operating in the Firth of Forth, along with the schooner *Ready; Chevington* and *Glendevon*, which were described as "proper transports but really decoys when empty," were working between Avonmouth and Rouen, directly under the control of the Admiralty; and *Duncombe* was sailing out of Scapa Flow.

Having read this note, Oliver pointed out that an additional three Q-ships were being fitted out by the Vice-Admiral, Eastern Mediterranean. One of them, the *Margit*, had been already given up.

The D.M.D. felt that locking up another four vessels was not justified, having regard to the shortage of tonnage at that time. Instead, when U-boats were reported, decoys should be ordered out as available to cruise in the localities where they would attract the most attention. As a sop to Webb's request, however, *Penshurst* and *Vala* were removed from the control of the C.-in-C., Home Fleets, at Scapa and handed to Bayly, with the proviso that "the main idea in bringing them south was that they

The fleet messenger *Redbreast*, which served as a Q-ship in the Mediterranean and was sunk there by *UC.38* in 1917. From *Q-Ships and Their Story*.

should operate from Pembroke on occasions when outward bound mercantile traffic was held up or on the point of being held up."

Webb was not satisfied with these measures and returned to the charge on 4th April, when he told the First Sea Lord:

> A study of the recent submarine activity off the entrances to the English and Irish Channel shows how consistently the enemy confines his operations to certain well defined areas representing the probable meeting point of the various trade routes of homecoming vessels. With the exception of *Manchester Engineer* and *Achilles* which were torpedoed without warning, and the *Inkonka*,[42] which was fired at but missed, all the vessels molested in the Soundings were attacked on the surface . . . the area of enemy operations thus offered an excellent opportunity for the working of decoys. It is urged most strongly that more of these vessels should be employed. Even if it led to the saving of one large ship, the expense to the Crown would be more than covered, while the demurrage* incurred by the vessels held up in port is very large indeed.

Four vessels from lines still trading with neutral ports should be taken up "and disguised either as neutral vessels of well-known British lines, or made to resemble types of British ships loading in U.S. ports. Enemy will be encouraged by recent successes and expand operations. Masters and crews of British vessels have, on the whole, shown great pluck and spirit in the past, but losses such as those which have recently occurred cannot but exercise a strong influence on them unless speedily checked."

Webb's arguments had their due effect. Everyone was convinced that the stranglehold on Britain's commerce must somehow be loosened.

---

*Compensation paid by the charterer to a shipowner for detention of a vessel beyond the time allowed for loading or unloading cargo.

"Four more ships would be an advantage," noted Oliver on the back of Webb's submission, "and it seems that they can be obtained from those working for neutrals. The Booth ships have lately been carrying German cargoes from the Amazon to U.S.A. and might now be requisitioned to help us instead of the Germans."

A meeting was held in the First Lord's room in the evening of 4th April and the pros and cons of the decoy system were no doubt discussed along the same lines as in an exchange of notes between Oliver and the First Lord on 5th April. The First Lord wrote:

> Looking through the report on enemy submarine losses prepared by the D.I.D.*, it is noticeable that except in one doubtful case, no submarines appear to have been sunk by any of the vessels . . . specially designed to deal with them, [that is, yachts and trawlers]. In these circumstances is it not very desirable that we should as much as possible develop the decoy system?

Oliver replied:

> The number of decoy ships is not common knowledge to officers in the Admiralty, and probably it is much under estimated . . . At the present time there are fourteen regular decoy ships and two decoy transports . . . Total 16. Six decoys are working in the Mediterranean, and the remainder in home waters, four in the vicinity of Queenstown, and four in the North Sea and Scottish waters. The decoy transports work between Avonmouth and Rouen.
>
> Four of the Mediterranean ships carry cargoes of coal, loading at Gibraltar, as it is not advisable to send them into a port like Cardiff to load. This involves double handling of coal. The coal carrying has not been a success, some of the ships having the same cargo on board for three months, owing to their being diverted to localities where submarines were active. Some of the ships have asked for wood cargoes in case they were torpedoed, but it has not been possible as yet to get the cargoes.
>
> There is no objection to having more decoy steamers provided modern guns can be got for them. They have about a minute and a half to get a hit in, and it is not fair to expect them to do it with old guns. They should be filled with empty casks, and wood, and have their bulkheads strengthened to give them a chance of going on with a fight, even after they are torpedoed, as they will get no quarter. Fifteen months with decoy ships points to the fact that they have on an average to cruise many thousand miles on the shipping routes before they see a submarine, and to make as good use of them as possible they must be kept at sea, and not be always going into harbour to load and unload, and they cannot load and unload at ordinary commercial ports without being found out. It is better to use them as decoy ships and not as carriers.

At the end of the meeting the First Lord approved of four suitable ships being acquisitioned. There were only three vessels readily available which seemed to be what was wanted, the *Perugia*, the *Intaba* and the *Barranca*, so it was proposed to requisition a fourth when a suitable vessel

*Director, Intelligence Division.

became available. *Barranca* would not be ready for use until 24th April, while *Intaba* was in the West Indies.

The three ships represented a new departure in Special Service vessels. They were "unsinkables," loaded with buoyant cargoes which it was hoped would keep them afloat if struck by a torpedo, and at over 4,000 gross tons were much bigger and much faster than previous Q-ships. Work began on converting them straight away. "It will probably cause delay on cruisers or other vessels building," it was noted, "but this will have to be accepted."

The First Sea Lord decided that the vessels should be allocated to Portsmouth, Devonport, and Pembroke. Accordingly *Perugia*, given the pendant number *Q.1* and renamed *Moeraki*, was allocated to Devonport for manning and storing. The designation of her letter and number marked the beginnings of the 'Q' nomenclature by which all the Q-ships were to be known for a time. As stated earlier, there was probably a close connection between Queenstown, from which so many decoys sailed, and the choice of the letter for the nomenclature. Gordon Campbell felt that to call all decoys by the same letter was bad for security. *Intaba*, pendant number *Q.2* and renamed *Waitoppo*, was to go to Chatham and *Barranca*, pendant number *Q.3* and renamed *Echunga*, to Portsmouth. It was noticed at this time that "one at least of these vessels, the *Barranca*, is so badly subdivided that she would sink at once if holed, and it will take at least a month to subdivide her."

Webb wrote to express the hope that the four Q-ships would be used for decoy work only, not for escorting important vessels, remarking that "If these vessels are used as convoy their presence will soon become known to the enemy . . . " He asked that all four should be allocated to the Vice-Admiral, Coast of Ireland, to work off the coasts of Ireland, in the approaches to the Irish and English Channels, the Bay of Biscay, and off the Spanish and Portuguese coasts as far south as the latitude of Cape Spartel, as Sir Lewis Bayly should direct.

Webb did not get all he asked for, but all three vessels were sent to Queenstown. They were fitted with a defensive armament of two twelve-pounder, twelve-hundredweight guns on S.2. mountings and one four-inch Mark VII B.L. gun on Mark VI mountings at Chatham Dockyard. Wooden magazines lined with thin steel were built in the hold to carry fifty rounds for the four-inch, and 100 each for the twelve-pounders. Communication between fore bridge and gun positions was by voice pipes, or telephone to the four-inch gun.

Bayly was very interested in the progress of the new vessels and on 8th May he submitted to the Admiralty that they should be supplied on commissioning with certain confidential signal books which he said were necessary to enable the Q-ships to intercept signals made by sloops, naval patrol vessels and merchant vessels. The fact of their being able to do this would very much reduce the amount of direct signalling that had to be made to them.

Like the many gadgets which were built into the Q-ships, their unsinkable nature has helped to foster their legend. Quite serious references are made to Q-ships which had been given a cargo of ping-pong balls—a cargo which, needless to say, would not have stood up to the explosion of a torpedo. There seems little doubt that the dockyards' efforts to make Q-ships unsinkable were much more

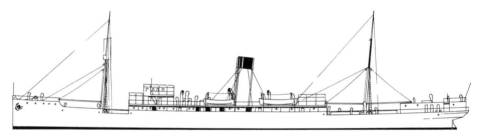

BARRANCA

successful than their attempts to give them impenetrable disguises. On 3rd December, 1916, *Perugia*, with a new alias of *Paxton*, was sunk by *U.63* in the Gulf of Genoa. W. H. Whiting, who gave evidence at the court of inquiry into the loss of *Perugia*, which opened its proceedings on 12th December, 1916, had something to say about the work done on them:

> The case of Q.1 . . . is one of some interest in that this is one of those vessels which have been carefully examined as to their watertight subdivision, and have been dealt with so as to give her without great expense or radical changes, the best chance of surviving damage. The result was, it is submitted, not unsatisfactory. The vessel probably had the engine and boiler room filled, as well as the shaft tunnel. In this condition she remained afloat four hours. The steps taken to improve her watertight subdivision, while fitting out at Pembroke, were as follows:
>
> The tween deck doors in all the main bulkheads were closed up and made quite tight. The decks at the ends of the ship, with the hatches, were also made tight. A considerable number of barrels were stored in the fore and after holds. The ship was also ballasted so as to ensure substantial initial stability. It will be noted that the ship kept on a fairly even keel.[43]

Yet some of the aspects of the fitting out of the *Paxton* seem less efficient than others. The barrels with which she had been loaded were, according to Lieutenant W. Mitchell, her mercantile master before she was taken up, "old oil barrels that had been long exposed to the weather." Her commander, challenged as to the inferiority of these barrels, replied: "Some of them were not good, but they were the only ones that could be got at the time."

Before we look at the second phase of the campaign to make Q-ships unsinkable, a campaign that had gathered momentum once it became the policy of the Admiralty and not just of the admirals, we must look at the

Admiral Sir John Jellicoe.

strangest chapter of the whole of the Q-ship war. No aspect of the Q-ship story reads more like an account of a Heath Robinson invention than does Jellicoe's attempt to disguise a Q-ship as a crashed Zeppelin; yet, had the conditions been right, there is no reason why the scheme should not have been successful.[44]

The inspiration for the Zeppelin decoy came from Commander R. G. Henderson, of the battleship H.M.S. *Erin*, then serving with the Second Battle Squadron in the Grand Fleet. He proposed that a well-armed trawler, suitably disguised as a disabled airship which had had to make a forced landing on the sea, should be sent out accompanied by one of the submarines of the Eleventh Flotilla. This was the first return to the idea of a Q-ship and submarine partnership after its initial trial in 1915. The Commander-in-Chief of the Grand Fleet, Admiral Jellicoe, took up the idea enthusiastically, and under the supervision of Commander Henderson, with the help of the complements of the fleet repair ship *Assistance* and *Erin* and with a very important contribution from Captain W. Whittingham, the Engineer Captain, Second Battle Squadron, preparations were begun on 15th June.

Vice-Admiral Sir Thomas H. Jerram, who commanded the Second Battle Squadron, suggested that what was wanted was "a trawler with a high forecastle, and funnel well aft," and that two light guns and two Maxims would be a suitable armament. Commander Henderson, however, decided to increase the armament to four six-pounder semi-automatics, one three-pounder, one twelve-pounder (12-hundredweight or 18-hundredweight), and two Maxims. The trawler chosen had the very Japanese-sounding name of *Oyama* but was in fact a British vessel owned in Cardiff. By 3rd July both her masts and all her gear except the winch for raising the trawl had been removed, and her funnel had been hinged and given a counterweight. The blacksmith and engineering department then fixed brackets to carry the ribs of the simulated Zeppelin. Balloon envelopes were despatched from Aberdeen, and kite balloon material was chosen for the covering of the "disabled Zeppelin."

The placing of the armament was complicated by the bulging envelope which would surround the *Oyama* once it had been shaped by gas piping fitted to the heel fitting of the ribs. Commander Henderson decided to retain the existing three-pounder Hotchkiss gun on the high forecastle. Four six-pounder semi-automatics were mounted, two on each side between the forecastle and wheelhouse. The twelve-pounder was placed on the centre line abaft the boiler room casing. "It is preferable,"

A steam trawler of similar design to the *Oyama*, on which was erected a dummy Zeppelin

wrote Henderson, "to place the six-pounder gun close to the ship's side and not on centre line, as it would entail clearing away too much envelope on wishing to open fire. This does not apply to after gun, as the envelope here is made to trail in water, and is not given the shape of a Zeppelin by the gas tubes . . . It is submitted that if there is any late information on the external markings or recognition marks that I may be informed in order to paint the envelope with the usual Zeppelin characteristic marks."

By 31st July a working party lent to Scapa Air Defences, where they were billeted, had begun the task of cutting and re-sewing balloon envelopes to suit the framework. This task took a week, and to hurry it on Henderson borrowed two private sewing machines, guaranteeing the owners that "if spoilt, which appears quite likely owing to the balloon texture, that the repairs will be made good at Government expense." The 2nd August was fixed as the day when *Oyama* was to proceed to Hunda Sound, where the skeleton frame would be shipped and tried in place. "During the process of rigging," wrote Commander Henderson regretfully, "no less than six other trawlers appeared and anchored in the vicinity."

Meanwhile the ship's complement for *Oyama* had been chosen. Jerram decided that Commander Henderson himself should command *Oyama* for the first trip, and that subsequently Lieutenant Fyffe, R.N.R., of H.M.S. *Erin* should remain in command. There was to be a complement of one lieutenant, R.N.R., as C.O., two mates, one chief petty officer, one signalman, three able seamen, R.N.R., two deck hands, one chief engineer, one second engineer, and two trimmers. When the Zeppelin ship set off on her maiden voyage she carried, in addition to the above, R. J. Cole, shipwright, and A. B. Richardson, plumber's mate, of *Assistance*, who had helped with the fitting out.

A C-class submarine, the *C.5.*, was selected to co-operate with *Oyama*, and all seemed ready for her first trip, which it had been estimated would be on 9th or 10th August "unless any unforeseen difficulties occur." Unfortunately they did, in the shape of an absence of "flexible wire belting as used for steam cutters' forced draught fans in 20 feet lengths with end connections, 22 in number lengths." These items were absolutely essential for the success of the project, though we do not know what they were to be used for, and on the forecast sailing day, *Oyama's* commander was still writing to ask "Whether any reply can be given to my letter of 23rd July as regards German kit and apparel? What would be the best number to paint on the envelope, i.e. in the recent air raids have any particular numbers been distinguished? If a yellow wash is considered the best colour, observing that the existing envelope is the same colour as aluminium paint. It is understood that Zeppelins vary a good deal—in fact from a brownish yellow to an aluminium colour."

It seems quite obvious that the *Oyama* project was one of those instances in the Q-ship campaigns where normal naval operations began to veer towards the sending out of a suicide squad. What would happen to the crew of *Oyama* if, dressed in German aviators' uniforms, and aboard a ship disguised as a Zeppelin with German markings, they did not overcome the U-boat, but were overcome by it?

The role cast for the new ship was outlined by Vice-Admiral Sir Thomas Jerram. She would be employed to the south during the hours immediately after a Zeppelin raid. She would return to Scapa as her base, without entering any other port, so as to preserve secrecy. Jellicoe himself had envisaged her making a first cruise "in the North Sea as far south as latitude 56° 0′ W., Long. 4° 0′ E."

On 27th August, *Oyama* set sail; ten days later Commander Henderson reported on his cruise.

> There was a long north-westerly swell in the Pentlands, which became serious when clear of the lee given by the Orkneys and Shetlands. The barometer was falling steadily. At 4 a.m. the wind was from north west, force 4–5. *Oyama* was at this time continually pooped, and carried away two of the after rollers complete. It was not until 6.30 a.m. on 28th instant that I was forced to return, having carried away further gear beyond the spares on board. Prior to this (about 5 a.m.) I hove to, but found that there was no improvement with a head sea, as regards the stern gear. *Oyama* arrived at the northern base at 6.30 p.m. 28th instant . . . I reported myself on board *Iron Duke** and informed the Commander-in-Chief that I did not consider that sufficient reliance could be placed in the vessel as fitted, if the area of operation was 24 hours' steaming, especially in view of the fact that autumn was approaching and that considerably worse weather conditions must be expected . . . Should the idea be worth consideration for a future occasion, I submit that a vessel with at least two feet more freeboard should be used. The failure was due to too little freeboard and too many outside fittings.

"The preparation of *Oyama*", wrote Jellicoe, "occupied a longer time than was expected, and the fine weather was missed. It is not proposed to repeat the experiment."

Unsinkability forced itself on the Admiralty's attention for a second time in the autumn, when it suddenly became obvious to Bayly that it would be necessary to provide an alternative to Welsh coal ballast for the Q-ships. The problem about coal, so far as the Royal Navy was concerned, was how to get enough of it rather than how to keep it safely in bulk for a long time; safe storage of coal was a task which had never fallen to Bayly during his service career up to then. As originally supplied, coal ballast appeared to be a great asset for a decoy, which could keep on steaming almost indefinitely by drawing on her ballast

*The Grand Fleet flagship H.M.S. *Iron Duke*.

supply once her bunkers were exhausted. *Q.1 (Perugia)* had been loaded with 1,800 tons of coal, of which 475 tons had been used by August, 1916; *Q.5 (Farnborough)* had 5,000 tons aboard, of which only 475 had been burned, *Q.6 (Zylpha)* had 2,400 tons, *Q.7 (Penshurst)* had 800 and *Q.8 (Vala)* had 700 tons.

But some of the greatest dramas of the sea have been played out when cargoes of coal have caught fire during a long voyage. Bayly became aware of the fact that coal was prone to spontaneous combustion. "Most of the Q-ship holds," he wrote, "are not intended for coal; they have no ventilating system to allow the gases to escape and owing to the necessities of the work on which they are engaged, long voyages at sea in various waters, possibility of being torpedoed, etc., their hatches are, or should be, closed down watertight." By the end of August, 1916, seventy-five per cent of the coal ballast of *Q.6* had to be removed to get to her bilge sections, which were choked with dust.

Bayly's predicament now suggested to Rear-Admiral Oliver that the ballast problem, which Bayly had suggested might be met by re-ballasting with shingle in very strong bulkheads, could be combined with a buoyant cargo. "It is suggested," he wrote, "that the Q-ships be sent over to Canada one or two at a time, and ballasted with timber. We shall then be quit of all trouble about them, and the timber will still be of use when the ships are eventually paid off. The coal can be discharged at Halifax and used for the squadron there, or else sold. The ships will float if torpedoed when timber loaded." Oliver showed a rather unscientific disregard for the flotation properties of various woods. He opted for spruce deals as cargo, but was not inclined to cavil at other kinds of wood. "The description of timber is not material," he wrote, "as long as it will go in the holds. Pit props or railway sleepers or fire wood or paper stuff would do."

Bayly was ordered to send his fleet across the Atlantic in instalments. *Q.1 Perugia* was not detailed, as she had other prospective duties, *Q.7 Penshurst* did not carry enough coal to cross the Atlantic, while *Q.8 Vala* was too small to cross, so Bayly despatched *Farnborough* and *Zylpha* to Halifax, Nova Scotia, on 12th September. They were to discharge all the coal they carried and reload with timber in a Canadian port, either Halifax or Quebec. The Admiralty had calculated that *Farnborough* could accommodate 95,000 standards of spruce deals, approximately twelve feet one inch long by three feet nine inches, while *Zylpha* could take 70,000 standards.* It was a completely unproductive cruise, except in so

*A standard of timber contains 1980 board feet, a board foot being a piece of timber one inch thick by twelve inches square; hence a standard is 165 cubic feet.

far as the two ships returned with wood cargoes to Queenstown in March, 1917. The two ships had patrolled American and West Indian waters in search of submarines, and Vice-Admiral M. E. Browning, Commanding North America, commented that *Farnborough* had a low speed and small radius of action, and that a larger vessel would be more suitable.

Captain Richard Webb, Acting Director of the Trade Division, had been largely responsible for the taking up of the new unsinkables, and in April, 1916, he was to play a large part in the expansion of another part of the Q-ship fleet, the adoption of sailing decoys. Webb pointed out that a large number of sailing ships had recently been sunk by U-boats in the approaches to British waters and attached a list of twelve of the vessels to prove his point. Once more the Admiralty reacted favourably to Webb's request for more protection for merchantmen, and the C.-in-C.,

The *Mary B. Mitchell* under sail, her guns all hidden behind the rails and in deck structures. From *Q-Ships and Their Story*.

Plymouth, directed the captain in charge at Falmouth to select a suitable ship. "Large, square-rigged ships would probably be of little use," he was told. "A barquentine or schooner would perhaps be most suitable, being handier and easier to manoeuvre during an engagement." An advantage in such a ship would be an auxiliary motor, to be used only during engagements with the U-boats.

Rarely has any request met with a more successful response. On 15th April, 1916, a telegram delivered at the Admiralty announced the selection of what was to be the best known of all the sailing Q-ships. "Have found suitable sailing craft for a trap ship at Falmouth, name *Mary B. Mitchell*, number 326 in Lloyd's Register, now here with cargo of china clay. Request authority to take her up immediately and arm her with two six-pounders and a twelve-pounder." The *Mary B. Mitchell*, a three-masted topsail schooner, was to become famous as *Q.9*. She was speedily armed with a twelve-pounder concealed in a dummy collapsible house on the poop, two six-pounders, one under each hatch, with swinging pedestals, and two Lewis guns. She also carried small arms and five boxes of hand grenades. Captain Valentine N. Mull, the captain in charge of Auxiliary Patrol Area XIV (Falmouth), suggested that she flew three different neutral colours and had three names. He submitted a list of suitable vessels of about the same tonnage which she might impersonate. He also suggested that she should be supplied with false papers, Bills of Lading, Bills of Health, and so forth, just in case a U-boat signalled for a boat to be sent to him with the ship's papers, while staying out of range of the Q-ship's guns. Looking through the list of nine neutral vessels, all of about 200–250 tons, Rear-Admiral Oliver did not feel that Mull's suggestion was a very good one. "This appears complicated," he wrote, "unless three varieties of Dago officer are carried to fit the respective neutral papers." It was obviously a very bad plan ever to let a Q-ship's lifeboat get within the grasp of a submarine, it would merely provide the U-boat with hostages. Later standing orders specifically state that this kind of situation must never be allowed to arise.

By 24th June, two days before she put to sea under the command of Lieutenant M. Armstrong, R.N.R., the *Mary B. Mitchell* had completely altered her appearance. Under cover of two trawlers she had been painted black with a yellow streak, and bore the name *Maria y José* of Vigo, with a covering plate over that bearing her own name, under which she left harbour. *Mary B. Mitchell* was a comfortable ship, in fine weather, at any rate. "There is ample accommodation for officers and men, and room for them to exercise in daytime. Gymnastic apparatus and boxing gloves have been provided."

How would the timbers and scantlings of the old ship, built in 1892, stand up to the discharge of the guns in 1916? Commodore J. M. Denison, R.N.R., Auxiliary Patrol, supplies the answer:

> During gun trials, carried out at night, a broadside was fired 11 seconds after the "bell for action" was pressed, hatches sliding off smoothly, and guns swinging smartly into position. This morning I inspected the vessel and found her clean, and a credit to her C.O. The guns were exercised, and I was astonished at the rapidity with which they were brought into action . . . these guns are hidden under hatches and swing into position through an ingenious design of Lieutenant-Commander Collett, R.N., who commands the base . . . In view of the proved success of these fittings, and the fact that until the guns are actually in action *nobody is visible on deck, except the normal crew,* I venture to suggest that a similar arrangement be fitted in other Special Service vessels . . . The fact that not a seam was sprung, nor so much as a glass cracked when the broadside was fired, speaks for itself, and is entirely due to the painstaking care with which the officers concerned supervised the strengthening of the deck and the gun supports.

Another useful addition to the sailing fleet was the 174-ton barquentine *Gaelic*, built of iron at Amlwch, Anglesey, in 1898. She had a length of 126 feet 8 inches, a breadth of 24 feet and a depth of 10 feet 8 inches. *Gaelic* had been selected by Vice-Admiral Charles H. Dare, in command at Milford Haven, who armed her with the guns taken out of the sailing trawlers *Strumble* (M 135) and *Kemes* (M105), two Q-ships which had proved unsatisfactory. This armament consisted of two eight-hundredweight twelve-pounder guns, and to these were added two twelve-hundredweight twelve-pounders and two Maxims. As *Q.22, Gaelic* was to have an eventful career.

Vice-Admiral Charles Dare was also responsible for the selection of another very famous sailing Q-ship, the three-masted schooner *First Prize*. This topsail schooner, formerly the *Else*, had sailed from Germany for England in August, 1914, being the first enemy ship to be captured, hence the name. *First Prize* had a great career as *Q.21*. She had a length of 112 feet 6 inches, a breadth of 24 feet 7 inches and a depth of 9 feet 2 inches. She was built of steel and iron, with iron decks at Westerbroek in 1901 with a net tonnage of 199. Dare decided to ballast her with 170 tons of copper slag and to arm her with three twelve-hundredweight twelve-pounder guns. There were two guns forward, one on each bow near the ship's side, and a third aft, mounted on the centre line and capable of being trained on either beam or astern, except where masked by the steering wheel.

Another of the Falmouth fleet of sailing Q-ships was the *Helgoland*. She had a length of 122 feet 9 inches, a breadth of 23 feet 3 inches and a depth of 9 feet 8 inches. Barquentine rigged, she was steel and iron built, had a net tonnage of 182, and had been built at Martenshoek, Holland, in 1895. *Helgoland* was such a successful bait for U-boats that she was attacked by three of them successively during her first cruise in September, 1916. She was left becalmed during the first attack and was narrowly missed by a torpedo in the third. Lieutenant-Commander J. A. Collett, in charge of the naval base at Falmouth, felt that if *Helgoland* had been such an attraction to submarines, then so would another vessel of the same type. He suggested to the Admiralty that he could use half the crew of the *Mary B. Mitchell* for the complement of the proposed vessel,

HELGOLAND

and recruit the rest from the Trawler Reserve in Falmouth. He proposed an armament of four twelve-pounders, two Lewis guns, "and if the build of the vessel allows it two torpedo tubes concealed," and strongly recommended wireless equipment of the type that would receive at a range of 150 miles and transmit for 30 miles.

H. E. Gecky of the Yacht Patrol, a rival and hitherto less successful branch of the Navy in the war against the U-boats, poured cold water on the idea. Falmouth, he said, already had three sailing Q-ships. "Their utility may not perhaps be so great as it was, for three German submarines recently attacked the *Helgoland* on sight. As none of them were sunk, the news that the Falmouth Area has this type of craft in service has now got back officially to Germany." He submitted that no further Special Service craft should be taken up.

"Concur with Y.P.," wrote Rear-Admiral Oliver. "The small sailing vessel will develop into a sailing line-of-battle ship with an electric light party reefing topsails and a seaplane hidden in the foretopmen's wash deck locker, and everybody sea sick."

As early as 3rd July, in fact, the Admiralty had decided not to acquire any more ships of the *Helgoland* type, a decision which brought a letter from Dare on 29th October, asking them to reconsider. He pointed out that sailing vessels could keep at sea for a much longer time than most steam vessels of the Auxiliary Patrol. It would not seriously handicap the carrying trade if a number of moderate sized sailing vessels were withdrawn from it. Sixteen vessels of the *Helgoland* type would only carry as much cargo as one 5,000-ton steamer. A number of suitable vessels were available, some British ones, others captured German sailing ships. Because of their roomy decks such vessels were well fitted for the construction of dummy houses to conceal their armaments. With no noise from the engines to worry about, sailing Qs could listen continually on the hydrophones, while they were so silent it was always possible that a U-boat, having failed to detect their presence because of the lack of engines, might break surface close enough to be exposed to a fatal shot. Dare added that what was wanted were iron ships of shallow draught, to avoid the risk of being torpedoed. *Helgoland* had had two torpedoes fired at her at close range, but they had passed beneath the Q-ship because of her 8 foot 3 inch draught. Of course a shallow draught had its disadvantages as regards weatherly qualities, but an auxiliary motor could be fitted to enable these vessels to get out of danger. Plenty of volunteers could be obtained from the Auxiliary Patrol, men who had sailing experience. If such vessels were to be sanctioned, concluded Dare, they ought to be fitted with a half kilowatt portable wireless set complete with petrol engine and dynamo.

Dare's letter got a less than warm response in Whitehall. He was told that there were three sailing decoys working from Milford and one from Falmouth, and forty-seven Q-ships altogether, ranging from motor drifters to medium-sized steamers. "Their success," wrote Rear-Admiral Oliver, "is mainly a question of the capacity of the captain and crew, very largely tempered by luck. The Granton vessels are very well commanded and manned, but they have had very poor luck for the last twelve months. The submarines are fairly well aware of the methods of Q-ships and there is no good case for a large increase in number." The most the

Admiralty would approve of was two more small sailing decoys for Milford, fitted with auxiliary motors.

As political arguments raged in Germany over whether unrestricted submarine warfare could be justified, Admiral Scheer recalled his U-boats from the Western Approaches and set them to work in the North Sea, where they attacked steamers, sailing vessels and fishing craft. And as the range of targets widened, so new types of craft seemed to offer possibilities for the Special Service.

On 1st May Admiral Sir Stanley Colville, who had moved his flag to

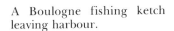

A Boulogne fishing ketch leaving harbour.

H.M.S. *Victory* as C.-in-C., Portsmouth, wrote to the Admiralty to draw their attention to the sinking of the *Jeannette* (118 tons), a French fishing ketch, on passage to the mackerel grounds off south west Ireland. She had been sunk twelve miles off St Catherine's Point by bombs placed aboard her. This incident demonstrated, said Colville, that the U-boats were still using weapons other than torpedoes against shipping. Why not take up a fishing Q-ship, if the French had not done so already, by hiring a ketch similar to the *Jeannette* from Boulogne, arming her with two twelve-pounder guns and using her as a decoy in the Channel?[45]

Shortly afterwards, Colville reiterated his request for fishing Q-ships and asked also for the taking up of two small steamers similar to the s.s. *Dresden* and s.s. *Pearl*, which had been captured and sunk by bombs placed on board in the Channel on 23rd September, 1916. To explain why he wanted to start his own line in decoys, Colville wrote: "German submarines have continued their old practice of sinking ships and West Country trawlers by gun-fire and bombs . . . At present any decoys for work in this area are sent from Queenstown, which is not satisfactory as they cannot instantly be got out on to the submarine area when required, and also I do not think Queenstown possesses any vessels of the type required."

Perhaps Sir Stanley had heard of the successes claimed for the Lowestoft smacks which had been fitted with three-pounder guns and sent off to the North Sea fishing grounds from the summer of 1915 onwards. One of the first to be hired as a decoy, the *G. & E.* (LT 649), attacked a U-boat which was thought to have been sunk on 11th August, 1915, and four days later the *Inverlyon* (LT 687) attacked another U-boat near the Smith's Knoll off the Norfolk coast.

"Decoy vessels have not been much of a success lately," wrote Oliver on 5th October, "but we are very short of patrol vessels in the Channel, as well as in most other areas, and any craft which can carry and use a gun is some use to make the sea unhealthy for submarines, and having a diversity of types of vessel is advantageous."

So *Brown Mouse*, a yacht built in 1908 on the lines of a Brixham trawler, was taken up, and after some search in Boulogne, Captain Stapleton Cotton reported favourably on a likely fishing vessel there, the *Bayard*. This craft was a sailing lugger of 220 tons gross, 143 net, built of wood and about sixteen years old. She had a length of 94 feet 1½ inches and a beam of 23 feet 10½ inches. *Bayard* was by no means ready for sea, as she had been fitting a new Swideraki heavy oil engine in Belgium just before the Germans moved in, and had escaped under sail. Colville decided to take up the lugger, arm her with a thirteen-pounder gun, and man her with a crew of Lowestoft fishermen with a naval gun crew.

The party sent to collect *Bayard* and sail her to her new port had a nightmare voyage to England.[46] When Lieutenant George Muhlhauser R.N.R., the captain, and his fifteen men arrived in Boulogne they were unable to get provisions, bedding, blankets or even a bucket to clean the ship either from the French or from the S.N.O., Boulogne. "The vessel herself was in a disgusting condition," wrote the Commodore in charge of the naval base at Lowestoft on 18th December. "Full of lice, bugs etc., and indescribably dirty, the motor unworkable and the joints to the steam pipe given out, and only one sail on board, namely the foresail." *Bayard's* complement, now verminous and starving after two twelve-hour spells without anything to eat during the voyage under tow to Lowestoft, suffered so badly from exposure that the commander had to be admitted to hospital on landing, with a temperature of 102°F.

This hardly augured well for her future career, but the new Q-ship was converted so that twenty men and three officers could be accommodated. *Bayard* was fitted with an armament of one thirteen-pounder, one three-pounder, and one Maxim, and Lieutenant W. F. Scott, D.S.C., R.N.R., took command.

As the fitting out of new decoys such as *Brown Mouse* got under way, the controversy about their value became apparent. Gecky of the Yacht Patrol felt that *Brown Mouse*, which looked just like a Brixham trawler, was of little value. Vice-Admiral Dare at Milford Haven had just paid off two similar craft, the sailing trawlers *Strumble* and *Kemes*, because they were unsuitable for the area. Severe weather conditions prevailed off Milford during the winter, and the two Q-ships had very low freeboard and took a big list in strong winds. It was very difficult in such conditions to get the eight-hundredweight twelve-pounder gun to bear to windward or leeward. The ships had a very limited range of vision, except when topping a high sea, and for six months of the year they just could not remain at sea for any length of time. This was unfortunate because *Strumble* and *Kemes* had undergone the usual expensive conversion process. They had been specially stiffened to fit them with their armament, their after companion had been removed and iron plates fitted in place there to carry a gun mounting pedestal. A light, movable companion had been built round the gun, and the boiler funnel had been made portable so as to be clear of the gun if required. The gun itself was concealed either by a dummy hatch or a fishing net. Beneath decks the fish hold had been converted to crew accommodation. Racks on the port side and after bulwark held five rifles and six lance bombs.

Charles Seymour took the view on 18th November that fishing decoys were of little use during the winter, and expressed the opinion that taking them up deprived the country of a valuable asset; a month later he had changed his mind. The U-boats had carried out a particularly violent strafe on fishing boats in the Channel, and representatives of the Brixham fishing industry had called on the Admiralty without appointment and had been given an opportunity of putting forward their views. Seymour now wrote to the Admiralty saying that he had changed his mind in view of the U-boat activity amongst the Brixham trawlers. He was going to approve a proposal by the C.-in-C., Devonport, to take up *Brown Mouse* and two other suitable smacks. They would be given one six-pounder each.

Colville outlined a proposal to use *Brown Mouse* to tow a submarine, basing her with the Brixham fishing fleet. So *Brown Mouse* underwent the conversion process at which the dockyards had become so skilful. Underneath where the gun was to be fitted the spaces between the deck beams were filled in with extra timber, and mild steel plate was fitted on the top and bottom with suitable supports from the deck to the keel. The galley was converted for use as a magazine under the gun, and messing accommodation for ten arranged. An auxiliary engine was fitted, and the six-pounder gun concealed "by means of a wooden covering the shape of a companion way, this covering to be built over the gun in two halves and fitted so that the halves can be parted and will fall clear of the gun at very short notice."

In spite of all this ingenuity and craftsmanship, the sudden end of *Brown Mouse* goes to show that you cannot make a purse out of a sow's ear. The rapid destruction of the vessel by fire on 28th February, 1918, showed the disastrous consequences which could result from the rapid conversion of civilian craft into naval ships. Reconstruction did not, in this case, put right inherent defects. The boiler and bunker of *Brown Mouse* had a wooden casing on which fell sparks from the chimney. In certain conditions any fire caused by these sparks would be fanned by a draught pouring in through the boiler room door, the frame of which twisted out of shape when the vessel was sailing in particular ways. On one tack the door would not close, on the other it would not remain closed. It was nobody's business to clean the chimney.

The final catastrophe was described by the commander of *Brown Mouse*, Lieutenant Henry Scott, R.N.R., at the inquiry into the loss of the vessel, which had been sailing with the Brixham fishing fleet.

> At 00.15, when in position ten miles S.E. x E. of Berry Head, I was called up, the vessel being on fire. I immediately got on deck and found the ship burning furiously in the boiler room. The skipper and crew were drawing water and trying to get the fire under.
>
> I ordered the chief motor mechanic to go below and use the Pyrene cylinder from the engine room, which he did. He remained below as long as it was possible. I then gave orders for the boat to be launched and made fast to the mizzen rigging. The wireless transmitter operator could not get to his cabin, being slightly scorched in making his escape from the forecastle when first called.
>
> We continued to endeavour to get the fire under until 01.00, and by this time the ship was all ablaze forward, the flames reaching up to the main boom. The ammunition room now being on fire, I gave orders to abandon the ship, handing a lifebelt to each of the crew.

Having first checked the set of the sails to ensure that the *Brown Mouse* was sailing a course which would not bring her into collision with other vessels, Scott himself abandoned ship. Half an hour later he and his crew were picked up by the smack *Ebenezer*.

During the latter part of 1916 there appeared a new answer to the U-boat, the convoy sloops of the Flower class. The earliest of these vessels to appear, the seventy-two vessels of the *Acacia*, *Azalea* and *Arabis* types, were all typical small warships and were classed as fleet sweeping sloops, many of them being fitted for minesweeping, though latterly their work as escorts and for anti-submarine patrolling was of much greater importance.

One of the *Azalea*-type sloops, the *Begonia*, was torpedoed on 29th March, 1916, while patrolling in the Atlantic, but she remained afloat and was towed into Queenstown. At the dockyard at Haulbowline she was reconstructed to resemble a cargo vessel at the same time that her torn hull was repaired, and in August she reappeared as a Q-ship, *Q.10*, her armament hidden. Subsequent convoy sloops of the *Aubrietia* and *Anchusa* types were built with merchant ship profiles, all the Flower class vessels being built along merchant ship lines for ease of production. In spite of there being at least eighteen variations of design among the forty vessels of the *Aubrietia* and *Anchusa* types, these convoy sloops did bear a strong family resemblance to one another. The first six vessels of the *Aubrietia* type, all ordered in January, 1916, became *Q.11* to *Q.16*, and a number of other units also bore aliases when serving as Special Service vessels.

All had their armament hidden behind false plating, but their guns could not be kept trained on the target before they were uncovered, so they had to be provided with rangefinders. These were considered to be

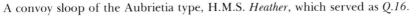

A convoy sloop of the Aubrietia type, H.M.S. *Heather*, which served as *Q.16*.

One of the PC class patrol boats which were built to resemble merchant ships and operated as decoys.

a great giveaway and no Q-ships had up to then been fitted with them, though they had often been asked for. Writing on 28th October of the new convoy sloops, Sir Lewis Bayly said "Their description has not apparently been circulated yet among the Germans. At the same time all, except *Q.10*, are handicapped by having only three guns and therefore a house on the poop in consequence, and this will react against them when they get better known. The flare on the bow has been considerably hidden by varying shades of paint put on there, so that the shadow is painted with a lighter shade than the better illuminated part of the bows."

Another useful anti-submarine vessel introduced at the same time as the Flower class sloops was the P class patrol boat, whose speed of 20 knots was a good three knots faster than that of the convoy sloops. With geared turbines driving twin screws in place of the triple-expansion engine driving the single screw of the convoy sloops, they were designed to be highly manoeuvrable, with a large rudder area and the hull strongly cut up aft to give rapid turning. The outline scheme for these boats stipulated that they should be of the minimum size consistent with sea-keeping qualities, simple in construction and with a shallow draught so that torpedoes fired at them might pass beneath their keels.

The first forty-four vessels of the P class were warships pure and simple; their low silhouettes could hardly be confused with anything else. Ten other P boats were, however, altered during building to resemble small merchant ships and were based at Pembroke Dockyard, from which they operated as decoys, this employment resulting in these ten and the further ten subsequently built in this disguise being known as "PQ" boats. In fact they were officially known as PC class patrol boats, being given numbers with the prefix PC. In these boats the after four-inch gun was hidden behind various forms of dummy deck loads such as bales, packing cases or trusses of hay, while in a few boats it was located within a collapsible pantechnicon furniture van or under a dummy boat.

Extending the principle of "unsinkability," the designers of the PC boats provided them with bulge protection and special fillings which were intended to keep them afloat at least long enough to dispose of their attackers, although it was hoped that their draught of only 8 feet or so would cause torpedoes to under-run them.[47]

As the convoy sloops first made their appearance under the aegis of the Q-ships it is not surprising that their officers and crews formed part of the Special Service, got the extra allowance which was the perquisite of Q-ship men, wore plain clothes, while carrying naval uniform on board, ready to put on before opening fire, wore the "War Badges" that the Special Service had adopted as an insurance against being shot as *francs tireurs* in the event of capture, and flew the Red Ensign, with the White Ensign to hand for raising during an action. Yet the convoy sloops were really only Q-ships by designation, with numbers, pay, and allowances. When, later in the war, these were all withdrawn, the convoy sloops and "PQs" lost their Q-ship status.

Allusion has been made more than once to the special pay of the decoy men. It had first been obtained by that forthright flag officer, Sir Lewis Bayly, for the Queenstown ships and subsequently extended to the rest of the Special Service. In a letter of 23rd November, 1916, Bayly suggested means of improving the efficiency of the Q-ships.

> The result of considerable experience with decoy ships, shows me that they are at present the most valuable form of defence (outside the North Sea) that we possess against submarines. But they labour under serious disadvantages, with the result that we do not get more than fifty per cent of their value, and in consequence there are more submarines afloat than there should be . . . The men are convinced (and I believe rightly) that if their ship is torpedoed, and any of them are captured, they will be shot. In order to make up for this, as well as to get the best volunteers, the officers and men should get submarine pay (Art. 1372, King's Regulations) . . . The work of these ships is strenuous and arduous; they spend eight days at sea out of twelve; their principal harbours (Queenstown and Berehaven) offer no decent attraction. When at sea, only two or three men can be on deck at a time (this is most important, so as not to give the ship away) and the weather from October to April is abominable.

This submission received a favourable reception at the Admiralty. At a meeting of the Standing Committee of the Treasury on 15th December,

1916, sanction was given to the payment, at the discretion of the Admiralty, of extra pay at the rate of six shillings (30p) a day for an officer, half a crown (12½p) a day for a chief petty officer, petty officer and leading seaman rating, and two shillings (10p) a day for men of the crews of these vessels.

Bayly had not merely asked for better pay for his men. He also wanted the Q-ships to be manned by volunteers, so that the men best fitted for this class of work could be taken. "Next to having all merchant vessels armed," he had written on a previous occasion, "I look upon Q-ships as our best protection against submarines, once they have been allowed to reach the open seas, but to obtain full value from these ships, it is necessary that officers and men shall be volunteers and be carefully selected. The gunlayers should be first-class shots with light guns, as it is necessary to be able to score hits with the first or second rounds with no aid from range finders, etc. At present officers and men appear to be drafted without any selection for the special duty." He had complained, perhaps too forcefully, about ratings sent to him such as one Henry Higgins, stoker, who was fifty and still suffering from "shock after being blown up in H.M.S. *Majestic* and *Ocean*." When he had complained about some of the officers sent to him the Admiralty, via Rear-Admiral Reginald Hutchinson, Devonport, had been obliged to tell him in self defence that they always sent him the best officers they could find, and that "officers appearing in a cheap, ready-made suit may not always give an impression of smartness. R.N.R. officers do not carry plain clothes

Penshurst cruising in search of U-boats. The man on deck keeping an unostentatious look-out is the gunlayer of the twelve-pounder concealed in the collapsible dummy boat on the main hatch, just visible on the left.

with them, and when detailed for Q-ships, have very often to get a suit at a moment's notice."

Not content with asking for more pay for the Special Service men, Bayly demanded that they should be given more recognition as well.

> More Distinguished Service Medals, etc., should be given to the men for engagements with submarines. Even if the submarine is not sunk, they run a greater risk of being sunk than any other class of ship, seeing that they try to close the submarine, and their turning powers, with a single screw, are none too good, whereas every other type of ship turns her stern to the submarine, except in the few cases where they try to ram her. The appreciation of their Lordships is satisfactory, but the men cannot wear it on their coats when they go home, and when they meet others who have got more for doing less.

Bayly's submission initiated a discussion in the Admiralty on his proposals. M. Seymour, Director of the Mobilisation Division of the Admiralty War Staff, felt that a call for volunteers, even though it involved some publicity, would probably be justified.

> This must be accepted—it is probable that the existence of these vessels is perfectly well known to the large majority of ratings in the Barracks and at sea. [In some cases, he added, the service part of the crews had already been obtained by volunteering, while] the mercantile ratings have always been replaced if they did not wish to sign on for this service, and have been allowed to leave if they felt unequal to the work after some time at it. [A crew made up of none but R.N. men would not be a good one.] The engineers have often been a long time in their ships and understand them thoroughly, and a Merchant Service mate understands keeping the ship thoroughly "trampy" in appearance . . . R.N.R. officers and men have done very well in many successful actions in the past. The great thing is to have keen volunteers.

Alexander Hunt pointed out that honours and medals had invariably been awarded when a submarine was considered to have been sunk. Moreover in such a case a reward of £1,000 was always paid to the ship's company. In other cases, a sum not exceeding £200 could be paid out; however, except in one case awaiting the King's approval, honours had not been awarded unless the submarine was considered to have been destroyed.

In the light of these deliberations a public call for volunteers was made. Commanders-in-Chief were circularised on 26th December, 1916, asking them to select a few men whom they considered suitable and invite them to volunteer. No more information was to be given to the selected men about their future duty than that "the service is a special service against enemy submarines; that it is dangerous, at periods monotonous, and not free from discomfort." The volunteers asked for were 320 seamen, 350 stokers, 40 engine room artificers, "men who understand commercial ship engines," and 2nd and 3rd class gunlayers, who "should be selected for their ability to estimate ranges and get on their target rapidly." If the open call for volunteers for special service did something to dissipate the secrecy that still in part hung round the Q-ships, and thereby made their task more difficult, there was evidence from other sources that the mystery ships were a mystery no longer.

"The fact that armed vessels flying the Red Ensign are in search of submarines being no longer secret," wrote Sir Lewis Bayly on 25th November, "I have issued an order that, in British harbours, the White Ensign is to be flown and officers and men are to wear uniform. This will assist in the maintenance of discipline, and is in accordance with the desires of the crews." Not merely the fact of disguise but even the methods of disguise were becoming known to the Germans. Keble Chatterton suggests that some of the Irish workmen employed at the Haulbowline dockyard were passing information to the Germans.[48]

However they had obtained the information, it was evident that they did know the secret of the Q-ships and that U-boat commanders had been briefed in the art of detecting them. On October 27th, the convoy sloop *Viola, Q.14*, sighted a U-boat which closed, shelling. Lieutenant Hogg at once stopped engines and put the panic party overboard into the boats. The submarine continued to close, still shelling. "The men on conning tower and manning both guns could be plainly seen," writes Hogg. "No action was taken, except about the boats, and a close range seemed a certainty, when suddenly the submarine, distant about 1,000 yards, turned to north, firing at high speed, and it appeared evident that the disguise of *Q.14* had been realised." Within a few seconds, the submarine had dived and escaped.

Yet the blowing of their security was only one of the new problems which Q-ships faced at the end of 1916. The U-boats had now adopted entirely different tactics. No longer, save in exceptional cases, did they boldly approach a merchant vessel, plant bombs on her, open the sea cocks, and then leave her to sink. Now they started to play the game back on the base line, sinking ships with gunfire from a distance of several miles, helped by their improved armament, particularly the 5.9 inch gun. The arrival of shells on the deck of a merchant ship, often from an invisible submarine miles away, served a double purpose. It protected the U-boat in case the merchantman was either a Q-ship or one of the new armed merchant ships, and it acted as a warning to the crew and officers of the ship to abandon her, though it was not a very successful warning if the first shell to arrive blew up the lifeboat. As an additional insurance, the U-boat commander tried to attack out of the eye of the sun, so as to make himself an even more elusive target. This technique had been introduced in the Mediterranean by the U-boat "ace" Arnauld de la

Perriere, whose French-sounding name betrayed his Huguenot origins.

At a stroke much of the Q-ship armament now became useless because it was outranged. "In the early days of Q-ships," reminisced Rear-Admiral Henry Oliver on 24th November, "a Maxim and ten good riflemen were supposed to damage the submarine personnel. For some time now, the actions fought have usually been beyond effective Maxim or rifle range."

It was from the hunting ground of Arnauld de la Perriere, the Mediterranean, that the commander of *Baralong*, now renamed *Wyandra*, J. M. Simon, commented on 15th July, 1916, on the new U-boat tactics.

> Owing to the extreme caution now being shown by enemy submarines in dealing with merchant ships, the chance of one of our "decoys" getting near enough to destroy them by gunfire is very remote, as the enemy will not approach a merchant vessel on the surface. Twelve months ago the enemy submarines would come within 1,000 yards fully buoyant. They no longer use these tactics. The destruction of the Norwegian s.s. *Aquila* quite recently is typical of their methods now. Attacked by gunfire at long range, the *Aquila* stopped. The submarine then signalled to send papers on board while she lay off from 3,000 to 4,000 yards in diving trim, and awaited the captain's lifeboat. After the papers had been examined the submarine approached the ship, and destroyed her by gunfire, taking the precaution of holding the captain of the ship on board as a hostage while the ship was boarded.

Was there a counter to this new submarine tactic? Simon thought there was. The ship's lifeboat which approached the U-boat to hand over the captain's papers would carry a torpedo. At the right moment it would

One of the many projects for an exploding lifeboat, redrawn from ADM 137/2133, page 122. "The boat is manned by two men with life belts on and proceeds towards the submarine as ordered. The torpedo being aft is safely out of sight even if the bow lifts to a choppy sea. When about twenty or thirty yards from the submarine the lanyard is pulled and the crew take to the water to be picked up by the other boat. The torpedo shoots forward to the dotted position with the warhead in advance and finally tows the boat. There is practically no possibility of a miss for direction as the towing of the boat will keep the torpedo straight and a good hit should result."

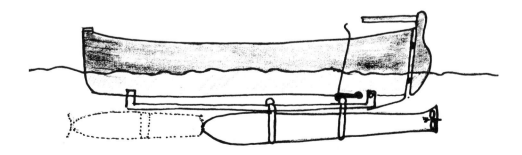

torpedo the U-boat. "I submit the above scheme is worth testing," he wrote. "As I patrol the Mediterranean in my present ship, armed with twelve-pounder twelve-hundredweight guns, I realise that, should I meet a submarine, my chances of destroying her are small under present conditions . . . The armament of decoys, however effective six months ago, has not changed with the changing tactics of the submarines and I submit my present armament is not suitable for the present conditions." The kind of armament that a decoy really needed, said Simon, was several four-inch Mark VIII or Mark VII guns. "If these were not available then 4.7 inch, although the bad sights on the latter guns caused inaccurate shooting and accuracy is essential on this work."

Under such adverse conditions, how could a Q-ship ever expect to make a kill? There were still several factors that might lure a submarine within range. The Marineamt (German Admiralty) was not prepared to accept its commanders' estimates of tonnage sunk. They wanted ships' papers as documentary proof, so these had to be procured whenever it was possible.

Another much more pressing reason why ships were still boarded was that Germany was running short of food as the British blockade bit harder and harder. Although the Germany Navy got better rations than civilians and although submariners in turn were better fed than their comrades in the surface ships, the food situation was so bad in the navy that cases of scurvy and beri-beri had occurred. Surface raiders were ordered to add to their food supplies, especially their supplies of fresh food, from ships they captured, and submariners apparently followed this practice as well.

Though successes were few, 1916 had not been devoid of Q-ship actions with the U-boats. *Margit* had fought a brisk action with a submarine on 17th January; *Redbreast* had caught a U-boat in the Cerigo Channel in the Mediterranean on 16th July; *Vala* had barely missed being torpedoed on 22nd November off Ushant; the convoy sloop *Viola*, *Q.14*, had had a duel with a submarine on 23rd November, while *Q.17*, the sailing Q-ship *Helgoland*, had engaged two submarines on 24th October twenty miles south west of the Lizard light; *Saros* had tackled a submarine near the Cani Rocks in the Mediterranean on 2nd November, while *Penshurst*, *Q.7*, had saved the s.s. *Wileysike* from a submarine on 29th November; and on the same date the indefatigable Lieutenant P. J. Hogg of H.M.S. *Viola* had been in action again. All these actions had been accompanied by reports of submarines probably sunk, and certainly damaged. Like many another Q-ship action, however, these successes were delusive ones. It is the function of submarines to sink, and in the list established by Campbell after the war, the only successes which could be claimed for the year were his own sinking of *U.68*, which has been described earlier in this chapter, and the destruction of *UB.19* on 30th November, 1916, by *Penshurst.*

About 4.30 p.m. on Thursday, 30th November, when in Lat. 49° 56 N. Long 2° 45' W., I engaged and sank the German submarine UB19, taking prisoners her commanding officer, two other officers, and thirteen ratings, one of the latter being badly wounded. Three others, including the commanding officer, had some slight cuts and abrasions. I was informed that seven other ratings were either killed, or went down in the submarine.

A little earlier, I had picked up the pilot and passenger (Flight Sub. Lieut. J. R. Ross, R.N., and A. M. W/T J. Redman) of British Seaplane No. 8379, belonging to

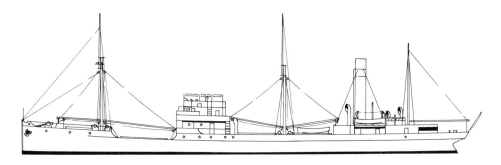

PENSHURST

Portland, which had "crashed" on the water close to the ship . . . The course of events was as follows. At 12 noon, when in Lat. 50° 11' N., Long 2° 31 W., steering N. 89° W., we intercepted a message from s.s. *Ibex* that a submarine had disappeared in position 20 Miles W.N.W. of the Casquets. Course was altered towards this position, and at 1.50 p.m. the conning tower of a submarine was observed about five miles to the southward, apparently chasing a steamer to the westward. A few minutes later the submarine appeared to turn East and then submerged, and at the same time a seaplane (No. 8379) was seen flying over her position in search of her (The pilot informed me later that he had dropped one bomb without effect). Since the presence of the seaplane excluded the hope of an action on the surface, and as we should probably have a decided advantage over the submerged submarine in the matter of speed, and our depth charges would be more effective than the seaplane's bombs, I decided to co-operate with the seaplane and ran down towards her.

At 2.22 p.m. in Lat. 50° N., Long 2° 48' W., the engines were stopped, and after some attempts at communication by signal, the seaplane alighted on the water alongside, and I arranged with the pilot to direct us and fire a signal light when we were over the submarine. Unfortunately, almost immediately after the seaplane had risen into the air to continue her search, she "crashed" on to the water, breaking a wing and knocking off her floats, and began to sink. The gig was lowered and brought her crew on board. I then went alongside the seaplane, grappled it, and was preparing to hoist it inboard when, at 3.14 p.m. a shell pitched 200 yards ahead of us. Two other shots followed in quick succession, and a submarine was sighted about 6,000 yards on the port quarter. The seaplane was at once cast off and sank immediately. The derrick was swung in. I had now the alternative of hoisting the gig on the port quarter in full view of the submarine, or of towing her alongside on the starboard side and risk her being seen. I chose the latter, and at 3.24 p.m., proceeded S.W. ½ W. at slow speed. As the submarine steered to come up right astern, the course had to be gradually altered, so as to keep her on the port quarter out of sight of the gig ... The submarine overhauled slowly, firing at intervals, and at 4.12 p.m. when she was within 1,000 yards of us, I stopped engines, the boat party abandoned ship, and the two boats pulled away to starboard. The submarine now took a sheer out to port, and came round in a sweep on our port beam, passed clear under the stern (with the object, I was informed later by her officers, of securing the ship's papers from the Master, who was supposed to be in the boats, before boarding the ship and sinking her with bombs) and, at 4.26 p.m., when she was on our starboard quarter and all our guns were bearing, I opened fire at 250 yards' range.

As the attention of all on the deck of the submarine was directed to our boats, no one was by her gun, and no attempt was made to return our fire. I was told that our second shot, fired from the starboard three-pounder, penetrated the engine room and prevented submersing. At this short range our guns were able to work at their maximum rapidity, nearly every shot took effect (we fired 83 rounds all told), the hull was soon fairly riddled with holes, large parts of the conning tower and hull plating were blown away by the twelve-pounder Lyddite shells, and the submarine sank bows first at 4.36 p.m.

The survivors of the crew on board were taken off by the boats just before the submarine foundered, and those who had jumped overboard were picked up.

I desire to bring to your notice the admirable steadiness displayed by all hands during the rather trying time (nearly an hour) we were being shelled without replying. Fortunately we were not hit, though a shell cut the whistle lanyard.[49]

Papers taken from the prisoners, and their replies to Grenfell's questions, established that that the submarine was the *UB.19*, built in 1915, armed with one 88 millimetre gun forward of the conning tower and with two bow torpedo tubes. She carried three torpedoes, one of which had recently been used to sink a Norwegian vessel, and two were still on board. The *UB.19* was 121 feet 4 inches long, and had a speed of ten knots on the surface and three to four under water. She had left her base, Zeebrugge, on 22nd November, 1916, and passed through the Straits of Dover. She was capable of remaining away from base for three weeks, and usually remained in harbour for eight to fourteen days. So much did Grenfell learn just in preliminary interrogation—Room 40 would no doubt learn a great deal more.

So, even after a rather slack year, caused partly by the interruption of submarine attacks and partly by the absence of the best Q-ship commander, Gordon Campbell, from the eastern side of the Atlantic for a large part of the year, the Q-ships were still earning their keep.

CHAPTER SIX

The *Strafe* of the Q-ships

I T NOW SEEMS reasonable to abandon the chronological account of the development of the Q-Ship campaigns and to look separately at two different strands which are revealed by the pattern of events in 1917. One of these is the continued successes of the mystery ships, the other contrasting strand is the deliberate and determined attempt by the U-boats to put an end to their operations, an attempt which succeeded to the extent that it reduced their 1916 number by a third.

It seems strange that no previous historian of the Q-ships has taken notice of this very definite pattern of events, but the relationship between the sinkings of 1917 is quite clear. The normal sequence of events was that the Q-ship was torpedoed without warning; any survivors were then taken prisoner and interrogated by the U-boat commander. An announcement was later made by the Germans that a Q-ship had been sunk, giving her name and number, indicating that this was a deliberate campaign against the Special Service. Sometimes there were no survivors, either because of the rapidity with which the Q-ship had sunk or, in one instance at any rate, as a result of the deliberate policy of *spurlos versenkt*—destroyed without trace. In order to demonstrate this pattern of intentional destruction of Q-ships, as opposed to the sinking of ships which were taken to be merchantmen, I shall take just a few examples out of many.

The first case to be considered is that of *Warner*, alias *Q.27*, a cargo decoy sunk by *U.38* west of Ireland on 13th March, 1917. An article appeared in the Hamburg *Nachrichten* commenting on the sinking, which was duly reported in the *Daily Express* and somewhat later in the *Fishing News* of 29th September.

> On a westward run from the coast, in order to lie in wait for the ships destined for England, one of our big U-boats, towards nine o'clock in the morning of a cold March day, sighted a smallish steamer of about 1,500 tons approaching with an eastward course, which excited remark not only by her high bridge and high deck erections, but also by the meaningless deviations from her route and her wild zig-zag course.
>
> The submarine put the last torpedo into the tube for the attack, and only now and again popped the conning-tower for a few moments above the surface, in order not to betray itself to the suspicious steamer, which was approaching at about twelve knots. In spite of the continuous change of course, it was possible to get the enemy within range, and the torpedo was launched without being noticed. It had scarcely

penetrated, with a powerful detonation, into the centre of the steamer when she began to sink, and after a second explosion in the boiler-house, she disappeared in less than three minutes.

The large number of the crew standing on deck, who only succeeded, in spite of the utmost exertions, in lowering one boat to the water, seemed to confirm the suspicion that this was a U-boat trap. In order to ascertain certainly if this were so, U-—— went up to the survivors, who were drifting about in the water, and fished out six men, who were clinging half benumbed to planks. The men were very well dressed, and had a good military carriage to which one is not usually accustomed in mercantile ships.

According to their statement, the steamer was bound from Africa to England. After denying it for a long time, they at last admitted that they belonged to the Navy. The sunk ship was, they said, the U-boat trap *Q.27*, H.M.S. *Warner*, and the captain and all the officers had perished in the boiler explosion.

Lieutenant Yuile, R.N.R., the senior officer from *Warner* to survive, reported her last moments after he and other survivors had been picked up by the British submarine *D.3* two days after the sinking and landed at Galway. He had been on the bridge when he suddenly observed the wake

Damage caused by a torpedo striking the engine room. The scale of the damage can be measured by the size of the men working among the shattered plating.

of a torpedo about 100 yards away. He rang "Full Speed Ahead" and gave the order "Hard a' Starboard", but even while he was giving the order the torpedo struck the ship on the port quarter, abreast of the magazine. The C.O., who had joined him on the bridge on hearing the order, gave the order to abandon ship, as there was no sign of the submarine. By the time Yuile had reached his station at the port lifeboat, the ship's stern was under the water. He asked the C.O. if he were coming to the boat as it floated off, but was ordered to carry on. At this time the C.O. was standing by the raft on the port side of the boat deck.

The starboard lifeboat was lowered away with Lieutenant Milne, R.N.R., in charge, but it was drawn in and capsized by the suction as the ship sank. It had taken exactly five minutes for *Warner* to sink. The U-boat's periscope appeared 800 yards away; she came to the surface and steamed towards the lifeboat. The following dialogue then took place.

"Where is your ship?" Replied, "Gone."

"Where is your captain?" Replied, "Gone down with the ship."

"What is the name of your ship?" Replied, "*Warner*, Clyde Shipping Co."

"Where were you bound?" Replied, "Destination unknown."

The U-boat commander then remarked that he was sorry he could not take all the survivors on board, but that he would take those survivors in the water. "As far as I am aware, the C.O., navigating officer, and three ratings were taken aboard the submarine," Lieutenant Yuile reported.

Yuile makes it quite plain that it was not *U.61*, as suggested by Dittmar and Colledge,[50] but *U.38* which had sunk the *Warner*. She steamed away in a north-easterly direction, and when about two miles distant "rigged up a dummy funnel abaft conning tower, which was painted black with a red band. She emitted black smoke from same."

The destruction of the *Aubrietia*-type convoy sloop *Tulip* was virtually identical with that of *Warner*. On 30th April *Tulip* was steaming 200 miles west of Ireland when a periscope was sighted. The commander, Norman Lewis, turned towards the submarine, intending to ram, but before the ship could answer the helm a torpedo hit her amidships, killing many of the engine room staff and wrecking the largest lifeboat. Lewis gave the order to abandon ship and threw overboard the iron box containing the confidential books. His steward, a butler in civilian life, apologised for leaving the captain's cabin in such a terrible state as the survivors got away in the three remaining boats.

The U-boat, *U.62* commanded by Korvetten-Kapitän Hashagen, closed the lifeboats, and a young officer asked for the captain. Lewis raised his hand and was ordered aboard. He was taken to Korvetten-

The convoy sloop *Tulip*, sunk by *U.62* on 30th April, 1917. From *Q-Ships and Their Story*.

Kapitän Hashagen who said: "Good afternoon, Captain. Do you have any papers or weapons on you?" Lewis said that he did not. "Very well," said Hashagen, "sit down and have a drink." Lewis had been expecting a rather different reception, but as he said later: "Being of a tactful nature, I had one."[51] He continued to be treated well in the U-boat and spent the rest of the war a prisoner at Freiburg. His men were left to a 200-mile row home; fortunately they were picked up the following day.

Later Hashagen reported that although *Tulip* was well disguised, his suspicions had been aroused by the way the merchant flag was hoisted and by the fact that *Tulip* appeared to have no defensive gun at a time when many British merchant ships were acquiring them.

Only a cargo of "firewood"* and heroic efforts by her officers and crew prevented *Q.26*, alias *Mavis* and *Nyroca*, from joining at the bottom of the sea other Q-ships torpedoed without warning. Commander Adrian Keyes, R.N., described how on 3rd June, after picking up survivors from a Greek steamer and sailing on through considerable wreckage, *Mavis* was torpedoed at 21.45 hrs twenty miles due south from the Wolf Rock light. Though the torpedo had been seen breaking surface

*Firewood—term used to denote a cargo of an assortment of cheap rough timber.

about forty yards from the ship, there was no time to take evasive action. It struck the ship abreast the engine room and penetrated inside before exploding.

> Nothing was seen of the submarine, which must have been directly in the path of the moon, and submerged. The explosion was very violent; the ship stopped at once, and the engine room and boiler room were flooded in a few seconds. The ship's company went at once to their stations, and everything was carried out as at drill. The firemen and non-combatants went away in the boats as if abandoning ship, and the armed boats prepared for attack . . . The emergency wireless was wrecked, and failed to give a spark. So after waiting half an hour with no sign of the submarine returning, I fired three rockets and surveyed the ship.
>
> The main engines were thrown right across the ship, and were lying against the port side; there was a very large hole on starboard side, with the plates blown outwards; the ship was listing about 10 degrees to port, and no water was making forward or aft of the engine and boiler room bulkheads.[52]

As usual the engine room staff had borne the brunt of the torpedo attack. One temporary Sub Lieutenant R.N.R., one leading fireman, and two firemen, who had been on watch in the engine room and stokehold at the time of the occurrence, had been killed. Most ships would have gone to the bottom at this point, but a lot of work had been done to make *Mavis* unsinkable. Her bulkheads at 26 and 90 stations had been made watertight and carried to the main deck, so that even if one section were flooded the rest would provide buoyancy. All her derricks, except on the forecastle, had been landed and stored, and they had been replaced by dummy ones, thus making her topworks very much lighter. The cargo hatches had been plated over, access to the holds being provided by manholes. Two nine-inch sea cocks, worked from the upper deck to No. 1 hold, and a steam ejector with a capacity of 200 tons an hour had been asked for as part of her fittings. In addition she had been ballasted with all the firewood available in Devonport, and as this had been done quite recently, in March, her cargo was still in good condition.

Nonetheless, but for the good weather conditions prevailing, a southwesterly swell and a bright moon, Keyes would probably never have got her back to port. When the destroyer *Christopher* approached, Keyes sent most of his men aboard her, only keeping four officers and five men to secure hawsers and throw the confidential books overboard. Under tow from two successive tugs, *Mavis* shaped a course for Plymouth. Towing gave the vessel such a further list that she took up an angle of 22°. As the list got worse, Keyes lashed the wheel and sent the officers and men into a lifeboat, which was towing astern. Gradually the list increased and the *Mavis* began to sink, but escorted by the *Christopher* and trawlers, *Mavis* arrived off Rame Head with a list of 45°. When the King's Harbour Master arrived in a tug, Keyes asked him to beach the *Mavis* in

Cawsand Bay, on the port hand in the approaches to Plymouth, before she capsized, and this was done.

The fate of *Paxton*, alias *Lady Patricia* or *Q.25*, the week before shows even more clearly how a Q-ship might reveal her true identity to the U-boats and thus become the target for not one but two torpedoes. When he returned from a prisoner-of-war camp after the close of the war her commander, Lieutenant-Commander George Hewett, R.N., told what had happened. On 20th May *Paxton* had been cruising about 100 miles west of the Fastnet light when she began to be shelled by a U-boat, which was invisible save for the flashes of its gun, at a range of some 6,000 yards. Hewett lit a smoke screen by dropping four smoke boxes, then altered course and waited for the submarine to close through the smoke screen. As the submarine showed no signs of closing he turned north-east and steamed on at a slow speed for twenty minutes before turning west. The U-boat surfaced again and began shelling *Paxton*, after twenty minutes hitting the Q-ship in the after hold. As the submarine showed no signs of closing, Hewett opened fire, whereupon the German vessel dived. Hewett reported:

> *Paxton* proceeded on a westerly course, my intention being to turn at 7.30 p.m. and return to position to try for submarines at daybreak. For this purpose I dismantled bridge house, removed crow's nests, painted ship all over a different colour, and painted in large letters on ship's side *TOSCA SVERIGE* as also Swedish colours on both sides. I also erected portable deck house on deck and a camouflaged cargo of wood (which had been fitted and carried for this purpose). These preparations were made in the hazy weather, and were completed by 5 p.m.

Had this change of make-up been accomplished while *Paxton* was watched through the periscope of a U-boat? It would seem so, because as the Q-ship continued on her original course she was struck by a torpedo at 7.15 p.m. It hit the port side, right aft, lifting the after gun house, killing two men and wounding two others. The ship settled down aft till the counter was awash. Of course the blowing overboard of the after gun house and the exposure of the four-inch gun would have cleared up any doubts that might still have existed in the U-boat captain's mind about the true nature of *Paxton*.

> The torpedo explosion caused wireless gear to be carried away, propellor shaft broken, and all sea connections from engine room to sea on port side of ship to be fractured and also blowing the wood cargo (in after hold) through the after bulkhead of engine room. This damage caused the ship to settle fast by the stern, and to flood the engine room. I ordered "abandon ship, stand fast twelve-pounder guns' crews." Telephoned to engine room to Acting Lieutenant George Augustus Prescott, R.N.R., to keep his watch with him and to do everything in his power to keep pumps going and to blow after ballast tanks, etc. . . . I also . . . ordered the W.T. operator to sway aloft a spare W/T aerial. These orders were carried out with

all haste and without panic and ship was abandoned by all hands except myself, Acting Lieutenant Ivor MacGregor, R.N., and Sub-Lieutenant Robinson, R.N.R., two twelve-pounder guns' crews and two marines.

I put out a W/T call for assistance, "Ship being abandoned." The officers and men remaining on board remained at their stations, out of sight of enemy, of whom nothing had been seen, ready for instant action. Meanwhile ship was settling very fast, and at 7.25 p.m. she was at an angle of about 30° up at the bow, with water over upper deck as far as the hold . . . Finding ship was likely to sink at any moment, I telephoned to Engineer Lieutenant George Prescott, R.N.R., who was at this time working up to his waist in water in the engine room, to evacuate the engine room. This order he carried out, so far as sending his men on deck, but he himself remained below, still attending to his duty in the face of certain death . . . and tried to keep pumps going after sending up his men. I ordered Lieutenant MacGregor to cast loose the rafts in fore waist, ready to float off when ship sank—this he did.

At 7.30 p.m. a torpedo was seen coming at right angles to port side of ship—no submarine visible—which struck engine room beneath twelve-pounder gun. Ship immediately started to sink by the stern, so I ordered: "Every man for himself" and in four minutes ship had sunk. I remained on board with Acting Lieutenant McGregor until we were washed overboard, and after swimming I gained a raft, whilst he was picked up by life boat. About ten minutes after ship had sunk, submarine *U.46* came to the surface and having taken Engineer Sub-Lieutenant Johnson, R.N.R., on board, came to my raft and took me prisoner. This submarine was *not* the submarine I had had action with at 10 a.m. Our treatment whilst aboard the submarine *U.46* was all that could be desired.[53]

Yet while Hewett and Johnson went off to captivity according to the rules of war, another fate was reserved for their comrades in the sea, as related in chapter one.

In sharp contrast to the honourable captivity of Commanders Lewis and Hewett was the fate of the master and the crew of the armed smack *Ethel & Millie*, the one instance of a Q-ship which we can prove to have been *spurlos versenkt*. After the wholesale sinkings of British fishing vessels by U-boats in 1916, whole complements of fishing craft volunteered for Special Service.

The *Ethel & Millie* (LT 200), a Lowestoft smack acting as a Q-ship and captained by William "Johnsey" Manning, was working in the North Sea with a companion smack, the *Nelson*, known in peacetime as the *G & E* (LT 649). One was armed with a six-pounder, the other with a three-pounder gun, but both were hopelessly outranged when attacked by a U-boat on 15th August, 1917.[54] What happened to the *Ethel & Millie* is unclear, for no survivors were picked up, although on 16th August the smack *Friendship* did pick up a pigeon with a message that the armed smack was being attacked by a U-boat. The *Nelson's* part in the story is well remembered, for her skipper, Tom Crisp, was awarded a posthumous Victoria Cross which was in due course presented by King George V to his son, Thomas Crisp, who was serving as second hand in his father's smack at the time and was himself awarded the D.S.M. The younger Tom Crisp told his story at the Court of Inquiry held at Lowestoft into the loss of the two armed smacks.

> On Wednesday 15th August at about 2.45 p.m. the trawl was shot and we were on the port tack. The skipper sang out "Submarine," and as soon as he had spoken a shot fell about one hundred yards away on the port bow. The submarine was between three and four miles away from us, coming up from the Northwest.

A Lowestoft smack leaving harbour. A number of sailing trawlers were employed as Q-ships and some successes were claimed.

> The skipper said "Let go your gear." We let go the warp and put a dan* at the end of it, firing at the submarine all the time. About the fourth shot from the submarine went through our port bow just below the waterline, and then the skipper shoved her round. About the seventh shot the skipper was mortally wounded, the shell passing through him from his left side, and then through the deck and out through the side of the ship. I took charge of the tiller then, keeping to the south east. All the time we were making water fast and sinking. The skipper

*A marker buoy.

122

just told me to send a message off. I told a seaman to put on the message: "Nelson being attacked by submarine, skipper killed. Jim Howe Bank. Send assistance at once."

After that we were making water fast, and had used nearly all our ammunition, only having five rounds left, and we had to leave the ship because she was sinking. I asked the skipper if we should take him in the boat with us, but he said: "No, throw me overboard." This I would not do, and so we had to leave him on board the smack as he was in too bad a condition to be moved. We got into the small boat, the smack sinking by the head about a quarter of an hour afterwards. All the shots were directed on the *Nelson* until she sank.

After our ship sank the submarine directed the fire on the *Ethel & Millie*. When we were in the small boat, the skipper of the *Ethel & Millie* beckoned us to go on board, but we would not go. We kept rowing in to the south east and we saw one direct hit on the *Ethel & Millie* and the *Ethel & Millie's* crew abandon her.

Then the submarine worked round to the south and came to the eastward of us. When the submarine was working round to the south we were working round in the opposite direction. The submarine left off firing at the *Ethel & Millie* and picked her crew up. We saw the submarine's crew line the *Ethel & Millie's* crew up on the submarine's fore deck. They tied the smack's boat up astern of the submarine and steamed to the smack. The wind being from the south south east was blowing the *Ethel & Millie* into the north north west until she was nearly out of sight. Just before the *Ethel & Millie* got out of sight a haze fell over her and we rowed into the southeast as hard as we could, the opposite direction in which the smack and the submarine were going. It was drawing in dusk then. After dark came on we kept pulling in to the southwest.

The next morning at daybreak we saw a buoy ahead of us and the wind freshened and blew us out to the eastward again. We still kept pulling to the westward. On Thursday we saw the *Dryad*.* It was about three o'clock in the afternoon. He came in sight of us and then directed his course to the northwest and went out of sight.

After the *Dryad* came a group of minesweepers. They got ahead of us, and then turned and went away in a southwesterly direction. All the time we had a large piece of oilskin and pair of trousers tied on two oars to attract attention, but they did not see us. As night came the weather became finer, and we kept pulling into the westward all night as hard as we could.

At daybreak we saw some smacks straight ahead of us, but there was too much wind from the westward, and we could not get to them, and they went away from us in a southwesterly direction. One of the chaps sighted a buoy which turned out to be the Jim Howe Bank buoy. We pulled up to it and made fast to it just as the tide turned about 10.30 a.m. on Friday. The wind was blowing hard.

About 1.45 p.m. the *Dryad* found us. When we sighted the *Dryad*, I climbed on top of the buoy and waved my handkerchief. I was told afterwards when I got on board the *Dryad* that they were just going to turn away from us.

Witnesses filled in other details of the fight between *Nelson* and the submarine, which had begun while the latter was still three or four miles away. The *Nelson's* gunner, Leading Seaman Percival Ross, said that though he had tried to increase the range on the gun several times, his

---

*An old torpedo-gunboat then based at Lowestoft for minesweeping duties.

shots fell consistently short of the U-boat. The gunlayer, A. B. Edward Hale, said that his gun training had been hampered by having no telescope to observe the fall of the shells. When the smack had begun to sink, the skipper had ordered them to abandon her, first to throw the pigeon cypher overboard. The first pigeon had been released half an hour after the action began. Three more had been released because the birds kept flying round and round the ship, apparently stunned by the noise of the continuous shelling and gunfire.

The Court of Inquiry decided that "*Nelson* was handled in a seamanlike and brave manner and continued firing till she was sunk by gunfire, being apparently out-gunned. Her Skipper, Mr T. Crisp, R.N.R., died in action giving orders up to the last minute." The court also decided that there was no evidence as to the ultimate fate of *Ethel & Millie*, "but it is presumed that she was damaged by gunfire and eventually sunk by bomb."

What happened to the seven men aboard *Ethel & Millie*? There was no record of Skipper "Johnsey" Manning, Edwin John Barrett, A. B., Spencer T. Gibson, 2nd Hand, John Lewis, Alfred Preece and Hugh

Harold Auten disguised as a tramp skipper. From *"Q" Boat Adventures*.

Thompson, Deckhands, being reported as prisoners of war, and on 23rd November their relatives were advised to consider them dead.[55] To be lined up on the deck of a U-boat was a most sinister augury. Had the U-boat submerged, leaving them floundering in the water?

Why did some Q-ships give themselves away to the enemy and others retain their disguise of innocent merchantmen down to the second they opened fire on the U-boat? It is a question to which there is no single answer. The former collier *Vala*, alias *Q.8*, was in action with U-boats no fewer than seven times and must have become well known to submarine commanders. Just before she disappeared with all hands in the Bay of Biscay in August, 1917, Vice-Admiral Sir Lewis Bayly recommended her commanding officer, Commander Leopold A. Bernays, and some of his men for decorations. What was more, as with so many Q-ships, there was that little detail about *Vala* which looked out of place.

On 6th August, 1916, the commanding officer of the French torpedo boat No. 313 reported to his superior at Cherbourg that he had closed a merchant ship flying the Red Ensign "and presenting the appearance of an ordinary cargo ship." When he had come a little closer, however, "I then noticed that there were masked gun ports on the side of the ship, and I realised that I was face to face with an armed vessel. The name *VALA* was still visible on the bulwark, covered with black paint."

Almost a year later, *Vala's* disguise was penetrated again. A broadcast from Berlin announced on 8th September, 1917:

> In the Atlantic Ocean, English Channel and the North Sea, German U-boats have sunk a total of seven steamers aggregating 19,500 gross registered tons. These included the English U-boat trap, *Q.8*,* the former English steamer *Vala*, an unknown steamer of about 4,000 tons, which, from appearance, and judging by the arms and searchlight carried and the uniform of the crew, was an auxiliary cruiser.

Harold Auten was sent out in command of the convoy sloop *Heather* to look for survivors of *Vala* after she had last been heard of at Queenstown on 20th August. He carried out an extensive search but found no survivors and no wreckage. *Vala* was officially paid off as from 25th August, 1917. Only after the war was it revealed that *Vala* had been destroyed by *UB.54* on 21st August.

Altogether no fewer than seventeen Q-ships were lost in 1917, all but one of them falling victim to submarine attack, and in addition six of the convoy sloops employed on Special Service were lost that year. One of these latter was the *Arbutus*, which sank in a strong westerly gale on 16th December after being torpedoed by *UB.65* in St George's Channel. Lost

---

*The official British monitor noted this as "QUACH" but this obviously stood for "Q. *acht*", "Q.8" in German.

The panic party preparing to leave the ship. From "*Q*" *Boat Adventures.*

with her were Commander C. H. Oxlade, R.N.R., and Lieutenant Charles Stewart, R.N.R., who had remained on board to attempt to get the ship to safety after the rest of the ship's complement had been taken off by an American destroyer. The Admiralty granted the usual "survivors' leave," even extending the usual ten days' leave to twelve "to take the survivors over Boxing Day."

The *Penshurst, Q.7*, met her end that Christmas and the last of the strafed Q-ships of 1917 was the U.S.S. *Santee*, badly holed by a torpedo on 27th December. Though the Q-ship was able to limp back to port, her services were lost for the next five months, during which she had virtually to be rebuilt. The *Santee*, formerly the *Arvonian*, was the only American Q-ship ever to be in action with a submarine. She had begun her life as a British Special Service ship on 28th August, 1917, and on 8th November she was offered to Admiral W. S. Sims, U.S.N., commanding U.S. naval forces in British waters, as a substitute for the *Pargust* which had been held up because of a delay in the delivery of machinery.

The first U.S. Q-ship was one of the most heavily armed decoys ever to be fitted out. She had "three four inch B.L. Mark IX guns on C.P. 1 mountings. Three twelve hundredweight twelve pounder guns on S.2 mountings to be fitted as a tilter. Two Maxims on beef block mountings, two pairs eighteen inch A.W. torpedo tubes with eight cold eighteen inch torpedoes and six collision heads." The four-inch guns were disguised by "being recessed and by lifeboat lockers, hatch covers, etc." The twelve-pounder gun aft was screened as in a defensively armed merchant ship, but it was on a tilting mounting for disguise if required. The two twelve-pounders forward were at the break of the fo'c'sle on either side on tilting mountings. The torpedo tubes were placed one on each beam, one firing right ahead and one firing right astern. In addition Sims was given "some deep running and circling torpedo gear" in the use of which his crew would have to be instructed by two British leading torpedo men and two seamen torpedo men. *Santee* was fitted with otter protection against mines and a ten-inch portable searchlight. She had a one and a half kilowatt wireless set with an emergency set in the saloon, and a tube coil set under the fo'c'sle. In every respect, save her speed, which was only eleven knots, she ought to have been more than a match for any U-boat which attacked her on the surface.

Like the other Q-ships which had been strafed by the U-boats, however, *Santee* never had a chance to defend herself. She had gone out to Bantry Bay to train her crew, and within five hours of leaving port she had been attacked. Her captain, Commander D. C. Hanrahan, reported:

> *Santee* was torpedoed by an enemy submarine at 8.45 p.m. in Lat. 51° 23′ N. Long. 8° 38′ W. It was a cloudy, moonlight night, visibility good, speed of ship 8½ knots, zig-zagging, wind was northwest, sea moderate. We were on route to Bantry for training, having left Queenstown at 4.00 p.m.
>
> The torpedo struck the ship on the port side, just abaft the engine room bulkhead in No. 6 hold, and at a point about 6 or 8 feet below the waterline, extinguishing all lights on the ship. The engine room watertight bulkhead was blown in on the port side, engine room and fire room filling immediately, water breaking into No. 4 hold. Holds No. 4 and No. 7 filled immediately, No. 4 had 18 feet of water in it when we arrived at Queenstown.
>
> There were no injuries to the personnel, and the behaviour of everyone was most excellent, all hands going to their stations when signal was given, guns and torpedoes were ready in regular drill time ... I immediately sent the crew to stations and called away panic party to abandon ship. The port after lifeboat was destroyed by the explosion, the panic party leaving in the other three boats ... There was a total absence of noise or confusion, the interior of the ship was black, lights being out, and the panic party got away in fine panicky style.

Hanrahan now swept the moonlit area of four hundred yards of clear visibility round the ship with his glasses, waiting for the U-boat to rise and attack him. It never surfaced and after two and a half hours he reluctantly sent an S.O.S. to Queenstown and tried to recall his lifeboats. One of them had been carried downwind so far it had to be retrieved by another vessel, the American destroyer *Sterett. Santee* had to be towed back to Queenstown by the tug *Paladin*. Her damage was so extensive, the estimated time for repairs so long, that Sims handed her back to the Royal Navy. Repaired and renamed *Bendish*, she was sent to Gibraltar as part of a special squadron of Q-ships intended for operations there during 1918.

There seems little doubt that *Santee* had been recognised for what she was and torpedoed by some U-boat which did not have a second torpedo to spare and dreaded a surface attack with a heavily armed Q-ship. How had her disguise been penetrated? Sims may have supplied the answer himself when he said that German U-boat commanders were issued with a handbook on "How to detect a Q-ship." It detailed the many tell-tale signs that might betray a decoy to inspection through a periscope. "In order to make the sides of the ships collapsible," wrote Sims, "certain seams were unavoidably left in the plates, where the detachable part joined the main structure. The U-boat commanders soon learned to look for these betraying seams before coming to the surface. They would sail submerged around the ship, the periscope minutely examining the sides, much as a scientist examines his specimens with a microscope."[56]

This survey of the *strafe* of the Q-ships in 1917 has not included the sinkings of the best known, such as *Prize*, and has not attempted to embrace all the known sinkings. Sufficient has been said, however, to suggest that by 1917 the true purpose of the Q-ships was no secret to the Germans, that they were determined to destroy as many of them as they could without giving them any chance to defend themselves, and that they were reasonably successful in this attempt. Yet, as the events described in the following chapter will show, the Special Service could still give a good account of itself.

CHAPTER SEVEN

The Year of Victories

I T MIGHT be assumed, in view of the difficulties mentioned in the previous chapters, the awareness of the U-boats of the Q-ship secret and their ability to penetrate disguise, that the Q-ship campaign would have ground to a halt in 1917. This indeed is what happened, but not till the end of the year, and not until the decoys had scored their greatest triumphs, five accredited kills.

They were only able to achieve this success because they deliberately adopted near-suicidal tactics, inviting the U-boats to torpedo them and even turning towards a torpedo if it appeared to be about to miss instead of trying to avoid it, voluntarily dooming part of the engine room complement to destruction in the hope that they might thereby be able to dispose of a submarine. It was not merely the adoption of new tactics that enabled them to have such a successful year, however, but the spread of their operations. Never before had there been so many Q-ships of different sorts.

Notable among the new decoys were numbers of fishing boats. The mass destruction of the fishing fleets by U-boats in 1916 had driven many fishermen to demand that some of their own craft should be enrolled in the Special Service. M. A. Neale, of Neale & West Ltd., steam trawler owners of Hope Street, Cardiff, wrote to the Director of Trade, Division D.A.M.S.,* Room Y, Admiralty House, Admiralty, Whitehall, on 15th December, 1916:

> The Admiralty have had seventeen of our trawlers and left us five with which to keep up the fish supply of Cardiff, ours being the only fishing boats which work to Cardiff at all. Of these five, three have been sunk by submarines, two during last month . . . We should be very glad if you will write to oblige us with some guns at once. We were promised them in the early days of the war, but the Admiralty then had none to spare. When the Commander of the Submarine sunk our last boat, he told our men that he knew the firm, that we had two more, and that he was coming back for them. We could have had submarines on various occasions if we had had real guns. We have been unmolested through putting wooden ones on until lately. Now they have found out they are wooden ones from spies. They told our men they knew they were wooden without going on board. If we have an immediate answer, we will have one boat fitted up next week, and another the week after.[57]

Rather than let Neale act alone, the Admiralty enrolled the crews of his trawlers *Suma* (CF 2) and *Asama* (CF 12), sent him some guns and

*Defensively Armed Merchant Ship.

gunners, and ordered him to go on fishing as usual. He could dispose of the fish he caught,[58] but the trawlers would be under Admiralty orders. *Asama* was given R.N. No. 515, *Suma*, 2516. Both were identical vessels, built in 1914, with a gross tonnage of 284, and they were given an armament of one three-pounder—not much, but better than a wooden gun. Neale's own workmen fitted the guns on board, and put an imitation boat cover round them "so as to conceal from inquisitive people".

Vice-Admiral Charles H. Dare, commanding at Milford Haven, issued general orders for the trawlers, stipulating that naval uniform was not to be worn, but to be carried on board so that all ranks could prove their identity in case of capture. The gun was to be kept concealed by placing an old trawl net over it or any other method. Fire was not to be opened on a U-boat until she had closed within six or eight hundred yards. If they were close to a merchant vessel which was attacked they had to proceed there at once to render all assistance either in attacking the U-boat or rescuing the crew. If the trawl was out, they were to slip or cut the warp without delay. To this end the trawl warp should be made fast to the winch by means of a light strop that would give readily when the warp was allowed to run out. Two good axes should be kept handy to cut the wire in case it jammed.

General Quarters, to be the subject of daily exercise, would be for the skipper to be in the wheelhouse, the gun's crew clearing away the gun, one deckhand at the wheel, the second hand and two deckhands supplying ammunition, and when all had been passed up they were to clear away the boat. The cook was to hoist the White Ensign and provide and load rifles; the first engineman and one trimmer to be in charge of the engine room, while the second engineman connected the fire hose, provided shot plugs and plugged shot holes where required.

Long before the "official" beginning of the all-out German attack on shipping Bayly's fleet had been engaged in a number of actions in which it was all too evident that the U-boat commanders were sticking to their new tactics of shelling at an extremely long range, and that they were able to recognise Q-ships for what they were once an action had begun. "I am of the opinion," wrote Lieutenant-Commander A. G. Leslie of the rebuilt convoy sloop *Begonia*, *Q.10*, relating an encounter of 3rd January, 1917, "that these ships are recognized at about 6,000 yards on a clear bright day, and that to abandon ship is to court disaster if this is the case."

"A disguised ship must always have the disadvantage of offering a bigger target than a submarine," commented Bayly. "Consequently submarines now frequently open fire at long range, since they have learned of the existence of Q-ships, and are afraid of getting too close to any ship for fear of being had . . . One device which might be tried at present is to have two or three buckets or mess tubs full of seaweed, rope-yarns or other similar material near each other on deck, and when the submarine opens fire, to throw red hot coal on these buckets so as to make a column of smoke with a view to inducing the submarine to close, thinking the ship is on fire."

On 14th January the decoys had their first success. Commander F. H. Grenfell of *Penshurst, Q.7*, succeeded in luring *UB.37* within 700 yards by sending off his panic party. Evidently this submarine had heard all about Q-ships and she did not intend getting any closer, as Grenfell reported.

> She stopped in this position, exposing her broadside and quickened her rate of fire (all told she fired 14 rounds) evidently with the intention of sinking us from this position by gunfire. It was now that we were hit twice in rapid succession. The first hit broke an awning ridge pole on the bridge, the second struck the angle of the

Commander F. H. Grenfell, fourth from left, and officers of the *Penshurst* in their naval uniforms. From *Q-Ships and Their Story*.

lower bridge, cutting the engine-room telegraph connections and the pipe connecting the hydraulic release gear with the starboard D-type depth-charge: this shot also, I regret to say, killed the gunlayer and loading number of the six-pounder gun and wounded the breech worker and the signalman standing by to hoist the White Ensign.

On perceiving the submarine's intention, I opened fire at 4.24 p.m. The first shot from the twelve-pounder gun (lyddite shell) hit the base of the conning-tower and caused a large explosion as though ammunition had been exploded. Large parts of the conning-tower were seen to be blown away, and a big volume of black smoke arose from it. The second shot from the twelve-pounder hit a little abaft the conning-tower and also visibly caused damage to the hull.

The starboard three-pounder gun hit the lower part of the conning-tower certainly four times and probably twice more. The submarine then sank by the stern, her bows coming appreciably out of the water.[59]

There is no doubt about the destruction of *UB.37*, but there were many occasions during the war when claims that a U-boat had been sunk turned out to be optimistic. Only after the war did the meticulous researches of Gordon Campbell into German naval archives and the painstaking comparison of Q-ship claims and German admissions of U-boat losses enable a true assessment to be made. Even now historians are not agreed over which U-boats were sunk and by what means.

Admiral Scheer gives us a chance in his book *Germany's High Sea Fleet in the World War* both to see the fight from the U-boat's point of view and to understand how much punishment a submarine could take without being destroyed. He quotes from the log of the *U.84* a somewhat graphic description of her duel with the Q-ship *Penshurst* on 22nd February, 1917.

1.50—Tank steamer, about 3,000 tons, with course 250 degrees, in sight. Dived. Torpedo fired from second tube; missed by 700 m.; had underestimated way. Steamer turns upon counter course. Went down. Rose to surface. Stopped her with gunfire. Steamer stops, blows off steam, crew leave the ship in two boats.

2.30 P.M.—Approached under water. No armament. Boats, about 8–10, are away from steamer.

2.49 P.M.—Rose to surface near boats which still try to pull away from U-boat.

2.49 P.M.—Steamer opens fire from four guns. Dive. Conning-tower hit five times: one shot through the bridge, one above the aerials, the third (4.7 cm.) goes through the conning-tower, explodes inside, nearly all apparatus destroyed. Second officer of the watch slightly wounded. Fourth shot smashed circulating water tubes; fifth shot hit a mine deflector. Abandoned conning-tower. Central hatch and speaking tube closed. As the conning-tower abandoned, the boat had to be worked from the central space below the conning-tower. The lifeboats throw depth charges to a depth of 20 m. Switch and main switchboard held in place by hand. Electric lamp over magnetic compass goes out. Boat is top-heavy and oscillates round the transverse axis [because the conning-tower was filled with water]. A number of connections between the conning-tower and hull do not remain watertight. Owing to short circuit the following fail in quick succession: gyro-compass, lamp-circuit [for lighting], main rudder, means of communication, forward horizontal rudder

The *Penshurst* with panic party rowing off, White Ensign being hoisted at the foremast and the guns about to open fire — but this was only a dress rehearsal. From *Q-Ships and Their Story.*

jams. In spite of being 14 degrees down by the stern and engines going full speed, the boat sinks by the bows to 40 m.; compressed air. To get rid of the water, rapid expulsion of air to 20 m. to 16 degrees to load aft. Tank No. 1 gets no compressed air. All hands in the bows to avoid breaking surface. Torpedo coxswain and No. 1 (petty officer) even counter-flood forward. Boat falls 8 degrees by the bow, and sinks to 35 m. depth. Compressed air on forward tanks.

Meanwhile the spray (from leaks in the conning-tower) is kept off the electric apparatus by sail-cloth, waterproofs, flags, etc. The watertight auxiliary switch-board is the saving of the boat. Boat sinks down by the stern again and threatens to break surface. Steering under water no longer possible.

3.10 P.M.—Compressed air on all tanks. Starboard electric engine breaks down. To the guns, clear oil motors, full speed ahead!

[The commander decided, as the boat could not remain under water, to rise to the surface and chance fighting the steamer.]

The steamer is 35 hm. (3,828 yards) off and opens fire at once. Shots all round the boat. One 7.5 and one 4.7 cm. shell hit the upper deck forward of the boat's 8.8 cm. gun. Second officer of the watch receives other slight wounds. Replied to fire, unfortunately without telescopic sight as the conning-tower is still full of water. Distance quickly increases to 50 hm. (5,468 yards). Then the steamer follows slowly. To starboard a destroyer which opens fire at 80 hm. (8,748 yards); shots fall short. Put on cork jackets. The intention is to continue gunfire till the boat can be sunk in the neighbourhood of a sailing vessel 8 sea miles away, to save the crew from a *Baralong* fate.

3.17 P.M.—The destroyer is a *Foxglove,** but cannot steam faster than the boat. At about 75 hm. (8,200 yards) replied to fire. The *Foxglove* soon begins to try and avoid shots; is hit twice, and increases the distance. Her guns only carry about 75 hm.

3.20 P.M.—Conning-tower can be made watertight; boat cleared; ammunition for gun cleared; except conning-tower, all damage can gradually be repaired.

*The Flower-class sloop *Alyssum*, which had been escorting the s.s. *Canadian*.

Course 165 degrees. The *Foxglove* follows in our wake. Steamer lost to view. At a pinch the boat can dive, but leaves a heavy oil track behind her. If no destroyer comes before night, the boat can be saved.

6.50 P.M.—The *Foxglove* has approached to 70 hm. (7,655 yards) and opens fire again. Return fire: hit. Enemy sheers off and falls back to over 100 hm. (11,000 yards)

8 P.M.—Twilight. Pursuit out of sight. On account of oil track zig-zag course. Run into another oil track, turned to port and gradually on course of 240 degrees.

The *U.84* returned to her base safely in spite of the damage she had received. Admiral Scheer, who inspected the vessel after her arrival, considered it was little short of a miracle she had survived—but survive she had.

The reports for January were so promising that Bayly announced: "Four submarines have been sunk during the first two weeks of January. In my letter of 15th January, 1917, I asked that six more Q-ships should be commissioned; I feel sure that we should get good value from them." Bayly had asked in addition that "Three of the six should be specially built (I would like to be consulted as regards their design)." Such demands for a purpose-built Q-ship resulted in the building of the *Hyderabad*, a unique vessel launched on 27th August, 1917, at the Woolston yard of J. I. Thornycroft. She came too late to affect the closing stages of the war against the U-boats.

So difficult was it to determine whether a submarine had been sunk or not that Captain J. L. Marx R.N.R. (who had retired from the Royal Navy as an admiral in 1911 but returned as an R.N.R. captain on the outbreak of war) had a brisk interchange with the Admiralty apropos of a U-boat which he claimed to have sunk in *Aubrietia, Q.13. Aubrietia's* shells

The purpose-built decoy vessel *H.M.S. Hyderabad*. She entered service too late to play a significant part in the anti-submarine campaign and in this picture is serving as a depot ship in 1919. *Imperial War Museum*

had blown away the conning tower completely, scattering the four men who were on it. Smoke in two colours had billowed from the submarine, and Marx had no hesitation in claiming this encounter as a sinking. The Admiralty had had their doubts, however, and at the part of Marx's report where the two colours of smoke were mentioned, someone had written in the margin "smoke screen."

These doubts proved justified when on 20th January a German broadcast from Berlin announced:

> One of our submarines sighted a steamer in the English Channel. The Danish neutrality indications, the Danish flag, and the words FAI, DENMARK, painted in large white letters, were clearly seen. The commander of the submarine thought he had to do with a harmless Danish steamer and approached, when suddenly the steamer dropped its mask. The boards of the aft wheelhouse fell down and a gun of between ten and fifteen centimetre calibre became visible, over which the Danish flag remained flying. At the same time several shots were fired from guns on the steamer. The U-boat succeeded in escaping from danger by quickly submerging. In the meantime it has been ascertained without doubt that we have to deal again with one of those shameless cases in which English steamers misuse the neutral flag in the most ruthless manner as U-boat traps.

Bayly, always very loyal to his subordinates, suggested that there had been two U-boats, and this was how the news of Marx's encounter had leaked out. The second U-boat had not torpedoed *Aubrietia* for some reason—possibly because she was out of torpedoes. Or perhaps there might be another explanation. "Q-ships," wrote Bayly, "are usually very elated after a success, and it is more than likely that tongues were loosed after arrival on shore and the information was made use of to discredit the victory." When Marx learned that the Admiralty proposed to reduce the usual £1,000 reward to the ship's company for a "certainty" to a £200 award paid out for a "possible" he wrote with some acrimony to state that the *Q.13's* assumed name had been KAI, not FAI. It was a lie that the Danish flag flew through the action: "this was not the case as the flagstaff falls down on the next deck at the time the gun is cleared away. As regards the commander of the submarine expressing his thoughts in Berlin, there is little doubt that he was on the conning tower when the shell hit it, and that he was one of the men whose pieces were seen in the air."[60]

It was becoming more and more difficult for a Q-ship to sink a U-boat. Commenting on Grenfell's action in *Penshurst* on 14th January, Sir Lewis Bayly referred to "the necessity of the most perfect discipline and organisation of Q-ships together with the danger of anything in the construction or design of the ship which would give her away. Thus the submarine fires her first shots at long range; she gradually approaches and orders a boat to be sent to her while the Q-ship stops, blows off steam, and gets boats ready. On the submarine's conning tower (this was seen by *Q.13*) is an officer or rating lying flat with a pair of glasses watching every movement of the Q-ship, and doubtless, should the Q-ship make one false move, should one man give the show away, the submarine could, with a slight movement of her helm, sink the Q-ship at once with a torpedo. The submarine approaches so as to get near enough to go on board and fix her bombs; the Q-ship delays with her boats etc., as much as she dares, so as to get the submarine near enough to make certain of her guns hitting. As they close the submarine gets suspicious; nervous of other ships approaching or angry at losing time and so missing other chances; and opens fire at the ship (as with *Q.7*) at a longer range than the Q-ship."

All sorts of factors were now forcing the long duel between Q-ships and U-boats into an impasse. By February, it had become obvious to Bayly that all Q-ships were undergunned, and that if they were really to stand up to U-boats they needed a four-inch gun. "It is increasingly difficult to get near enough to submarines for the twelve-pounder guns in the convoy sloops to be effective. Experience has shown that the modern German submarine makes fair shooting at 6,000 yards in good conditions of weather and light." Yet the four-inch guns were difficult to disguise, which was why he had discouraged them hitherto.

In spite of the difficulties, the Q-ships continued taking their toll of the U-boats, as Gordon Campbell demonstrated by his sinking of *U.83* by *Farnborough, Q.5*, in the action of 17th February. The first intimation that the *Farnborough* was under attack was the track of a torpedo approaching on the starboard beam, Campbell reported.

> It was evident it would hit the ship, so I put the helm hard aport to try to avoid the engine room. The torpedo struck the ship in No. 3 hold, bursting the bulkhead

between that hold and the engine room. I regret that an Engineer Sub-Lieutenant, R.N.R., was slightly wounded by the explosion. No signal was sent, as I feared some ship arriving before we had done our work. Action stations had in the meantime been sounded and all hands went to stations previously arranged for such an emergency; the ship was abandoned by every available man except those required on board; two lifeboats and one dinghy full of men were sent away and the fourth boat partially lowered. The Chief Engineer reported the engine-room filling and I ordered him to hang on as long as possible and then hide, which he did.

While we were doing this the submarine was observed on the starboard quarter about 200 yards distant, watching the proceedings through his periscope. He then came past the ship on the starboard side, about five yards off the lifeboats and ten yards off the ship, so close that I could see the whole hull of the submarine distinctly. The temptation to open fire was almost unbearable. He passed close across the bow and broke surface about 300 yards off on the port bow at 10.5 a.m. and I then made the signal "Torpedoed." He came down on the surface past the the the port side; I waited till he was on the only bearing on which all my guns could bear, and opened fire at point blank range. The first shot—from the six-pounder—hit the conning-tower and, according to the prisoner, removed the captain's head. The submarine apparently never recovered from his surprise as he remained on the surface whilst we shattered his hull. His conning tower was continually hit, some of the shells apparently going clean through it. Altogether 45 shells were fired in addition to the Maxim. He finally sunk with his conning tower open and shattered, and with the crew pouring out. When the submarine had disappeared I ordered "Cease fire"; there were about eight men in the water and one of my lifeboats went to their assistance, and were in time to save one officer and one man. The water was thick with oil and blood, and air bubbles were very conspicuous. No number was visible but it is believed to have been *U.83*.

I recalled the boats and inspected the ship. The engine and boiler-rooms, Nos. 3, 4 and after holds were rapidly filling, and I considered she was sinking by the stern. I therefore signalled for assistance and placed all hands on the boats, except a few men I kept on board, and I also gave orders to destroy all confidential and valuable books and charts etc.

Opposite: A Sutton-Armstrong bomb thrower concealed in a dummy hatch on the *Hyderabad*.
Imperial War Museum

Right: The after deck of the *Hyderabad* showing a quick-firing gun on disappearing platform.
Imperial War Museum

The destroyer *Narwhal* arrived in a short time to succour the sinking *Farnborough*, and while she took off the crew the convoy sloop *Buttercup* took the stricken Q-ship in tow. The water gained rapidly and one of the depth charges aboard exploded, making *Buttercup* cast off. In spite of this mishap the *Farnborough*, kept afloat by the timber in her holds, was towed to Berehaven in Ireland by the sloop *Laburnum* and was beached at Mill Cove the following day.

In order to achieve success, Campbell had had to allow his ship to be torpedoed, and he had nearly been blown up by the armaments of his own ship exploding. He was, nonetheless, satisfied with what he had achieved. Leutnant zur See Ferdinand Boenicke, gunnery officer and one of the two survivors of the *U.83*, told him that the submarine had been captained by Korvetten-Kapitän Hoppe and armed with the 5.9 inch (150 mm.) gun with which the Germans could do such good shooting at 6,000 yards. In addition she had five 45 cm. torpedoes. She had a speed on the surface of over sixteen knots and submerged, of ten. The crew numbered thirty-one, not including the officers.

The *U.83* had left Heligoland about three weeks earlier for what was expected to be a five-week cruise. They had come northabout through the Fair Island Channel. For most of the voyage, they had been working round the Scillies, where on the 7th they had engaged a trawler, but had

Left: *Farnborough* in a sinking condition after having sunk the *U.83*, seen from one of the escorting naval vessels.

Opposite: *Farnborough* beached in Mill Cove after being towed into Berehaven by the sloop *Laburnum*. Both pictures are from *My Mystery Ships*.

been forced to submerge. They had sunk a steamer, name unknown, about a week before the encounter with the *Farnborough*.

The next successful encounter, in which the cargo-type Q-ship *Privet* sank *U.85*, again demonstrated only too clearly that no longer could a Q-ship expect to destroy a submarine except by running the risk of her own loss and incurring heavy casualties. *Privet*, *Q.19*, was on a passage from Land's End to Alderney on 12th March when a torpedo passed under the ship below the engine room. Ten minutes later the U-boat which had fired the torpedo surfaced and began to shell *Privet*, the fourth shot passing through a depth charge aft. Gradually the submarine closed the range from 2,400 yards to 1,800 yards, scoring five hits with the first nine rounds, one shell bursting among the "abandon ship party", causing many casualties and destroying both boats. Fourteen minutes after the start of the action the port battery had been hit and the engines disabled. Lieutenant-Commander C. G. Matheson, R.N.R., sent off an S.O.S. and the next minute opened fire at 2,000 yards. The submarine was able to return only one more round and was hit four times before she sank. Although the evidence at the time seemed no more conclusive than in so many other cases, Campbell afterwards established that *U.85* had in fact been lost.

Meanwhile the *Privet* was in a bad way. The engine room was filling up from a hit which had occurred about 3.18 p.m., and communication between bridge and engine room was impossible except by telegraph because of the noise of escaping steam from the damaged whistle connection. As the chief engineer reported that water was over the plates

and rising, the first lieutenant attempted to plug the shell hole with hammocks and timber, but owing to the size of the hole and its inaccessibility, this proved to be impossible. It was feared that the bulkhead might give at any moment, so Lieutenant-Commander Matheson ordered the crew, with the wounded, into the remaining boats, one lifeboat and a skiff. A quarter of an hour later the destroyer *Christopher* arrived, followed by another destroyer, the *Orestes*, but the after bulkhead gave way and water rose so fast that it was obvious that nothing could be done, so the confidential books were passed overboard and the depth charges put to "safe". Matheson went aboard *Orestes*, only to return to make a desperate unsuccessful attempt to tow *Q.19* into port. She sank in Plymouth Sound opposite Picklecombe Fort in four and a half fathoms.[61].

On 28th April, 1917, the Q-ship era came to an end, as far as official nomenclature went, when the Admiralty made a signal that all 'Q.' prefixes were to be abolished and that "the vessels will be known in future

The hole made by a torpedo in the engine room of the *Pargust*, seen after she had been taken into dry dock. From *My Mystery Ships*.

as SPECIAL SERVICE SHIPS". A list of names replaced the old 'Q.' numbers. So it was under the name of *Pargust* that Campbell's latest ship won its success over *UC.29* on 7th June, 1917.

Being in Latitude 51° 50' N., Longitude 11 50' W., steering east (true) eight knots and disguised as an armed British merchant vessel (dummy gun mounted aft attended by a man in uniform) a torpedo was seen approaching the starboard beam, at the time it was misty, raining heavily, with a fresh southerly breeze and a choppy sea. The torpedo was apparently fired at very close range—it jumped out of the water when 100 yards from the ship—and struck the engine room near the water line, making a large rent and filling the boiler room, engine room and No. 5 Hold. The starboard lifeboat was blown in the air, pieces of it landing on the aerial. The helm was put hard-a-starboard to get a lee for the lifeboat.

The alarm had previously been sounded and "Abandon Ship" ordered—the three remaining boats, one lifeboat and two dinghies, being lowered full of men. Lieutenant F. R. Hereford, D.S.C., R.N.R., (acting as Master) went in charge of the lifeboat and greatly distinguished himself by his coolness and cunning. At 8.25 a.m. (the last boat then shoving off) the periscope was observed just before the port beam about 400 yards distant—he turned and steered straight towards the ship. At 8.25 a.m. when about 50 yards off the ship and close to the stern of the lifeboat, he submerged. Periscope was again sighted directly astern a few minutes later and he steamed to the starboard quarter, then turned round and went across to the port beam, turned again towards the ship and lifeboat, and at 8.33 a.m. when about 50 yards or less off the ship he partially broke surface—the conning tower and ends being visible.

He was heading parallel and opposite to the ship—the lifeboat in the meantime was pulling away and round the stern.[62] The submarine followed, passing close under the stern, and by the time the lifeboat was on the starboard beam, the submarine was close astern abaft my beam—one man was on top of the conning tower and kept shouting down directions through the conning tower. I watched this man carefully, as, as long as he was on top, I knew I could withhold my fire.

Lieutenant Hereford, knowing that I could fire at any minute now, pulled towards the ship. This action apparently annoyed the submarine, as when on the beam he came right up and started to semaphore to the boats—a second man apparently had a rifle or Maxim trained on the lifeboat. At 8.36 a.m., the submarine bearing one point before the beam distant about 50 yards, as all guns would bear, I opened fire—a torpedo was also fired on the offchance but missed astern. The first shot from the four-inch gun hit the base of the conning tower and also removed the two periscopes.

The close range enabled many hits to be obtained, nearly all in the conning tower. The submarine almost immediately on opening fire assumed a list to port and several men came out of the hatch abaft the conning tower. She steamed slowly across my bow with a heavy list to port, stern nearly under water, oil squirting from her side and the crew coming out of the conning tower and the after hatch.

When close on the port bow they held up their hands and waved. I ordered "Cease Fire"—no sooner had the order been carried out than she started to move off at a fair speed, with a heavy list to port and stern under water, apparently to get away in the mist. I was therefore obliged to open fire again, though it was obvious she was crippled.

I continued to fire until 8.40 a.m. when an explosion took place forward and she sank about 300 yards from the ship, falling over on her side—the last seen of her being the sharp bow, end up, about three feet out of the water.

During her swift rush of a few hundred yards the men abaft the conning tower were washed into the sea and others came up the fore hatch, one man clinging to the bow as she went down. There were several men in the water in the midst of the thick oil and I sent my boats to their assistance. They had a pull to windward, but managed to save one officer and one man.

In all 38 rounds were fired from the guns, nearly all of which were hits. H.M.S. *Crocus* arrived at 12.30 p.m. and took me in tow in a very seamanlike manner, and towed ship to Queenstown, arriving there at 3 p.m. on June 8th . . . It was a great strain for those on board to have to remain entirely concealed for 35 minutes after the ship was torpedoed, especially for instance the foremost gun's crew, who had to remain flat on the deck without moving a muscle. The men in the boats, especially the lifeboat, ran a great risk of being fired on by me if the submarine closed them.[63]

Nothing perhaps speaks more strongly about the suicide squad nature of the Special Service than this admission of Campbell's that rather than lose the U-boat he would fire on her when she was closing the lifeboat, yet the men in the lifeboat would not have had it otherwise. If German propagandists had been able to get their hands on the story of *UC.29's* end they would doubtless have made great play of shots being fired on a U-boat crew who had already raised their hands in surrender. Yet the submarine had been steaming away into the mist, apparently making a determined attempt to escape. The stationary and helpless *Pargust* would have had no chance of chasing an escaping U-boat.

Leutnant zur See Hans Bruhn and petty officer Stelan made no protests as they were hauled aboard *Pargust*. Bruhn admitted that the submarine was sunk but refused to say anything else, saying he was not allowed to do so. The other man was more communicative, as Campbell noted in his report.

Gave his name as Stelan, a mechanician of sorts, did not speak English very well, said number of submarine was *U.92*—then *UC.29*—this latter not borne out either by its appearance or by his statement that she carried no mines. Spent 10 days at Hamburg—left on Saturday—had been 21 days "in the sea." Had sunk some French and Norwegian ships and was homeward bound—wanted to sink a Britisher first. Said we were very kind and warned us (in return) that a submarine was close to westward of us.

Asked if his Captain had been saved, if so he wanted to jump over the side—delighted to hear his Captain had gone. Said he would talk if no other crew were saved. Said his father was a Russian and pro-English, also himself. Wanted to know if he would be forced to go back to Germany after the war.

There is only time to glance briefly at the suggestions which continued to arrive at the Admiralty for new kinds of Q-ships. They included a suggestion by Lieutenant Ivan B. Franks, R.N., for an exploding lifeboat, containing a 200lb charge of T.N.T. with a fuse set to

PARGUST

forty seconds to enable the boat's crew to jump overboard and swim to safety. Lieutenant R. Bowyer, commanding the destroyer H.M.S. *Paragon*, wanted a Q-ship with external saddle tanks so as to make her immune from torpedo attacks. When chased by a submarine she would flee, laying mines in quincunxes* on the track the U-boat would follow. Bowyer also suggested a "Fitting Ship" to take two one-man submarines in a contained dock in the double hull. These would be released to torpedo the U-boat. Perhaps Lieutenant Bowyer's idea did not fall on deaf ears. The PC boats did have shallow bulge protection against torpedoes, and *Hyderabad* was to have carried a coastal motor boat, an early form of motor torpedo boat, if not one-man submarines.

Lieutenant T. Hardy, R.N., submitted an idea for equipping fishing Q-ships with torpedoes under their keels, and fishing boats equipped with torpedoes did come into use. On the only occasion when one of them had a U-boat in the sights of his torpedo tube he refrained from firing until the U-boat had shown her hostile nature by beginning to shell

*Quincunx—Five mines laid one at each corner of a rectangle and one in the centre.

him, for fear she might be a British submarine. By that time it was too late to achieve success.* Proposals for the use of seaplanes with Q-ships were also put forward, and Lieutenant Harold Auten, R.N.R., himself a Q-ship officer, brought forward the not wholly novel idea of a derelict as a Q-ship. The derelict was to be towed by a tug, then abandoned on sight of a submarine.

Submarine and Q-ship partnerships suddenly returned to favour and towing trials were undertaken. Captain M. Nasmith, a British submarine "ace", proposed the use in conjunction with a submarine of a wholly unarmed sailing Q-ship. The schooners *Mana* and *Result* were sent to sea for trials with submarines, but Sir Lewis Bayly put a stop to this idea. "I consider," he wrote, "that with the present methods of enemy submarines and the suspicion they show for everything afloat, to send these unarmed ships out would be a useless waste of life; and I do not propose to allow these ships to sail from this harbour under present conditions. Also to send such ships as these out on the Atlantic or anywhere else but coasting from port to port would at once label them as enemies or lunatics." In the face of Bayly's determination the Admiralty had to climb down, but the Q-ship and submarine partnership had a more thorough trial in northern waters, without, however, producing any results.

More productive, in appearance at least, were the sailing decoys which appeared in increased numbers during the last year of the Q-ship campaign. They were more uncomfortable to sail in than any other kind of mystery ship, and were always at risk, as the *Mary B. Mitchell* showed when she just escaped disaster in a January gale. On 7th January, 1917, her commander, Lieutenant John Laurie, was making for Torbay when sudden squalls made it impossible to come to anchor. By 8th January the squalls had turned into a full gale.

"At 9.30 p.m.," reported Laurie, "foremast and spars fell over the port side, taking the mainmast with it. Wreckage was then cut adrift, none of which could be saved. The mizzen mast being left standing intact, the ship lay-to, comfortably." Amidst mountainous seas, a steamer offered to take the *Mary B. Mitchell* in tow. A line was passed but it parted. Laurie refused to leave his ship, and the following day help appeared in the form of a Norwegian steamer which at last passed another line to the *Mary B. Mitchell* and brought her into Brest.

It was not only from storms that the sailing decoys were at hazard. *Bayard, Q.20,* was cut in two by the steamer *Tainui* during the night while

---

*Caution was necessary. The Q-ship *Cymric* sank the British submarine *J.6*, having mistaken her for an enemy.

A Q-ship action portrayed by Charles Pears in a series of paintings reproduced at the time of the action in the *Illustrated London News*. Above, the *U.93* shells the Q-ship *Prize* and, below, the panic party abandons ship in the lifeboat.

Above: As the submarine closes the *Prize* the crew remaining on the Q-ship hoist the White Ensign and open fire with their twelve-pounders.

Below: In the final stage of the duel the U-boat submerges, leaving her commander and two other men in the water. Although it was believed at the time that the U-boat had been sunk, she escaped under the command of her First Lieutenant and returned safely to her base at Emden.

cruising off the Isle of Wight. Lieutenant Scott, the commander, was drowned with fourteen of his crew in spite of valiant efforts by his second-in-command, Sub-Lieutenant Keith Morris, R.N.R. Morris caught hold of a rope which dangled from the starboard anchor of *Tainui*, climbed on board her and launched one of her boats to pick up survivors.

Another sailing Q-ship, the *Merops*, caught fire because of the backfiring of the engine. The engineer had to be hauled on deck with a rope as the fumes overcame him, the second engineer was severely burned as the paraffin tank exploded, a petty officer was overcome by the gas given off by burning lyddite explosive in the magazine and the leading telegraphist nearly succumbed to the fumes in saving him.

Yet with all their dangers, sailing Q-ships had endeared themselves to all who sailed them by such actions as that of 30th April, 1917, in which *Prize* lured *U.93* within range and then, after a shelling which had left the Q-ship a sinking and apparently helpless cripple, blasted the submarine with thirty-six shots at point-blank range until she disappeared under water, stern first, four minutes after the action began. The captain of the U-boat, Kapitän-Leutnant E. Freiherr Spiegel von und zu Peckelsheim, the navigating warrant officer and a stoker petty officer had been blown from the deck and were picked up by *Prize's* panic party. The Germans immediately gave their word not to try to escape or to capture the ship and assisted their captors in the all-important work of saving the *Prize* as she limped towards the Irish coast, with all hands at the pumps.

Yet, incredible though it sounds, *U.93* had not sunk. She had merely submerged, and finding it impossible to navigate underwater, escaped on the surface in the darkness. She reached Emden in safety under her second-in-command, Leutnant zur See Zeigler, who was promoted and personally decorated by the Kaiser. *Prize* must have become as much a household word in Germany as she was in British messes. Quite apart from the mark that her gallant exploits had put on her in U-boat eyes, there was something else about her which courted disaster, an aerial which was disguised as part of her rigging but not so skilfully, it was said, that the practised eye of a seaman trained in sail could not detect the imposture.

In the autumn of 1917, to bring us back to the point that had been reached in this chronicle of the successes of the year, *Prize* sailed in company with the submarine *D.6*. On Monday, 13th August, the sailing Q-ship engaged *U.48* in 55° 58′ North, 19° 33′ West. She scored five direct hits at 200 yards, range, and the enemy submerged with a heavy list. The following day *Prize* blew up, presumably from a torpedo attack. There were no survivors and although *D.6* attacked the U-boat responsible, said by Keble Chatterton to have been none other than *U.48*, her attack was unsuccessful.

We now come to the action which in many ways was the crux of the Q-ships campaigns, the encounter between *Dunraven*, commanded by Gordon Campbell, and *UC.71*

On 8th August, at 10.58 a.m., G.M.T., when in lat. 48° 00′ N., long. 7° 37′ W., steering N. 27° E., 8 knots, disguised as an armed British merchant ship and zigzagging, a submarine was sighted two points before the starboard beam, on the horizon. Zigzag course was maintained and submarine steered towards the ship. At 11.17 a.m. she submerged. At 11.43 . . . submarine broke surface on the starboard quarter about 5,000 yards distant and opened fire. I at once opened fire with my after gun (2½ pdr.) and ordered the remainder of the crew to take "shell cover." I ordered much smoke to be made but at the same time reduced speed to seven knots (with an occasional zigzag) to give him a chance of closing (had I been a merchant ship I could probably have escaped). I was steaming head to sea and the submarine's firing was very poor, shots were right for direction but bad for elevation, nearly all falling over. At 12.10 he ceased firing and came on at full speed: owing to the sea he was apparently unable to fire whilst chasing me. At 12.25 he turned broadside on and reopened fire; in the meantime my gun was intentionally firing short.

During this period I made *en clair* signals for the submarine's benefit such as "Submarine chasing and shelling me," "Submarine overtaking me, help, come quickly," "Submarine (position). Am abandoning ship." At 12.40 shells were now falling close. I made a "cloud of steam" to assume boiler trouble and ordered "Abandon ship," at the same time stopping, blowing off steam and turning my broadside so that he could see me abandon ship (to add to the panic we let go a boat by the foremost fall on his side).

He closed and continued shelling. A shell went through the poop, exploding a depth-charge and blowing Lieutenant Chas. G. Bonner, D.S.C., R.N.R., out of his control. Two more shells followed into the poop and he then ceased fire and closed. He was coming along nicely from port to starboard to pass 400 or 500 yards off. In the meantime the poop was on fire and clouds of dense black smoke issuing and partially hiding the submarine from view.

It was obvious to me (the magazine and depth-charges being in the poop) that an explosion must soon take place, so I had the option of opening fire on an indistinct object with a minimum chance of success or waiting till he got on the weather side—I waited.

At 12.58, when the submarine was passing close to my stern, a large explosion—probably two depth charges and some cordite—took place, the four-inch gun and gun's crew complete were blown in the air, the gun landed forward on the well-deck and the crew in various places—one man in the water—four-inch projectiles were also blown about the ship. This was indeed a misfortune as the submarine had only to steam another 200 yards and I should have had three guns bearing at 400 yards' range. The explosion started the "open fire" buzzers at the guns and the gun on the after bridge—the only one bearing—opened fire. The submarine had already started to submerge after the explosion, but it is possible that one hit was obtained on the conning-tower as he disappeared.

Realizing that a torpedo would probably follow, I ordered the doctor to remove

Blown apart by the explosion of her own depth charges, the *Dunraven* is a stricken vessel with her decks awash. From *Q-Ships and Their Story.*

all the wounded and lock them up in cabins, etc., so as not to spoil the next part, hoses were also turned on the poop which was one mass of flames, the deck being red hot and the magazine still apparently intact. I also signalled to a man-of-war, who had answered my signal for assistance when the explosion took place, to keep away, as I realized the action was not yet ended. At 1.20 a torpedo was seen approaching from the starboard side, about 1,000 yards, and struck abaft the engine-room. I then ordered, "Q. abandon ship," guns were left visible, and an additional party of men sent away on a raft and a damaged boat.

At 1.40 a periscope was sighted on the starboard bow, and from then until 2.30 he circled round us at various ranges, also in and about between the boats. During this period boxes of cordite and four-inch shells were going off every few minutes and the fire in the poop was still burning fiercely. At 2.30 the submarine broke surface directly astern (no gun bearing) and shelled me at a range of a few hundred yards, at the same time apparently using a Maxim at the boats. Nearly all the shells either hit the ship or fell close to the boats. Two shells burst on the bridge and did much damage. He was slowly steaming towards my port quarter, but as only one gun would bear I waited for him to get on a good bearing. At 2.50 he ceased shelling and submerged; I therefore decided to try my torpedoes. He steamed past the port side about 150 yards off (with only a small part of periscope showing) at an estimated speed of 7 knots, parallel to the ship. At 2.55 I fired a torpedo when "on" set at 22 feet (maximum depth) the bubbles passing just ahead of the periscope. He did not notice it, as he steamed very sharp round the bow—according to the boats his periscope only missed it by about six inches—and he came very slowly down the starboard side.

At 3.2, allowing a speed of 3 knots, another torpedo was fired, the bubbles passing a couple of feet abaft the periscope—maximum depth was on, but suppose it must have passed over the top. The submarine saw it and at once submerged. I therefore signalled for urgent assistance as he would probably have either torpedoed or shelled me till we sank; but pending arrival of assistance I arranged if necessary for me to jump overboard in a "panic" and leave one gun's crew aboard.

Almost immediately after U.S.S. *Noma* arrived and fired at a periscope a few hundred yards astern of me; H.M.S. *Attack* and H.M.S. *Christopher* also arrived. Boats were recalled, the fire extinguished (the poop being completely gutted and all four depth charges and the ammunition having gone—the last thing to explode after the crew returned being a box of tubes), and arrangements made for towing.[64]

The *Dunraven* was taken in tow, but it was obvious she was a stricken ship. At 1.30 a.m., with seconds rather than minutes to spare, Campbell and the remnant of the crew were taken off by H.M.S. *Christopher*, and the *Dunraven* went down.

Captain Gordon Campbell inspects damage caused by a U-boat's shells to the bridge of the *Dunraven*. From *Q-Ships and Their Story*.

The last moments of the *Dunraven*, sinking while under tow. From *Q-Ships and Their Story.*

Campbell's report has been worth quoting at such length if only for one important particular. In the report he says he sent an uncoded signal containing the ship's position, whereas in his book *My Mystery Ships* he says he sent out an uncoded call for help, but omitted the position. This is a matter of some moment, as will be seen shortly, but there is nothing sinister in the discrepancy. Campbell had simply forgotten what he had written when, years after, he came to construct his memoirs. Other Special Service men have had similar lapses of memory.

The struggle between the *Dunraven* and her anonymous assailant (later identified as *UC.71* by Dittmar and Colledge) had been magnificent, but it was hardly war. A very expensive ship, crammed with the most modern and valuable equipment, had been sent to the bottom, and the U-boat had gone off without a scratch. Worse still, eleven of the crew had been wounded, one mortally, and during the final stages of the conflict they had had to lie in the cabins and staterooms with shells exploding all around them, and only such attention as the surgeon probationer and their comrades could give them. It goes without saying that, as Campbell himself says, "When I visited them after the action they thought little of their wounds, but only expressed their disgust that the enemy had not been sunk."[65]

All these sacrifices would not have been too heavy to outweigh the destruction of a submarine. Campbell himself said "By losing a few men we might save thousands not only of lives but of ships and tons of the nation's requirements."[66]

Unfortunately the whole technique of Q-ship warfare had become so complicated as to be self-defeating. If Campbell radioed an S.O.S., uncoded, and gave his position, he risked British or American ships hurrying to his assistance and thus frightening the U-boat into submerging. But if he sent out an S.O.S. and omitted his bearings, this would look very suspicious if it were intercepted. If he later radioed for help, in code, and then cancelled the help, again in code, the U-boat would wonder why a seeming merchant ship was sending coded messages for help in a naval code. If Campbell held his fire until the U-boat had got really close, he might just be able to sink her, but by doing this, as has been seen, he had enabled the U-boat to immobilise his ship, thus rendering all his armaments useless except the torpedoes, and to turn the *Dunraven* into an inferno of exploding ammunition. Stalemate had now been reached in the Q-ship campaign.

These points were taken up, mentally, by those who attended a conference held twenty days after the sinking of the *Dunraven* in the room of Captain William Fisher, R.N., Director of the Anti-Submarine Division of the Admiralty War Staff, the others present including Captain Alexander Farrington, Captain Walwyn, Captain Gordon Campbell and Lieutenant-Commander Edmund Lockyer, R.N. The agenda was, significantly, "The Future Role of Q-ships and a General Policy regarding these Vessels." It was agreed initially that it was much more difficult for a mystery ship to make a kill than three months earlier, "and after the recent actions of *Bergamot* and *Dunraven*, it is likely that these difficulties will even be increased in the future." Lockyer felt that Q-ship service was unproductive in Home Waters, though it might still work in the Mediterranean or somewhere else where Q-ships were unknown. Captain Campbell pointed out that *Dunraven* and *Chagford* had nearly achieved success, and Captain Fisher added that there had been some very near misses during the last day or so with *Acton*, *Penshurst* and *Cullist*.

Lockyer's contention was supported and it was felt that there were only two openings left for the Q-ship, to act as a fast merchant vessel outside a convoy or to invite attack, hoping the submarine would make a faulty move. Yet, as it was pointed out, this latter case was a hazardous one for the Q-ship, as if the U-boat commander had any suspicions, he could after torpedoing the ship lay off and shell the decoy from a bearing on which no gunfire could be returned, as had happened in the case of *Dunraven*. It was decided to relegate convoy sloops and PQ.s (fast escort vessels) to escort duty only. They were not to go out alone to invite torpedo attack, because they were too valuable to be lost. Merchant Q-ships should be retained for home waters as long as they could be spared and the dockyards could fit them out, sailing Q-ships should be increased in numbers, and the Q-ship force in the Mediterranean strengthened.

Depth charges were to be removed from all merchant Q-ships of less than twelve knots because of the danger from shellfire. "These ships frequently come under fire, and in fact invite it, and usually from after bearings, which particularly exposes the charges carried aft. In the case of *Dunraven*, Captain Campbell was very emphatic that but for the explosion of his depth charges his ship would not have been lost." Sailing mystery ships which made doubtful and unsuccessful attacks should return to port at once and alter their rig or disguise. Whenever possible a Q. steam vessel would accompany convoys, and when in the danger zone drop astern as if unable to keep up.

After the strategic came the administrative decision. The men of the convoy sloops had their special privileges withdrawn from them. Admiral Francis Miller, commanding at Buncrana, County Donegal, and Bayly were invited by Lord Fisher to put their own points of view. Under Admiralty Letter M.010358/16, the convoy sloop men drew a special rate of pay, "the increase in the case of Officers being 6/- *per diem*, and the lowest ratings 2/- *per diem*." Originally it had been felt that both the men of the Q-ships and those of the convoy sloops would do the same job, but by the autumn of 1917 the convoy sloops and PQ.s were employed on escort duty and submarine hunting, being considered too valuable to invite torpedo attacks as the Q-ships did. "It appears, therefore, that the conditions of service in these ships are quite different from the conditions of service in the Merchant Q.s. Invidious situations have

Waves break over the after deck of the sinking *Dunraven*. In this photograph, taken from the boat deck, the wreckage of the poop can be clearly seen. From *My Mystery Ships*.

already arisen. For instance in the same escort may be found a sloop and a convoy sloop carrying out precisely the same work, running the same danger, and yet working under different scales of pay."[67] So the following year saw large numbers of ships and men moved out of the Q-ship category and returned to ordinary naval status.

Before that had happened, the mystery ships had scored their last success. On 17th September Commander Maurice Blackwood of *Stonecrop*, an alias of the collier *Glenfoyle*, sighted a submarine and simulated flight, under a hail of shells. "I lit the smoke apparatus," wrote Blackwood, "the effect of which was particularly good; the phosphorus leaked out of the container and caught fire outside it on the deck. The port side of the after deck house was a mass of flame and being before the wind the whole ship was enveloped in smoke." Blackwood then sent his panic party over the side, not forgetting two men in naval uniform to impersonate the naval gunners carried by most merchant ships of the day.

The submarine closed; Blackwood hesitated, considering whether to try to torpedo her, but decided against a torpedo attack. The U-boat surfaced completely 600 yards off the starboard quarter. "We looked at each other for three minutes, but he showed no signs of opening the conning-tower hatch, and as I thought his propellers were moving and he was pointed for our boats, I gave the signal and opened fire with four-inch and all howitzers at 6.10 p.m." The U-boat was hit eleven times; she submerged, water running out of the shot holes in her hull as she dived stern first. Then she came to the surface again for a few seconds, and Blackwood felt that she was trying to surrender, but that the conning tower hatch had been damaged by a hit from a four-inch shell and would not open. "She hung in this position for a few seconds, five at the most, and then sank rather by the stern and still with a list."

Campbell was convinced that *Stonecrop* had sunk her submarine that day and that the U-boat in question was *U.88*. He affirmed this belief in *My Mystery Ships*, page 292. The Admiralty also believed that *Stonecrop* had sunk a U-boat on that occasion and the action appeared in the printed account of successful Q-ship actions (ADM 186/430 8729). In the margin of the Public Record Office copy of this document has been written in pencil "*U.88,*" but below it appears another pencilled note "*U.88* hit a mine in N.Sea on Sept.7." Robert Grant, the author of *U-boat Intelligence 1914–1918*, does not consider that *Stonecrop* sank a U-boat on this occasion, while he records that *U.88* (Commander Schweiger) was sunk by a mine in position 54° 10′ N, 04° 45′ E.

Stonecrop herself was sunk the day following this action, 18th September, 1917.

The Epilogue

THE DAY of the Q-ships was over but they continued to exist, in diminishing numbers. They escorted important vessels, tried to prevent gun running to disloyal elements in Ireland, and were used against German surface ships. Apart from the sinking of *U.34* by *Privet* on 9th November, 1918, in what Campbell calls "more of a destroyer action" than a regular Q-ship encounter, they sank no more U-boats.

It seems reasonable to ask at this point why for the rest of the war they were a spent force, a weapon brandished in empty air which never fell on an opponent, and to go also into the wider question of what they failed to achieve, and what they they really did achieve. In a letter written to the Admiralty on 2nd February, 1918, Vice-Admiral Charles Dare, commanding at Milford Haven, set out some of the reasons for the Q-ships' failure to decoy U-boats.

> The tactics of the enemy have completely altered with the improved and universal arming of all merchant ships, and the chances which these Special Service ships have of securing the definite destruction of submarines are very remote.
>
> Their offensive weapon is gun power only and an opportunity seldom offers for its use, and when the occasion does arise they rarely secure a definite hit. On the other hand the chances of the enemy effecting their destruction is considerable since they are always operating in the most dangerous areas and their slow speed makes them an easy prey for the torpedo.
>
> When torpedoed, there is some risk of a portion of the armament being placed out of action as result of the explosion. The engines are generally disabled and the ship rendered more or less impotent ... These Special Service vessels lock up a number of men who would be more advantageously employed in manning new fast craft or relieving crews for rest, etc. They occupy in addition, the attention and time of H.M. Dockyards, in the matter of repairs and coaling, which could be more usefully directed to other work.[68]

The coming of the convoy system in May, 1917, meant that there were few vessels sailing independently and it became impossible for a Q-ship to move to its new station without an escort. These convoys were guarded by destroyers, the ships which—as one U-boat prisoner had confessed to Campbell—the German submariners really dreaded.

For a U-boat to torpedo a ship in a convoy was hazardous enough. For it subsequently to surface and attack its victim by gunfire would be suicidal. Any ship which moved outside the protection of the convoy was so suspect that it would be accorded the compliment of a torpedo from a safe distance.

Dazzle painting, or camouflage as it is now called, had made it very difficult for a Q-ship to alter her disguise continually, impersonating a

Swede in the morning, a Norwegian at night, and an American the following day. No disguise, however tempting, could allure a U-boat which began shelling from a distance of four miles and did not leave off till the victim had sunk. As Dare had pointed out, every merchant ship was to carry a gun, so there would be no surprise element if it shelled the U-boat.

The U-boat commanders had developed a flair for spotting Q-ships in disguise. They must literally have been able to scent them, because gallons of fresh paint were lavished on each new disguise. Details which never occurred to ship converters in the dockyards stood out clearly when viewed with the eyes of apprehension through a good pair of glasses.

Great attention was paid to zig-zagging by the Q-ships. Did their captains develop a "regulation" zig-zag which became identifiable as that of a Special Service ship? There was one moment of a mystery ship's day when she had to reveal her identity, when she exercised her guns. General orders specified that this was to be done with an empty horizon—but there were no empty horizons where a periscope was concerned. The moment when disguise was changed was another perilous time. We have already seen how one Q-ship was sunk just after she had "cast her skin."

If there was one moment of a cruise which was even more dangerous than the two which have been mentioned, this was the time when a Q-ship changed course and, after having apparently been making for Ireland from America, suddenly turned round and began sailing back to America again.

The Q-ships never came under a single unified command, and were at first used in penny numbers, like the tank, so that the value of their secrecy was frittered away. The early Q-ships had failed because they did not have the right kind of captains. The first commanders of mystery ships had seamanship and courage, but not all of them that infinite patience and cunning that were needed to achieve success. "There are not many Campbells," Bayly had written. Not everyone can be made into a fly fisherman, and this was what the captain of a mystery ship had to be.

Compared to their adversaries, the Special Service were, until almost the very end, when it was too late, ill-found in ships and guns. Dittmar and Colledge have said that "many otherwise unsuitable vessels saw active service as decoys."[69] Yet the expensive conversion of elderly tramps, unseaworthy vessels at a danger from every gale, whose guns bore for only a few seconds in every roll, was no substitute for proper, purpose-built Q-ships. It is true that the *Aubrietia* and *Anchusa* types of convoy sloops had been purposely built to resemble merchant ships, but

The *Lothbury* in dazzle painting. The dummy hatch which hid one of her guns can be seen abaft the bridge structure.   *Imperial War Museum*

their disguise would only bear a passing glance. Contrast with these vessels the *Hyderabad*, built specially as a decoy, made to appear deeper in the water than she really was by a false rudder top visible below her hull, and with twin screws set in tunnels in the after part of the ship. It was intended that torpedoes fired at her should run beneath her; though it is only fair to add that many torpedo attacks on normal Q-ships failed because of an error in the depth setting. A fleet of *Hyderabads* might have written a very different chapter in the history of the Q-ship campaigns, and so might a consistent use throughout the war of that very promising partnership of Q-ships and C. and later E. class submarines. It was extremely difficult for a Q-ship to sink a U-boat by gunfire, but there is no record of a U-boat surviving a torpedo hit from a British submarine.

It might be thought from what has been said that the outlay of lives, effort and courage by the Special Service did not receive a proportionate return, and indeed this view has been expressed more than once. Only eleven U-boats are known to have been sunk by Q-ships. It would be wrong, however, to look on the U-boats sunk merely as an exchange for Q-ships; what had been exchanged was the tonnage of merchant shipping that was *not* sunk. *U.36*, the first U-boat sunk by an unaided Q-ship, had sunk thirteen ships in the week before she was accounted for by *Prince Charles*.

As the total known kill of U-boats by every method was 145, Q-ships had thus accounted for about eight per cent of all U-boats sunk, a very respectable total.

Campbell argued that an encounter with a Q-ship made the U-boats use up their limited supply of torpedoes and thus return to base earlier than they might have done if they had had the opportunity of destroying ships by gunfire on the surface. This argument could only apply to the days before the introduction of the 5.9-inch gun. Encounters with Q-ships did fluster the U-boat commanders, as Campbell suggests. One attacked by Lieutenant-Commander W. Olphert, R.N.R., became so confused that he steamed towards his attacker. Even a fright that lasted an hour or so and made the submarine keep below the surface might well save several ships.

The real effect of the Q-ships, however, does not lie in any of the directions which have been mentioned. Their real importance was as an irritant to the Germans. Even the Admiralty was eventually forced to conclude that, so far as the Hague Convention was concerned, the

A feeling of real indignation rose in the German breast at the thought of being fired on by someone wearing a Great Eastern Railway guernsey — Commander Godfrey Herbert on the bridge of the *Antwerp*, with the mercantile chief officer and quartermaster in the foreground. From *Q-Ships and Their Story*.

earliest Q-ships had been pirates. This is a mere technicality. The U-boats never scrupled to disguise themselves as something other than what they were. They impersonated steamers, fishing boats and British submarines, and they wantonly flouted international law by omitting to show markings, numbers or even their own naval ensign. Again and again Q-ship commanders reported about a U-boat "She flew no colours."

But a feeling of resentment does not grow any less for being irrational. The *Baralong* affair was paraded before the whole world as an infamous atrocity perpetrated on German submariners who had surrendered. The Germans regarded the Q-ship officers and men as *francs tireurs*. They did not massacre all they caught, as they did with Belgian *francs tireurs*, but they did make away with the crew of *Ethel & Millie* if no more. A feeling of real indignation rose in the German breast at the thought of being fired on by someone wearing a Great Eastern Railway guernsey, even if he did have a Special Service badge instead of a regular naval uniform.

The Germans objected strongly to being attacked under a neutral flag. This did happen on one occasion, because the commander of *Q.16*, the convoy sloop *Heather*, Lieutenant-Commander William Hallwright, was killed before he could give the order to strike the Norwegian flag and colour boards. To the German mind, too, the despatch of a panic party over the side appeared as a surrender. Yet the men in the lifeboats were armed to the teeth, just like those left concealed aboard the Q-ship. Did the men in a Q-ship lifeboat ever attack a U-boat? No such case is known, but Lord Fisher conceived that it might happen and at one stage ordered that weapons be removed from the Q-ship lifeboats.

> After careful consideration and review of the general situation it has been decided that in the event of a Special Service ship being torpedoed and abandoned by the crew, it is inadvisable that any hostile action against the enemy submarines should be taken by means of the boats from the torpedoed ship. It is conceivable that the opportunity might arise in which the crews of these boats would be in a position to carry out an attack on the enemy, by means of torpedoes, machine guns, or grenades, should she subsequently come to the surface.
>
> Although boats with shipwrecked crews have generally speaking been hitherto immune from deliberate violence by gunfire, there is little doubt that in the event of an unsuccessful attack as outlined above, the indiscriminate massacre of the occupants of boats from abandoned merchantmen would result.

Though this letter was followed by an order for the "military bombs" to be removed from the lifeboats, for some reason this order was subsequently rescinded.

"The use of Q-ships," writes Antony Preston, "had put the U-boats in the position of having to attack without warning; the use of neutral flags, although historically regarded as a legitimate *ruse de guerre* for unarmed

A stern view of the *Margaret Murray* showing a four-inch gun aft and twelve-pounders forward.   *Imperial War Museum.*

merchantmen, tempted U-boat commanders to treat all neutral ships as Allied ships in disguise."[70] Dittmar and Colledge remark: "This method of warfare was used as an excuse for increasing the ferocity of submarine attacks."[71]

The atrocities of the U-boat campaign, many of which can be explained in reference to the U-boat reaction to the Q-ships, took place on the doorstep of the western world. "The ocean south of Ireland," wrote the American consul at Queenstown, Wesley Frost, "is the most crowded highway of commerce in the world, and on a fine day I have seen merchant ships in all directions like a vast parade. As consul at Queenstown for the three years ending last June, I reported to our Government on the destruction by submarines of eighty-one different ships carrying American citizens. I collected at first hand much of the evidence upon which America has entered the war and placed this

160

evidence on record in legal form." Frost's indictment of the U-boats was drawn up under several heads. First came the submarines' tactic of warning steamers by bombarding them from a great distance. Even when the men were in the boats the shelling continued. Next Frost turned to the cases, "scores if not hundreds," where ships were torpedoed in some vital place and sunk in ten minutes. If there was any suspicion that a ship was a Special Service vessel then the only safe course as far as the U-boats were concerned was to send her to the bottom with a torpedo. If a ship appeared to float, then torpedo it again; it might be a mystery ship with a buoyant cargo and strengthened bulkheads. This might explain the fact, inexplicable to Frost, that some ships were torpedoed twice or even several times. He cites the case of a horse-transport which was torpedoed four times in succession, the torpedoes exploding among the lifeboats while the crew were dropping into them.

"Why torpedo passenger ships?" Frost asks. Passenger ships had been compromised since the earliest days of Q-ship warfare and the use of the *Vienna/Antwerp*, a ship whose existence was perfectly well known to the Germans.

"Why sink ships hundreds of miles out to sea, and then refuse to tow the lifeboats?" asks Frost. Again the answer to this may be stated in Q-ship terms. The lifeboats might explode, and if they did not, the S.O.S. from the steamer would bring Bayly's fleet swooping down to the position of the U-boat.

"Why stand by while women and children drown in the water?" asks Frost. The U-boat reply would have been "are they really women and children?" Harold Auten tells of Q-ship legends, unfounded apparently, of Special Service men disguised as captains' wives hurling bombs disguised as babies down the hatches of conning towers. Certainly some men were disguised as women. No German U-boat commander would have paid great heed to the signal "Women aboard," for had it not been recommended, and presumably used, by the captain of the infamous *Baralong*?

Against the background of the Q-ships, as revealed by their archives, the stories that Frost has to tell become explicable, if not excusable. In the face of the account that Frost had to give of surrendering ships and crews blown to pieces, lifeboats raked with shrapnel, an American captain's body brought ashore in fragments in a gunny sack, of boatloads of survivors driven by a howling gale into the Ballinskelligs rocks, American public opinion compelled President Wilson to choose between neutrality and belligerence. It was the U-boats which had lost the war for Germany, it was the Q-ships which had brought them to the position in which they did so.

References and Notes

The numbers prefixed by Adm are those of Admiralty documents preserved in the Public Record Office.

1. Adm 137/2233.

2. Adm 137/1931.

3. Adm 137/1162.

4. Adm 137/1270.

5. Adm 137/1270.

6. Adm 137/1931.

7. Richard J. Scott, *The Saga of the Mary B. Mitchell* in *Ships Monthly* Volume 2, No. 6.

8. Adm 137/3091.

9. Not a real woman but a seaman dressed in woman's clothing from the waist up. Special Admiralty sanction was required for this impersonation.

10. Written during the earlier part of the campaign. With the fitting of larger guns to the later types of U-boat it became usual for the U-boat to begin to shell the abandoned ship from a distance of three or four miles.

11. Selected from "General Instructions for vessels acting as Decoys", Adm 137/1931, "Hints . . . to new Commanding Officers", Adm 137/1270 and "Standing Sailing Orders for Special Service Vessels", (May 1917) Adm 137/1438.

12. Adm 137/1270.

13. Adm 137/1267.

14. Adm 137/3656. Keble Chatterton in *Q. Ships and their Story*, page 104, suggests that four of the original eleven reached Manchester safely. The same author in *Danger Zone* records that three officers and eight men were picked up next day by U.S.S. *Wadsworth*, other men being rescued after a week by a trawler and by an American steamer.

15. Richard Humble, *Before the Dreadnought*, pages 174, 175.

16. R. H. Gibson, *The Navy*, December 1931, Volume XXXVI.

17. R. H. Gibson, op. cit.

18. Adm 137/1050, page 363.

19. The steamers operating between Harwich and the Continent adopted a coat of overall grey, but it seems that the *Vienna* had retained the peacetime black hull and white upperworks, with black-topped buff funnels.

20. Adm 137/1050.

21. Adm 137/1931, section: "Trawlers towing Submarines".

22. Adm 137/1933, page 200.

23. Adm 137/1933, No. 13, page 212.

24. Poldhu was an English radio station in Cornwall, originally set up by G. Marconi in 1904 for his early transatlantic transmissions, and Nordeich was a German radio station near Juist, in East Friesland.

25. Adm 137/1099, page 40.

26. Adm 137/1933, page 261.

27. "Memorandum of the German Government in regard to incidents alleged to have attended the destruction of a German submarine and its crew by His Majesty's Auxiliary Cruiser *Baralong* on August 19, 1915 and reply of His Majesty's Government thereto presented to both Houses of Parliament by command of His Majesty, January 1916", in Adm 1/8473, 255A.

28. The six witnesses were: J. M. Garrett, Charles D. Hightower, Bud Emerson Pallen, Edward Clark, R. H. Cisby and James Curran. All said they had been muleteers aboard *Nicosian.*

29. "Griff." *Surrendered. Some Naval War Secrets.* Published by the Author, Cross Deep, 1927, page 12.

30. Sir Julian S. Corbett. *Official History of the War. Naval Operations.* Longmans, 1923, Volume III, page 133.

31. E. Keble Chatterton, *Gallant Gentlemen.* Hurst and Blackett, London 1931, pages 172–173.

32. E. Keble Chatterton, *Amazing Adventure.* Hurst and Blackett, London, 1935, pages 138–140.

33. Admiral Scheer, *Germany's High Sea Fleet in the World War.* Cassell, 1920, page 227.

34. Commander Norman Lewis of H.M.S. *Tulip,* some years after his return from captivity, invited Korvetten-Kapitän Hashagen of *U.62* to England, a courteous gesture which aroused some unfavourable comment at the time. But, as described in chapter six, Hashagen had behaved impeccably towards his prisoner after taking him from one of the *Tulip's* boats and in the circumstances such a gesture was to be expected.

35. During 1915 no fewer than thirty-three such colliers were lost, all but seven being victims of submarine attack. See *Losses of H.M. Ships and Auxiliaries during the War from 4th August 1914 to 11th November 1981,* published in *British Vessels Lost at Sea 1914–18,* Patrick Stephens, Cambridge, 1977.

36. M.F.A. = Mercantile Fleet Auxiliary. *Baralong* had been taken up as a squadron supply ship with the pendant number Y9.5 on the outbreak of war in August, 1914.

37. The *Leicester* was an iron steamer built in 1891 and formerly owned by the Great Central Railway, hired as a store carrier in 1914.

38. The Lowestoft smacks *G & E, Glory* and *Inverlyon* were hired by the Admiralty in July and August, 1915, and armed with concealed three-pounder guns.

39. Adm 137/1099.

40. Berthon boats = folding boats of canvas on wooden frame invented in 1849 by E. L. Berthon.

41. Adm 137/1162, page 63.

42. The *Manchester Engineer* (4,302 tons) was sunk on 27th March, 1916; the *Achilles* (7,043 tons) on 31st March, 1916. The *Inkonka* (3,430 tons) was attacked on 25th March, 1916, but the torpedo missed her.

43. Adm 137/3164.

44. Adm 137/1944, page 580.

45. Adm 137/1162, page 378.

46. For an account of this voyage see G. H. P. Muhlhauser, *Small Craft.* John Lane The Bodley Head, 1920.

47. *Jane's Fighting Ships*, 1920 etc.

48. E. Keble Chatterton, *Danger Zone.* Rich and Cowan, 1934, page 133.

49. Adm 186 430. 8729.

50. F. J. Dittmar and J. J. Colledge, *British Warships 1914–1919.* Ian Allan, London, 1972, page 129.

51. Arthur G. J. Whitehouse, *Subs and Submariners.* Frederick Muller, London, 1963.

52. Adm 137/1267.

53. Adm 137/648. Hewett's report has been interpolated with a letter recommending Prescott for a posthumous decoration.

54. For an account of the action in the words of Ted Fenn, cook of the *Nelson* at the time of her loss, see David Butcher, *The Trawlermen.* Tops'l Books, 1980.

55. Adm 137/3813.

56. Rear-Admiral William Sowden Sims, U.S.N., *The Victory At Sea.* John Murray, London, 1920, page 149.

57. Adm 137/1162.

58. A different practice was followed at Lowestoft, according to David Butcher, op. cit. Elsewhere, as at Aberdeen, Special Service trawlermen sold their fish for their own benefit.

59. Adm 186/430.

60. Adm 137/467.

61. Adm 186/430.

62. Lieutenant Hereford deliberately brought the lifeboat round to the starboard side to entice *UC.29* into a position in which the *Pargust's* guns would bear. This is made clear by Gordon Campbell in *My Mystery Ships.* Hodder and Stoughton, London, 1928, page 221.

63. Adm 137/649, pages 27–28.

64. Adm 186/430.

65. E. Keble Chatterton, *Q. Ships and their Story.* Sidgwick and Jackson, London, 1922, page 207.

66. Gordon Campbell, op cit. page 259.

67. November 30th, Adm 137/1440, page 486.

68. Adm 137/1213.

69. F. J. Dittmar and J. J. Colledge, op cit, page 126.

70. Antony Preston, *U-Boats*. Arms and Armour Press. London, 1978, page 68.

71. Dittmar and Colledge, op cit.

72. Rear-Admiral Sir Douglas Brownrigg, Bt, *Indiscretions of the Naval Censor*. Cassell, London, 1920, page 74.

The midship four-inch gun of a Q-ship ready for action. From *"Q" Boat Adventures*.

Chronology of the Q-ship Era

1870–71. The Franco-Prussian War. A lasting hatred and fear of fighters out of uniform is implanted in the German mind. The *francs tireurs*, members of rifle clubs enrolled into French irregular units, armed with modern rifles but without uniforms, harass the Germans at every step, holding up movements and destroying reconnaissance parties. Those *francs tireurs* caught by the Germans are shot without mercy.

2nd August, 1914. The Germans invade Belgium and later Northern France. They are on the look out for *francs tireurs*, and anyone suspected of being one is dealt with mercilessly.

4th August, 1914. Germany begins the war against Britain with twenty U-boats available for war service.

22nd September, 1914. Otto Wedingen in *U.9* sinks the British cruisers *Aboukir*, *Cressy*, and *Hogue* in a matter of minutes, thus revealing the capabilities of the submarine.

The crew of *U.9* receive a heroes' welcome at Wilhelmshaven after showing the potential of the submarine by torpedoing the British cruisers *Aboukir*, *Cressy* and *Hogue* in the North Sea on 22nd September, 1914.

November, 1914. The German Chief of Naval Staff, Admiral von Pohl, orders "unrestricted" U-boat warfare against British shipping.

26th November, 1914. Winston Churchill, First Lord of the Admiralty, inaugurates the Q-ship era by sending a telegram to the Commander-in-Chief, Portsmouth, Sir Hedworth Meux: "It is desired to trap the German submarine which sinks vessels by gunfire off Havre. A small or moderate-sized steamer should be taken up . . . "

December, 1914. Germany has twenty-nine U-boats on a war footing.

January, 1915. The first of seventeen coastal U-boats, the UB. type, puts to sea.

January, 1915. A new class of 15 UC class minelaying submarines is ordered.

January–December, 1915. U-boats sink 39,025 tons of British shipping a month.

5th February, 1915. The Kaiser orders the sinking of any merchantmen in waters round the British Isles.

April, 1915. The Cunard liner *Lusitania* is sunk by *U.20*, commanded by Schweiger. Many of the 1,200 passengers drowned are American. Immense indignation is caused in America.

May, 1915. Ten new UE. type U-boats, ocean-going minelayers armed with the new 15cm (5.9 inch) gun, are ordered.

6th June, 1915. In response to American protests over the *Lusitania*, U-boat commanders are ordered to spare passenger ships and use the gun, rather than the torpedo, to sink other ships.

23rd June, 1915. First Q-ship success, as *U.40*, commanded by G. Fürbringer, is sunk by British submarine *C.24*, partnered by *Taranaki*.

20th July, 1915. *U.23*, commanded by Schulthess, is torpedoed by British submarine *C.27*, partnered by Q-ship *Princess Louise*.

24th July, 1915. Rear-Admiral Henry F. Oliver, Chief of War Staff, decides that Q-ships must be commissioned as tenders to naval vessels, otherwise they will be pirates under the Hague Convention.

24th July, 1915. *Prince Charles* sinks *U.36*, commanded by Graeff.

August, 1915. Admiral Tirpitz decides to divert the U-boats to the Mediterranean, thus making it much more difficult for Q-ships to achieve "kills."

12th August, 1915. Germany complains to Britain about the attack on a U-boat by a Q-ship flying neutral colours.

19th August, 1915. *U.27*, commanded by Kapitän-Leutnant Wegener, is sunk by Godfrey Herbert of the *Baralong*. Some German submariners die in such suspicious circumstances that the *Baralong* affair becomes the British atrocity of World War One in German eyes. Germany demands that Herbert and his crew should stand trial for the murder of Wegener and his men. Britain offers to submit the incident to an international tribunal if the Germans permit the investigation at the same time of three very recent U-boat "atrocities"; the Germans refuse the offer.

30th August, 1915. U-boat commanders are ordered to give passengers and crews of merchantmen time to abandon ship and to ensure that no neutrals are sunk unless they are actually taking cargoes to Britain.

17th September, 1915. Oliver decides to commission some un-commissioned Q-ships.

18th September, 1915. Orders are given for the ending of unrestricted warfare by U-boats on shipping. Shipping losses fall immediately. So do the chances of Q-ships.

24th September, 1915. *U.41*, commanded by Hansen, is sunk by the *Baralong*; her second success.

4th March, 1916. The Kaiser agrees to the renewal of unrestricted warfare by the U-boats, due to start on 1st April, but this decision is modified to exempt passenger ships. America threatens to break off diplomatic relations unless "there is a modification of Germany's submarine operations."

22nd March, 1916. The *U.68*, commanded by Kapitän-Leutnant Guntzel, is sunk by *Farnborough*.

5th April, 1916. Discussion of the possibility of giving Q-ships buoyant cargoes which will delay their sinking even if they are torpedoed, in the hope that even though sinking they may dispose of their attacker.

July, 1916. Working in the Mediterranean, Kapitän-Leutnant Arnauld de la Perriere perfects the technique of destroying ships at long range, beginning at 6,000 yards and finishing at 3,000, with the new 10.5cm gun which is replacing the old 8.8cm. This technique enormously increases the difficulties of the Q-ships.

8th July, 1916. Carrying a cargo of strategic importance, the German submarine *Deutschland* reaches America. Q-ships *Q.1*, *Q.2*, *Q.3*, *Q.4*, *Q.5*, *Q.6*, *Q.7*, and *Q.8* are sent out to try to intercept her on her return to Germany.

20th July, 1916. War Service Badges are to be worn by all officers and men serving in Special Service. These badges, to which are later added certificates, will, it is hoped, prevent any Special Service men who are captured being shot as *francs tireurs*.

September, 1916. It is decided to send some Q-ships to Canada to embark buoyant cargoes.

October, 1916. 119 U-boats in service.

6th October, 1916. U-boats ordered to carry out attacks against merchant shipping subject to prize regulations, i.e. no torpedoing without warning. This restricted campaign runs to 31st January, 1917.

30th October, 1916. There are forty-seven Q-ships afloat, ranging from motor drifters to medium-size steamers.

1–31st October, 1916. 353,600 tons of Allied and neutral shipping sunk.

November, 1916. A special Anti-Submarine Division (A.S.D.) is set up at the Admiralty.

30th November, 1916. *UB.19*, commanded by Noodt, is sunk by *Penshurst*.

1–31st January, 1917. 368,500 tons of shipping of all nations sunk.

January, 1917. Thirteen Flower class sloops, *Anchusa* type, are ordered, due for completion in June and September, 1917. These sloops are to be the successors and the supplanters of the Q-ships as effective submarine hunters.

9th January, 1917. With effect from 1st February, 1917, the Kaiser approves an unrestricted U-boat campaign against shipping in the hope that Germany can cripple Britain before America enters the war.

14th January, 1917. *UB.37*, commanded by Gunther, sunk by *Penshurst*, her second success.

February, 1917. Vice-Admiral Sir Lewis Bayly, Commanding on Coast of Ireland, commands ten Q-ships operating from Queenstown (the first letter of which is probably the origin of the Q. nomenclature), Berehaven, Milford Haven, Devonport, and Bermuda.

February, 1917. Bayly sends *Q.13*, *Q.15*, and *Q.10* to prevent "an anticipated attempt to land arms on the West Coast of Ireland for the *Sinn Fein*." This is merely one example of diversions of Q-ships from their task of hunting submarines.

169

17th February, 1917. *U.83*, commanded by Hoppe, is sunk by *Farnborough*.

1–31st March, 1917. 594,000 tons of shipping sunk by U-boats.

March, 1917. "German submarines are now very cautious as to approaching a merchant ship, even when stopped and abandoned. Torpedoing ships without warning has become much more common, and, when a torpedo is not used, the ship is shelled at long ranges for a considerable period."—Lewis Bayly.

12th March, 1917. *U.85*, commanded by Petz, is sunk by *Privet*.

6th April, 1917. United States declares war on Germany.

10th April, 1917. Each of the Lowestoft-based decoys is to be supplied with 50 Mills bombs, two Lewis guns and 1 Maxim (except that *Q.s9, 2, 22, 23, 28* and *29* do not get Maxims).

28th April, 1917. Captain James Startin, Senior Naval Officer, Granton, Scotland, has nine Q-ships under his command.

May, 1917. The convoy system is introduced. This cuts the disastrous shipping losses, but almost eliminates the role of the independent command Q-ship sailing in search of trouble. Henceforward all ships sail in convoy. The convoy sloops and "PQ." or PC. boats now take up the role of the Q-ship, sailing at the head, tail, or flanks of a convoy, and looking enough like merchantmen to invite attack by an unsuspecting U-boat.

May, 1917. There are sixty-three Q-ships operating in British waters.

1st May, 1917. Discontinuance of the use of Q. numbers. Henceforth the decoys have names, which are continually changing.

7th June, 1917. *UC.29*, commanded by Kapitän-Leutnant Rose, sunk by *Pargust*.

13th July, 1917. Renewed discussion of Q-ships towing submarines.

20th July, 1917. Bayly's fleet numbers eleven.

August, 1917. There are seventy-two Q-ships, convoy sloops, and "PQ.s" (PC. boats) in use or fitting out.

3rd August, 1917. Bayly's command has risen to twelve ships.

2nd September, 1917. Depth charges having shown a tendency to explode while U-boats shell Q.s or while they are sinking, it is decided to remove them from the slower merchant Q-ships.

17th September, 1917. Sinking of *U.88* by *Stonecrop*, a "kill" authenticated by Gordon Campbell in *My Mystery Ships*, but disallowed by Robert M. Grant in *U-Boat Intelligence, 1914–1918*.

October, 1917. Convoy sloops and PQ.s sail regularly with convoys.

9th November, 1917. Bayly's fleet has dropped to nine.

A Special Service joke, from *Q-Ships and Their Story*. As *Penshurst* is shelled by a U-boat one member of the panic party semaphores to another "Did yer make the tea afore we left 'er?"

23rd January, 1918. "Convoy sloops and the Special Service P class patrol boats are no longer to be commissioned as decoy vessels, but are to be treated in all respects as ordinary sloops or P class patrol boats."

8th February, 1918. Bayly's fleet is reduced to three: *Eilian, Stock Force* and *Wexford Coast*.

February, 1918. The Dover Straits are closed to U-boats by minefield and net barrage.

October, 1918. There are 179 operational U-boats.

15th October, 1918. In response to President Wilson's demand that the U-boat campaign must cease before armistice talks can begin, Admiral Scheer orders all U-boats to return to harbour.

15th October, 1918. Q-ship *Cymric* sinks British submarine *J.6* by mistake.

9th November, 1918. Two days before the Armistice Q-ship *Privet* sinks *U.34*. Though authenticated by Campbell from German records after the war and published in *My Mystery Ships*, this claim has also been contested by Robert M. Grant.

11th November, 1918. Armistice Day finds Startin commanding the largest Q-ship fleet ever assembled, twenty ships.

5th December, 1918. Bayly sends in his last weekly report from Queenstown. The Q-ships, no longer a secret, go on show to the public in the shape of *Suffolk Coast* and *Hyderabad*.

VISIT OF THE "Q" SHIP TO LONDON

How the "Stock Force," Herself in a Sinking Condition, Sank the German Submarine

An item from the *Illustrated London News* records the visit of the Q-ship *Suffolk Coast* to London and relates the story of the *Stock Force* engaging a U-boat in spite of being in a sinking condition.

The Q-ships, 1914–1918

THIS list contains the names of more than two hundred vessels known to have served as Special Service ships during the First World War. There have been considerable difficulties in compiling this list, and it has proved impossible to avoid discrepancies.

The Q-ship was the nautical equivalent of the secret agent and constantly concerned to conceal her real identity. So successful were the "covers" used by some decoys that they have remained unpenetrated to this day. Some vessels assumed the names of other decoys, while some bore the same names as others serving in the Special Service: there are two *Violas* in the list.

A starting point for any such list must be the authoritative work of F. J. Dittmar and J. J. Colledge, but the reader will find many differences between their list of decoy vessels and this one. The bulk of this index had been compiled from documents in the Public Record Office, but a search of the records set aside by the Naval Historical Branch for conservation reveals that these represent only a part of the whole, and not a very large part, one suspects. Entries have been drawn up either from scattered references to individual ships or from documents attempting to list Q-ships such as Adm. 137/1931, Grand Fleet, Secret Packs Vol. LI, drawn up on 1st May, 1917, which lists ninety-six decoys. Other documents which proved useful include Adm. 186/430, 8279 Actions between Special Service Vessels and Enemy Submarines.

Outside of the Public Record Office the most important single source has been the collection of log cards in the Naval Historical Branch Library, Ministry of Defence. These cards are résumés of the logs of individual ships and often provide precise dates for the employment of the vessels on Special Service, but they are at best only a source of partial information.

The vessels employed on Special Service include several very varied types, the largest categories being steam merchant vessels and store carriers, of which seventy-one are listed, and steam (and motor) fishing vessels, of which fifty-four are listed. Forty merchant sailing vessels and twenty-four sailing fishing craft appear in the list, and so do thirty-three convoy sloops and thirteen PC. boats, which were built as warships. For a time the crews of these warships received special rates of pay while these vessels were employed in the Special Service, but on 23rd January, 1918, this special pay was withdrawn from the complements of convoy sloops and PC. boats. Sloops and PC. boats commissioned after that date are not included.

Name	Alias	Tonnage	When built	Type	Armament	Service	Comments
Acton	Q.34 / Gandy / Harelda / Woffington	1,288 GT	1901	Cargo steamer	1 - 4 inch / 1 - 6 pdr / 4 submerged 18 inch torpedo tubes / 4 - 200lb bomb throwers	On S.S. 22.3.17-11.11.18	
Airblast, see Spiraea							
Albert H. Whitman	A. H. Whitman	94 GT	1916	American schooner	1 - 12 pdr / Lance bombs / Type G depth charge	6.7.17-22.11.17	
Albert J. Lutz	Arthur J. Lutz	95 GT	1908	American schooner	1 - 12 pdr / Lance bombs / Type G depth charge	6.7.17-22.11.17	
Alcala, see Privet							
Aldebaran, see Rosskeen							
Alduych, see Eglantine							
Alistair, see Arvonian							
Allie		1,127	1883	Steamship			"Inspected, not suitable," 26.10.15.
Alma	Vera Elizabeth			Schooner	1 - 4 inch / 1 - 12 pdr	21.9.17-29.4.18	Prize. Handed over to new owner in May, 1918.
Amaris, see Mary B. Mitchell							
Amber, see Remo							
Ameer, see Remo							
Amy B. Silver		129 GT	1912	Schooner	1 - 12 pdr / Lance bombs / Type G depth charge	17.7.17-22.11.17	
Anchusa	Ard / Cashel / Patrick / Winstree	1,290 displacement	1917	Flower class convoy sloop Anchusa type	2 - 4 inch / 2 - 12 pdr	26.5.17-16.7.18	First of 13 convoy sloops ordered in January, 1917. Sunk by U.54 off the West Coast of Ireland, 16.7.18.
Anchusa, see Lady Patricia							
Antic, see Auk							
Antwerp ex-Vienna		1,753 GT	1894	G.E.R passenger steamer	2 - 12 pdr	27.1.15-5.4.15	Had been accommodation ship at Harwich in 1914; became armed boarding steamer in 4.15.

Name	Other names	Tonnage	Year	Type	Armament	Service dates	Notes
Arbutus	*Sprigg*	1,290 displacement	1917	Flower class convoy sloop *Anchusa* type	2 - 4 inch 2 - 12 pdr	27.10.17-16.12.17	Sunk by *UB.65* in St George's Channel, 16.12.17.
?*Archangel*		2,448 GT	1910	G.E.R. passenger steamer			
Ard, see Anchusa *Argo, see Lothbury* *Ariadne GY 173*		225 GT	1906	Steam trawler	1 - 6 pdr		Submarine partner for British submarine *C.33*. Hired from Consolidated Steam Fishing and Ice Company (Grimsby) Ltd, employed mainly on mine-sweeping duties.
Arius, see Mary B. Mitchell *Arthur J. Lutz, see Albert J. Lutz*							
Arvonian	*Alistair* *Balfame* *Bendish* *Dorinda* *Girdler* *U.S.S. Santee*	2,794 GT	1905	Collier	3 - 4 inch Mark IX on SP1 mountings 3 - 12 pdr 12cwt 2 Maxims 4 - 18 inch torpedo tubes	19.8.17-21.4.19	Service with R.N. until 26.11.17 when she commissions as U.S.N. vessel under name of *Santee*. After being torpedoed and reconstructed again commissioned as HM ship and took name of *Bendish*.
Asama CF 12		284 GT	1914	Steam trawler	1 - 3 pdr	1.17-7.17	Owned by Neale and West of Cardiff. Sunk by U-boat gunfire west of Ushant, 16.7.17.
Aubrietia	*Q.13* *Kai* *Winton* *Zebal*	1,250 displacement	1916	Flower class convoy sloop *Aubrietia* type	2 - 4 inch 1 - 3 pdr	29.8.16-11.11.18	
Aubrietia, see Viola							
Auk H 755	Armed Trawler Decoy No. 422 *Antic* *Bennaris* *Claymore* *Girdler* *Glen Afric* *Hope* *St Gothard* *Spica*	168 GT	1903	Steam trawler	2 - 12 pdr 2 - 6 pdr 1 - 7.5 inch howitzer	S.S.3.17-11.18	Operating with *W. S. Bailey*, October, 1917. Hired from Kelsall Brothers and Beeching Ltd, Hull
Auricula	*Hempseed*	1,290 displacement	1917	Flower class convoy sloop *Anchusa* type	2 - 4 inch 2 - 12 pdr	27.11.17-1.3.18	

Name	Alias	Tonnage	When built	Type	Armament	Service	Comments
Balfame, see Arvonian							
Ballantrae, see Underwing							
Ballistan, see Bradford City							
Baralong	Mercantile Fleet Auxiliary No. 5 *Wyandra*	4,192 GT		Three-island tramp	3 - 12 pdr 12 cwt	3.15-9.11.16	Sank *U.27* on 19.8.15 and *U.41* on 24.9.15
Baron Rose ex-*Samuel S. Thorp*	*Sieux* Tender to *Gunner*	524 GT	1881	American three-masted auxiliary schooner	1 - 4 inch 2 - 12 pdr	9.4.18-14.6.19	
Barranca	*Q.3* *Echunga*	4,124 GT	1906	Cargo	1 - 4 inch Mk VII 2 - 13 pdr 2 - 12 pdr	18.4.16-15.5.17	Acquired from Elders and Fyffes. Torpedoed 26.4.17, but towed into Portsmouth.
Baryta, see Devonport							
Bayard	*Q.20* *Ledger No. 898* *Syren*	220 GT	1908	French sailing fishing boat, auxiliary lugger	1 - 13 pdr 1 - 3 pdr Hotchkiss 1 Maxim	12.16-29.6.17	Fishing number B 2783. Run down by s.s. *Tainui* in English Channel, 29.6.17.
Begonia	*Q.10* *Dolcis* *Jessop*	1,200 dis-placement	1915	Flower class convoy sloop *Azalea* type	3 - 12 pdr 2 - 3 pdr A.A.	S.S. 9.8.17-6.10.17	After torpedoing reconstructed at Haulbowline to resemble a merchant ship. Sunk by U-boat in Atlantic, 6.10.17.
Bellmore, see Merops							
Bellona II INS 403	*Birch* GY 677	82 GT	1907	Steam drifter	1 - 6 pdr		*Birch* was minesweeping trawler mined off Yarmouth, 23.8.16.
Bendigo II, see Rosskeen							
Bendish, see Arvonian							
Ben Hur				Steam trawler			Partner for submarine *C.27*.
Bennaris, see Auk							
Bergamot		1,290 dis-placement	1917	Flower class convoy sloop *Anchusa* type	2 - 4 inch 2 - 12 pdr	14.7.17-13.8.17	Acts as partner for submarine *E.48*. Sunk by *U.84* in Atlantic, 13.8.17.
Betsy Jameson BK 7		45 GT	1900	Motor drifter	2 - 6 pdr		
Billy, see Peggy							
Birch, see Bellona II							
Bird, see Nelson							
Birdwood, see PC.56							
Blessing				Yorkshire fishing coble with auxiliary engine	1 - 3 pdr Mined nets 300 yards long and 30 feet deep	30.4.16-3.17	Unsuitable, returned to owners.

Bolham, see Sarah Colebrook						
Bombala, see Willow Branch						
Boy Alfred, see Ethel & Millie						
Boverton, see Dunraven						
Bracondale Chagford	2,095 GT	1903	Collier	1 - 4 inch 2 - 12 pdr 1 howitzer 2 Maxims 2 - 18 inch above-water torpedo tubes	18.6.17-7.8.17	Submarine partner; commissioned as independent command. Sunk by U-boat in Atlantic, 7.8.17.
Bradford City Ballistan Saros	3,683 GT	1910	Collier	2 - 4 inch 1 - 2½ pdr 1 Maxim	16.10.15-26.8.17 (official paying off date)	Sunk by U-boat in Straits of Messina 16.8.17.
Breadwinner LT.1095 S.7. Seagull	57 GT	1907	Trawling smack	1 - 3 pdr	2.17-11.11.18	
Brig 1, see Emilia C.						
Brig 2, see Rosina Ferrara						
Brig 3, see Sant' Anna						
Brig 4, see Margaret and Annie						
Brig 5, see Salomea K.						
Brig 10, see Helgoland						
Brig 11, see Gaelic						
Brigand, see Cowslip						
Brine, see Mary B. Mitchell						
Brise, see Mary B. Mitchell						
Britannia, see Willow Branch						
Brown Mouse Spinoza BM 276	43 GT	1908	Smack yacht	1 - 6 pdr	12.17-28.2.18	Destroyed by accidental fire in Lyme Bay, 28.2.18.
Bryony	1,290 displacement	1917	Flower class convoy sloop Anchusa type	2 - 4 inch 2 - 12 pdr	19.12.17-1.4.18	
Burlington, see PC.60						
Burmah, see Coot						
Bywater, see Heather						
CB, see Telesia						
Candytuft Paritt	1,290 displacement	1917	Flower class convoy sloop Anchusa type	2 - 4 inch 2 - 12 pdr	9.8.17-18.11.17	Torpedoed twice by U-boat off Cape Bigli, Mediterranean, drifted ashore, 18.11.17.

Name	Alias	Tonnage	When built	Type	Armament	Service	Comments
Caird, see Ceanothus							
Caleb, see Spiraea							
Cancalais, see Mary B. Mitchell							
Capulet, see Result							
Carrigan Head	*Q.4* *Carrighan Head* *Carrington Head*	4,201 GT	1901	Cargo	1 - 4 inch Mk VII 2 - 13 pdr 2 - 12 pdr	10.7.16-25.9.17	Had been squadron supply ship since 4.8.14; became commissioned escort ship in 1917.
Cashel, see Anchusa							
Cassor, see Devonport							
Ceanothus	*Caird* *Linksman*	1,290 displacement	1917	Flower class convoy sloop *Anchusa* type	2 - 4 inch 2 - 12 pdr	1.9.17-11.11.18	
Century	*Penhallow*	4,318 GT	1913	Collier	2 - 4 inch 1 - 12 pdr Some smaller	10.15-23.5.17	Buoyant cargo loaded. Was not suitable—ship given up and crew transferred into *Huayna.*
Chagford, see Bracondale							
Champion, see Commissioner							
Champney, see Duncluha							
Charing, see PC.43							
Charyce, see Stock Force							
Chatsgrove, see PC.74							
Cheerio, see Energic							
Cheriton, see Tay and Tyne							
Chesney, see PC.61							
Chevington		3,876 GT	1912	Collier employed as mechanical transport		21.9.15-27.6.16	"Mechanical transports but really decoys when empty."
Children's Friend *LT 174*	*S.6*	60 GT	1900	Trawling smack	1 - 3 pdr	7.2.17-11.11.18	
Chintz, see PC.67							
Chiswell, see Maresfield							
Chromium, see Eilian							
Chrysanthemum		1,290 displacement	1917	Flower class convoy sloop *Anchusa* type	2 - 4 inch 2 - 12 pdr	12.17-11.11.18	Still in service as R.N.V.R. guardship on Embankment, London.
Claymore, see Auk							
Cockedge, see Harmonic							

Name	Tonnage	Year	Type	Armament	Dates	Notes
Commissioner GN 18 / Champion / Recorder / Roller	161 GT	1905	Steam trawler	2 - 12 pdr, 1 - 6 pdr, 1 - 7.5 inch howitzer	3.17-1919	Hired from Thomas L. Devlin, of Edinburgh, whose other vessels included *Champion* GN48 and *Controller* GN 79.
Commodore, see *Telesia*						
Connaught	2,632 GT	1897	Irish Sea packet			Owned by City of Dublin Steam Packet Co.
Convolvulus	1,290 displacement	1917	Flower class convoy sloop *Anchusa* type	2 - 4 inch, 2 - 12 pdr	2.7.17-11.11.18	
Coot H 897 / Burmah / Dora / Kia Ora / Lorne	172 GT	1906	Steam trawler	1 - 12 pdr, 1 - 6 pdr, 1 - 7.5 inch howitzer		Partner for submarine *C.7*. "Based on Granton and fishes down to River Tyne." Owned by Kelsall Bros and Beeching, who also owned *Burmah* H 86
Coral, see *Hyderabad*						
Coreopsis	1,290 displacement	1917	Flower class convoy sloop *Anchusa* type	2 - 4 inch, 2 - 12 pdr	27.10.17-11.11.18	
Cormorant IV / Nadine GY 345	162 GT	1897	Steam trawler	1 - 6 pdr		As Q-ship, took identity of trawler *Nadine* GY 138, which had been mined in North Sea in 1915.
Cortes	1,275 GT	1885	Cargo			Taken up as store carrier 14.9.15; discharged 1.12.15.
Cowslip / Brigand	1,290 displacement	1917	Flower class convoy sloop *Anchusa* type	2 - 4 inch, 2 - 12 pdr	4.12.17-25.4.18	Sunk by *UB.105* off Cape Spartel, 25.4.18.
Cranford, see *Viola*						
Craven, see *Ooma*						
Cullist ex-*Jurassic* / Hayling / Prim / Westphalia	1,467 GT	1913	Cargo	1 - 4 inch, 2 - 12 pdr, 2 - 14 inch torpedo tubes above water	S.S. 12.5.17-11.2.18	Taken up as store carrier in 1914. Sunk by U-boat in Irish Sea off Drogheda 11.2.18.
Culloden, see *PC.42*						
Cymric / Olive	226 GT	1893	Iron barquentine	1 - 4 inch, 2 - 12 pdr, 1 - 7.5 inch howitzer	23.2.17-8.4.19	Sank British submarine *J.6* on 15.10.18.
Dag, see *Result*						
Damaris, see *Viola*						
Danton, see *Wellholme*						

Name	Alias	Tonnage	When built	Type	Armament	Service	Comments
Dargle	Q.29 / *J.J. Bibby* / *Grabbit* / *Peggy*	176 GT	1902	Brigantine	1 - 4 inch / 2 - 12 pdr / 1 - 3 pdr	23.2.17-9.3.20	"She was originally built as a training ship, has heavy spars and is of a type not usually seen in these waters" (Orkneys and Shetlands). Damages a U-boat which afterwards surrenders to trawlers from the Tyne.
Dargle, see Peggy							
Dartmore		1,579 GT			1 - 12 pdr / 1 - 6 pdr	13.6.17-11.11.18	
Defender				Trawling smack			Temporary name, original name not known.
Derwent, see Duncombe *Desmond, see Superb* *Deverill, see Polyanthus*							
Devonport	Q.35 / *Baryta* / *Cassor* / *Ouse* / *Puma* / *Rule*	1,004 GT	1911	Cargo	1 - 4 inch / 2 - 12 pdr / 2 - 14 inch torpedo tubes / 2 Lewis guns in each boat	13.3.17-11.11.18	"Merchant ship converted."
Diana, see King Lear							
Dianthus	*Dhoby*	1,290 displacement	1917	Flower class convoy sloop *Anchusa type*	2 - 4 inch / 2 - 12 pdr	23.11.17-1.4.18	Later employed as convoy escort.
Djerissa	*Mallina*	3,723 GT	1910	Collier	2 - 14 pdr / 2 - 12 pdr / 1 Maxim / "6 pdrs or 3 pdrs optional"	9.11.16-18.5.18	
Djerma, see Marispeed *Dolcis, see Begonia* *Donlevon, see Glenfoyle* *Donlevon, see Ravenstone* *Dora, see Coot*							
Dorando Pietri LT 295	S.5	54 GT	1911	Trawling smack	1 - 3 pdr	7.2.17-11.11.18	
Dorinda, see Arionian *Dorothy, see Imogene*							

Name	Alt name	Tonnage	Year	Type	Armament	Dates	Remarks
Dorothy G. Snow		98 reg	1911	American schooner	1 - 12 pdr; Lance bombs; Type G depth charge	4.7.17-22.11.17	
Downton, see *PC.61*							
Dreadnought II	Ledger No. 897			Trawling smack		6.17-11.11.18	Temporary name, original name not known.
Dunclutha	*Champney Stamford*	3,975 GT	1910	Collier	4 - 12 pdr	18.12.16-23.6.18	
Duncombe ex-*Derwent*	*Derwent Duncome*	830 net	1888	Collier	2 - 12 pdr 12cwt; 2 - 6 pdr	19.10.15-30.9.17	"Rather small vessel" — "armed and disguised collier" — 30.9.17 "employ her as collier, retaining present armament".
Dundreary, see *Tay and Tyne*							
Dunraven ex-*Boverton*	*Boverton*	3,117 GT	1910	Collier	1 - 4 inch; 4 - 12 pdr; 2 - 14 inch torpedo tubes	25.6.17-10.8.17	Acquires crew from *Pargust*, 28.7.17. Foundered in tow 10.8.17 after being torpedoed by *UC.71*.
Dunsany, see *Hartside*							
Earl of Powis		116 GT	1882	Steam tug		11.5.16-20.1.17	
Early Blossom LT 16	*S.2*	57 GT	1908	Trawling smack	1 - 3 pdr	23.11.16-11.11.18	
Echunga, see *Barranca*							
Edith S. Cummins, see *Fresh Hope*							
Eglantine	*Aldaych Hickory*	1,290 displacement	1917	Flower class convoy sloop *Anchusa* type	2 - 4 inch; 2 - 12 pdr	1.9.17-11.11.18	Ends war as convoy escort.
Eider, see *Mary B. Mitchell*							
Eilian	*Chromium*	140 GT	1908	Three-masted auxiliary schooner	2 - 12 pdr; 1 Lewis gun	24.9.17-1.2.19	
Eleuthera ex-*Elizabeth*	*Elizabeth* Tender to *Gunner*	156 GT	1892	Three-masted schooner	1 - 4 inch Mk IX; 2 - 12 pdr 12cwt; 1 - 7.5 inch howitzer; 1 - 3 pdr	1.5.18-1.2.19	
Elixir, see *Sailer Thyrza*							
Elsa		114 net	1891	Two-masted schooner			Requisitioning telegram 17.4.19.
Else, see *First Prize*							

Name	Alias	Tonnage	When built	Type	Armament	Service	Comments
Emilia C.	*Brig 1* *Emiliac* *Marguerite*	123 GT	1907	Auxiliary barquentine	2 - 2 pdr 2 Lewis guns	10.11.17-16.10.18	
Emma M, see Rosina Ferrara							
Energic LT 1195	*S.1* *Cheerio* *Mascot*	59 GT	1912	Trawling smack	Mined nets	20.1.16-11.11.18	Caught U-boat in mined nets, 23.4.16.
Ethel & Millie LT 200	*S.3* *Ledger No. 929* *Boy Alfred* *? Ethel and Emily*	58 GT	1908	Trawling smack	1 - 6 pdr	1.2.17-15.8.17	1.2.17 with *G & E* claimed to have sunk two U-boats. Sunk by U-boat in North Sea 15.8.17.
Ethelwulf II, see Rosskeen							
Excel BK 188		40 GT	1898	Motor drifter		2.17-3.17	Built as a sailing vessel.
Extirpator, see G & E							
Fairfax, see Hartside							
Fairfield				Collier			"Unsuitable for decoy and can be reallocated to coaling service," 31.10.15.
Fairlight, see Harmonic							
Fame LT 1020	*Revenge*	39 GT	1906	Trawling smack		21.1.16-19.11.16	In action in North Sea 6.3.16. Sunk in collision off Lowestoft 19.11.16.
Farnborough ex-*Lodorer*	*Q.5* *Lodorer* *Sandyford*	3,207 GT	1904	Collier	5 - 12 pdr 2 - 6 pdr 1 Maxim	6.4.16-25.2.18	Sank *U.83*, 17.2.17. Torpedoed 22.10.17 but beached. Sold 1919.
First Prize ex-*Else*	*Q.21* *Else* *Prize*	227 GT	1901	Three-masted auxiliary schooner	3 - 12 pdr	6.4.16-14.8.17	Owned by William Garthwaite after being seized as prize. Partner for submarine *H.5* 28.7.17. Sunk by U-boat in Atlantic 14.8.17.
Fisher Lassie II BK 114		44 GT	1903	Motor drifter	2 - 6 pdr	1.1.18-5.12.18	There is also a *Fisher Lassie* in M.O.D. Naval Hist. Library Log Cards but this is BF 1069.
Fizzer ex-*Violet* LH 183	*Violet*	90 GT	1907	Steam drifter	1 - 6 pdr	7.9.16-11.11.18	"Based Granton and fishes off East Coast, Scotland." Ended war inspecting nets on patrol.
Flashlight, see PC.67							
Flower of the Fleet BM 33		18 net	1914	Motor drifter		12.8.15-1919	
Foam Crest, see G & E							

	Tonnage	Built	Type	Armament	Service dates	Notes
Fort George GN 77 *Robina*	180 GT	1902	Steam trawler	1 - 12 pdr 1 - 6 pdr		28.4.17 "due to leave today, to fish on the Aberdeen Banks." *Robina* A 903 was another Granton-owned steam trawler.
Fresh Hope *Edith S. Cummins* *Iroquois*	574 net	1889	American three-masted schooner	2 - 4 inch 2 - 12 pdr 1 - 3 pdr 1 - 7.5 inch howitzer	8.11.17-6.6.19	
Frixwell, see Pargust						
G & E LT 649 *Bird* *Extirpator* *Foam Crest* *I'll Try* *Nelson*	61 GT	1905	Trawling smack	1 - 3 pdr	8.8.15-9.15 22.1.16-15.8.17	11.8.15 hit *UB.6*, which escaped. 1.2.17 with *Ethel & Millie* claimed to have sunk two U-boats. Sunk by U-boat in North Sea, 15.8.17.
Gaelic *Q.22* *Brig 11* *Gobo*	224 GT	1898	Auxiliary barquentine	4 12 pdr 8cwt 2 Lewis guns	10.16-11.12.18	Owned by W. Thomas & Sons, Amlwch, Anglesey.
Gaillardia	1,250 displacement	1917	Flower class convoy sloop *Aubrietia* type	2 - 4 inch 1 - 3 pdr	20.10.17-22.3.18	Sunk by explosion, whether mine or torpedo unclear, 22.3.18.
Gandy, see Acton						
Gardenia	1,290 displacement	1917	Flower class convoy sloop *Anchusa* type	2 - 4 inch 2 - 12 pdr	18.2.18-11.11.18	Ends war on escort duty in Mediterranean.
George L. Muir *ex-Cholmondeley* *Cholmondeley* *G. L. M.* *George L. Munro* *Padre*	65 GT	1883	Auxiliary ketch	1 - 12 pdr 1 - 6 pdr	7.17-11.11.18	Built as mission smack *Cholmondeley* for R.N.M.D.S.F., converted for trading between Kirkwall and Firth of Forth. "Not suitable for heavy weather."
Girdler, see Arvonian *Girdler, see Auk*						
Glen *ex-Sidney* *Sidney* *Athos*	113 GT	1897	Auxiliary schooner	1 - 12 pdr 1 - 6 pdr	27.2.17-18.12.18	
Glen Afric, see Auk						
Glendale *ex-Speedwell II* *H 481* *Q.33* *Speedwell II* *Vanda*	273 GT	1899	Steam trawler	1 - 4 inch 2 - 12 pdr 1 - 6 pdr 2 - 14 inch torpedo tubes	27.7.14-15.7.18	Owned by Great Northern Steam Fishing Co, Hull. "Disguised as coastal vessel." 28.4.17. Ran ashore on Stone Rock, Prussia Cove, Penzance, in gale 15.7.18.
Glendevon	4,169 GT	1907	Collier employed as mechanical transport		21.10.15-27.6.16	"Mechanical transports but really decoys when empty." Paid off because unsuitable for decoy work.

Name	Alias	Tonnage	When built	Type	Armament	Service	Comments
Glenfoyle	Domlevan Domlevon Stonecrop	1,680 GT	1913	Collier	1 - 4 inch 1 - 12 pdr 1 - 6 pdr 4 howitzers 4 - 18 inch torpedo tubes	22.4.17-18.9.17	Sank *U.88* on 17.9.17. Sunk by U-boat in Atlantic, 18.9.17
Glen Isla		786 net	1878	Collier	Not known	13.10.15-20.13.16	"Old fashioned in appearance," had many defects and in unsatisfactory condition.
Glenmay, see *Stormount*							
Glory LT 1027		58 GT	1906	Trawling smack	1 - 3 pdr Lance bombs	2.8.15-9.15	
Gobo, see *Gaelic*							
Goblin, see *Mana*							
Good Hope H 722		256 GT	1903	Steam trawler	1 - 12 pdr 1 - 6 pdr	1.17-2.17	
Goodwin, see *Underwing*							
Granmer, see *Laggan*							
Grantley		1,869 GT	1908	Collier			Released as unsuitable.
Graveney, see *Stormount*							
? *Great Southern*							Owned by Great Western Railway Co.
Gunner	*Q.31* No. 31 *Planudes*	276 GT	1915	Admiralty trawler, Military class	2 - 12 pdr 12 cwt 2 - 6 pdr 1 howitzer 2 - 14 inch torpedo tubes	2.15 onwards	28.4.19 "disguised as coastal vessel."
Harelda, see *Acton*							
Harmonic	*Cocksedge* *Fairlight* *Tricord*	2,826 net	1905	Collier	1 - 4 inch Mk VII 4 - 12 pdr 2 - 6 pdr	14.8.16-11.2.18	Owned by Howard, Jones & King, Cardiff. On 10.7.17 described as "no longer any use for employment as decoy."
Hartside	*Dunsany* *Fairfax* *Trica*	2,740 net	1909	Collier	1 - 4 inch 4 - 12 pdr 2 - 6 pdr	25.8.16-2.18	Owned by the Charlton Steamship Co. Ltd. Newcastle-upon-Tyne.
Haying, see *Cullist*							
Heather	*Q.16* *Bywater* *Lisette* *Lizette* *Seetrus*	1,250 displacement	1916	Flower class convoy sloop *Aubrietia* type	2 - 4 inch 2 - 12 pdr 1 - 3 pdr A.A.	9.16-11.11.18	Ends war departing from Queenstown with the new minesweeping sloop *Sir Bevis*.

Name	Tonnage	Year	Type	Armament	Dates	Notes
Helen M. Coolen	94 GT	1914	American auxiliary schooner	1 - 12 pdr Lance bombs Type G depth charge	13.7.17-6.2.18	Sold as unsuitable.
Helgoland Q.17 *Brig 10 Hoogzand II Horley*	182 net	1895	Auxiliary brigantine	4 - 12 pdr 12cwt 1 Maxim	1.6.16-21.12.18	Built at Martenshock, Holland, and owned by H. & G. Grayson, Liverpool.
Hempseed, see Auricula						
Hester, see Lisette						
Hibiscus *Palette*	1,250 displacement	1917	Flower class convoy sloop *Aubrietia* type	2 - 4 inch 1 - 3 pdr A.A.	21.12.17-11.11.18	Ends war at Genoa.
Hickory, see Eglantine						
Hilcollav, see Marshfort						
Hildebrand, see Marshfort						
Hobby Hawk, see Telesia						
Holkar LT 596	61 GT	1905	Trawling smack		8.16-9.16	Sunk by gunfire by U-boat 8 miles N. from Trevose Head, 6.2.18.
Hope, see Auk						
Huayna, see Marshfort						
Hunter, see Rosskeen						
Hurter, see Prevalent						
Hyanthus, see Ooma						
Hyderabad H.M.S. 966 *Coral Nicobar Thornycroft*	624 displacement	1917	Purpose-built decoy ship	1 - 4 inch 2 - 12 pdr 1 - 2½ pdr 4 - 3.5 inch howitzers 2 - 18 inch torpedo tubes 4 depth charge launchers	24.9.17-5.20	Commissioned as an independent command from Lowestoft. 22.4.18 temporarily out of action at Milford. Put on exhibition at the end of the war. Refitted as depot ship, 1918, and sold in 1920.
Ianthe *Manon*	212 GT	1910	Three-masted auxiliary schooner	5 - 12 pdr 1 Lewis gun	15.9.17-2.12.18	"To be used to protect coal trade."
I'll Try, see G & E						
I'll Try LT 379 G & E	59 GT	1901	Trawling smack		21.4.16-?1916	Sunk by U-boat when fishing 14 miles N.N.E. from Haisbro light-vessel 27.7.18.
Ilma, see Merops						

Name	Alias	Tonnage	When built	Type	Armament	Service	Comments
Imogene	Dorothy, Jeanette, Strathendrick	189 GT	1882	Barquentine	1 - 4 inch, 2 - 12 pdr, 1 - 7.5 inch howitzer	24.2.18-15.5.19	
Imperator ex-Impregnable LT 1118		108 GT	1911	Steam drifter	1 - 6 pdr		Owned by E. Catchpole, Kessingland.
Imperieuse, see Merops							
Intaba	Q.2, Waitomo, Waitoppo	4,832 GT	1910	Cargo liner	1 - 4 inch Mk. VII, 2 - 13 pdr, 2 - 12 pdr 12cwt	18.4.16-11.7.17	Owned by the Union S.S. Co. of New Zealand.
Inverlyon LT 687		93 GT	1903	Trawling smack	1 - 3 pdr	2.8.15-9.15	15.8.15 attacked and believed sank U-boat in North Sea. Sunk by U-boat gunfire 15 miles N. × W. of Trevose Head, 30.1.17.
Iroquois, see Fresh Hope							
Island Queen, see Privet							
Izaak Walton SA 47		252 GT	1907	Steam trawler	1 - 4 inch, ?1 - 12 pdr	7.18-11.18	Owned by the Izaak Walton Fishing Co, Swansea.
Jeanette, see Imogene							
Jeanette, see Mary B. Mitchell							
Jessop, see Begonia							
J.J. Bibby, see Dargle							
John G. Walter		258 GT		Three-masted schooner		21.3.18	Requisitioned for S.S. but captured by U-boat 20 miles S.W. from Smalls before commissioning, 24.3.18.
Juggernaut, see PC.55							
Juggler, see Willow Branch							
Jurassic, see Cullist							
Kemes M 105		45 net	1911	Trawling smack	1 - 12 pdr 8cwt, 1 - 6 pdr	4.5.16-11.12.16	
Kent County LT 1129	Kentish Knock	86 GT	1911	Steam drifter			Sunk by mine near Cross Sand 8.12.16.
Kia Ora, see Coot							
Kidner, see Lychnis							

Name	Tonnage	Year	Type	Armament	Dates	Notes
King Lear H 871 Trawler No. 78 Diana Enid Xenia H 861	311 GT	1906	Steam trawler	1 - 4 inch Mk VII 4 - 12 pdr 2 - 3 pdr	14.3.15-1918	Owned by Hellyer's Steam Fishing Co, Hull. "Special Service trawler operating from Longhope disguised as RE 148 Diana." Lent naval ratings in 1915. RE are registration letters for Reykjavik, Iceland.
King Stephen GY 1174	162 GT	1900	Steam trawler		2.16-4.16	Owned by Consolidated S.F. and Ice Co, Grimsby. Sunk by U-boat in North Sea, 25.4.16.
Kullen			Steamship			
Lady Olive ex-Tees Trader Q.18	702	1913	Steam coaster	1 - 4 inch 4 - 12 pdr 18cwt	18.12.16-19.2.17	Torpedoed after action of 19.2.17 with U-boat in the Channel.
Lady Patricia Q.25 Anchusa Paxton Tosca	1,372 GT	1916	Cargo	1 - 4 inch 2 - 12 pdr	6.2.17-20.5.17	Torpedoed by U-46 in Atlantic, 20.5.17.
Laggan ex-Pladda Q.24 Granmer Pladda	1,334 GT	1907	Cargo	1 - 4 inch 2 - 12 pdr	12.2.17-terminated S.S. 11.18	"Merchant ship converted."
Lammeroo, see Remembrance						
Laureate, see Taranaki						
Lee Lee			Motor coaster		Commissioned 12.2.17	At Brightlingsea, Essex, for some time.
Leicester	1,001 GT	1891	Store carrier			Owned by Great Central Railway. Taken up as store carrier, 1914. Mined 12.2.16 off Folkestone.
Linksman, see Ceanothus						
Lisette Hester	116 GT	1873	Auxiliary schooner yacht	3 - 6 pdr		Requisitioned 14.5.17. Returned to owner as unsatisfactory 30.4.18
Lisette, see Heather						
Lodorer, see Farnborough						
Lorimer, see Ooma						
Lorne, see Coot						
Lothbury Argo Sarusan Stead	661 GT	1906	Store carrier	1 - 4 inch 1 - 15 pdr 2 - 12 pdr	23.9.17-11.11.18	15.7.18 paid off and recommissioned; none of officers and men taken for recommissioning and cell punishment awarded to some of crew. Appears in Granton Command 16.3.18. In Leith Roads at Armistice.
Lothian GN 5	131 GT	1904	Steam trawler		8.8.17-11.11.18	Owned by General Steam Fishing Co, Edinburgh.

Name	Alias	Tonnage	When built	Type	Armament	Service	Comments
Lowtyne ex-*Slingsby*		3,231 GT	1892	Collier		7.6.18-10.6.18	Sunk by U-boat in North Sea 10.6.18. In official list *Navy Losses* published 1919 is listed under "miscellaneous", not as Special Service ship nor as collier.
Luigi F., see *Rosina Ferrara*							
Lychnis	*Kidner Willangil*	1,250 displacement	1917	Flower class convoy sloop *Aubrietia* type	2 - 4 inch 1 - 3 pdr A.A.	15.11.17-11.11.18	Commissions for Mediterranean and ends war escorting convoy to Gibraltar.
Lyons	*Lyon*	537 GT	1885	Salvage vessel	4 - 12 pdr	5.8.14-17.4.16 and 7.12.17-20.5.19	
Mallina, see Djerissa							
Malta ex-*Weelsby*				? Steam trawler			Renamed 31.7.15. *Weelsby* GY 299 was a trawler built in 1891; *Malta* GY 325 was a trawler built in 1897 and, as an armed patrol vessel, mined 1.9.15.
Mana	*Goblin*	91 GT	1912	Wooden whaler-built schooner		24.9.17-3.1.18	Paid off.
Manford, see Penshurst							
Manon, see Ianthe							
Maracaibo, see Merops							
Maresfield	*Chiswell Sequax*	4,716 GT	1910	Collier		9.11.16-15.5.18	
Margaret and Annie ex-*Vera*	*Brig 4 Vera*	212 GT	1903	Brigantine		6.4.18-11.11.18	
Margaretha	*Margaretta*			Steam trawler	"Usual trawler armament." Bombs and Lewis guns	19.9.18-11.11.18	British trawler disguised as a Dutch vessel.
Margaret Murray	*Sarah Jones* Tender to *Research* (depot ship at Portland)	184 GT	1885	Three-masted auxiliary schooner	1 - 4 inch 3 - 12 pdr 12cwt on tilting mountings 1 depth charge thrower	16.7.18-18.10.19	
Margit	*Wellholme Werribee Woganella*	2,490 GT	1911	Collier	2 - 12 pdr		Given up by 1916.
Marguerite, see Emilia C.							
Maria y José, see Mary B. Mitchell							
Marie Therese, see Mary B. Mitchell							

Name	Other names	Tonnage	Year	Type	Armament	Service	Notes
Marispeed	*Djerma*	4,716 GT			"Armament from station, will have 1 - 12 pdr and 1 Maxim."		Ends war refitting at Belfast.
Marjoram		1,290 displacement	1917	Flower class convoy sloop *Anchusa* type	2 - 4 inch / 2 - 12 pdr	2.4.18-11.11.18	
Marshfort ex-*Huayna* ex-*Hildebrand*	*Hilcollow* *Hildebrand* *Huayna* *Senley*	1,988 GT	1893	Cargo vessel	2 - 4 inch / 2 - 12 pdr / 1 howitzer / 2 torpedo tubes	22.4.17-13.5.19	
Martin II ex-*Martin* H 187		242 GT	1897	Steam trawler	1 - 12 pdr	Minesweeper from 11.14. S.S. 5.5.16-11.11.18	Owned by Kelsall Brothers and Beeching Ltd, Hull.
Mary B. Mitchell	*Q.9* *Amaris* *Arius* *Brine* *Brise* of St Malo *Cancalais* *Eider* *Jeannette* of La Houle *Jeannette* of Lake Uleaborg *Jeannette* of Lake Ulealong *Maria y José* of Vigo *Marie Therese* *Mitchell* *Neptun* *Neptune* of Riga	227 GT	1892	Three-masted auxiliary schooner	1 - 12 pdr / 2 - 6 pdr / 2 Lewis guns / Mills bombs / Small arms	25.4.16-24.3.19	
Mascot, see Energic							
Master, see Quickly							
Mavis	*Q.26* *Nyroca* *Nyorca*	1,295 GT	1903	Cargo	1 - 4 inch / 2 - 12 pdr	S.S. 19.3.17-30.6.17	Torpedoed and beached, 3.6.17; "paid off into dockyard hands" 30.6.17.
Meg	*Z.1* *Zeduhale*	237 GT	1915	Steam whaler	2 - 12 pdr 12cwt		Taken up 2.8.15. French crew paid off 13.1.16. Recommissioned with British crew as tender to *Attentive* (leader, 6th Destroyer Flotilla at Dover). Goes to Granton 14.1.16 as tender to *Columbine* (base ship at Rosyth). Partners *Lorne*, alias *Coote*, 6.17. Considered unsuitable during original commission in S.S.

189

Name	Alias	Tonnage	When built	Type	Armament	Service	Comments
Meredith, see PC.60							
Merops	Q.28 *Bellmore Imperieuse Maracaibo Steady Toofa*	324 GT	1892	Auxiliary barquentine	1 - 4 inch 2 - 12 pdr	2.17-11.2.19	Fitting out at Granton in 2.17. Caught fire in 7.17 and eight of crew were badly gassed by Lyddite fumes from burning ammunition.
Meryl, see Sarah Colebrook							
Methyl, see PC.55							
Milfoil, see PC.65							
Mistletoe		1,290 displacement	1917	Flower class convoy sloop *Anchusa* type	2 - 4 inch 2 - 12 pdr	25.4.18-11.11.18	Ends war undergoing basin trials at Liverpool.
M. J. Hedley		449 GT	1891	Store carrier		27.6.18-4.10.18	Capsized and sank while coaling in Barry Docks, 4.10.18.
Moeraki, see Perugia							
Moderley, see Underwing							
Mona	Zeus			Auxiliary yacht	"To be armed from station" (Malta).		Partner for submarine *E.2*. "Mistaken by *E.2* for enemy, officers of *Zeus* abandoned and destroyed ship." According to official publication *Navy Losses Mona* was "blown up to avoid capture in Mediterranean off Cape Passaro," 4.7.17.
Mongibello, see Rosina Ferrara							
Montbretia		1,250 displacement	1917	Flower class convoy sloop *Aubrietia* type	2 - 4 inch 1 - 3 pdr A.A.	1.12.17-11.11.18	Ends war in Dundee, cleaning and refiting.
Morning Star				Steam drifter	1 - 6 pdr	19.4.15-11.11.18	"Based at Granton and fishes off East Coast of Scotland." Ends war "on patrol at Fidra line of nets."
Mornington, see PC.62							
Mortmain, see PC.43							
Nadine, see Cormorant IV							
Nelson, see G & E							
New Comet, see Rossken							
Nicobar, see Hyderabad							
Nigel					2 - 12 pdr 12cwt	27.2.15-6.4.15	Given up as unsuitable.
Nyroca, see Mavis							

190

Name	Other names	Tonnage	Year	Type	Armament	Service dates	Remarks
Ocean Fisher YH 345		96 GT	1913	Steam drifter	1 - 3 pdr		Mined in North Sea 16.6.18.
Oceanic II ex-*Oceanic* H 449		168 GT	1895	Steam trawler	1 - 12 pdr	11.14-1919	
Olive, see Cymric							
Ooma		3,427 GT	1899	Collier	2 - 4.7 inch 2 - 12 pdr	18.1.17-9.10.18	
Orisroot, see PC.62							
Ouse, see Devonport							
Oyama CF.23		257 GT	1908	Steam trawler	1 - 12 pdr 4 - 6 pdr 1 - 3 pdr 2 Maxims Depth charges	S.S. 6.16-6.9.16	Owned by Neale and West, Cardiff. Experimental Q-ship disguised as a crashed Zeppelin.
Pamela, see Resolute							
Panache, see PC.56							
Pargust	*Friswell* *Pangloss* *Snail* *Vittoria*	2,817 GT	1907	Collier	1 - 4 inch 4 - 12 pdr 2 - 14 inch torpedo tubes 1 - 11 inch bomb thrower	28.3.17-28.7.17 Recommissions 16.5.18	Sank *U.C. 29* on 7.6.17. Ended war in Mediterranean. Loaned to US Navy, 10.17-4.18.
Parramatta H 445		168 GT	1891	Steam trawler	1 - 6 pdr		"To be employed with fishing fleet as its protection."
Parritt, see Candytuft							
Patrick, see Anchusa							
Paxton, see Lady Patricia							
PC.42	*Culloden* *Mallory*	682 displacement	1917	PC class patrol boat or "PQ"	1 - 4 inch 2 - 12 pdr	Due to commission end of July, 1917.	Ends war in Pembroke Dock.
PC.43	*Charing* *Trego*	682 displacement	1917	PC class patrol boat or "PQ"	1 - 4 inch 2 - 12 pdr	Commissions 23.8.17-11.11.18.	
PC.44	*Mortmain* *Rolask*	682 displacement	1917	PC class patrol boat or "PQ"	1 - 4 inch 2 - 12 pdr	Due to commission July, 1917. Survived war.	July 25, 1917, at Wellington Quay, Newcastle. Ends war at Milford Haven.
PC.51		682 displacement	1916	PC class patrol boat or "PQ"	1 - 4 inch 2 - 12 pdr	Due to commission end of August. 1917. Survived war.	

Name	Alias	Tonnage	When built	Type	Armament	Service	Comments
PC.55	Juggernaut Methyl	682 displacement	1917	PC class patrol boat or "PQ"	1 - 4 inch 2 - 12 pdr	On trials June, 1917. Served to 11.11.18.	Ends war refiting at Milford.
PC.56	Birdwood Panache	682 displacement	1917	PC class patrol boat or "PQ"	1 - 4 inch 2 - 12 pdr	Due to commission end of July, 1917. Commissions 18.8.17.	
PC.60	Burlington Meredith	694 displacement	1917	PC class patrol boat or "PQ"	1 - 4 inch 2 - 12 pdr	26.6.17-11.11.18	Ends war cleaning boilers in Pembroke Dock.
PC.61	Chesney Downton	694 displacement	1917	PC class patrol boat or "PQ"	1 - 4 inch 2 - 12 pdr	1.8.17—survived war.	On patrol in October, 1918.
PC.62	Kingsnake Mornington	694 displacement	1917	PC class patrol boat or "PQ"	1 - 4 inch 2 - 12 pdr	18.8.17-11.11.18	Ends war at Pembroke Dock.
PC.63	Orrisroot	694 displacement	1917	PC class patrol boat or "PQ"	1 - 4 inch 2 - 12 pdr	Due to commission mid-August, 1917.	
PC.65	Milfoil	694 displacement	1917	PC class patrol boat or "PQ"	1 - 4 inch 2 - 12 pdr	Due to commission end of September, 1917. Survived war.	
PC.67	Chintz Flashlight	694 displacement	1917	PC class patrol boat or "PQ"	1 - 4 inch 2 - 12 pdr	Due to commission end of June, 1917. Survived war.	
PC.74	Chatsgrove	694 displacement	1918	PC class patrol boat or "PQ"	1 - 4 inch 2 - 12 pdr	Survived war.	Also served in Second World War as Chatsgrove.
Pearl GY 1121	Ruby GY 1136	198 GT	1899	Steam trawler	1 - 6 pdr		Under command of Rear-Admiral, Stornoway. Ruby was name of trawler torpedoed 17.10.17 off Ushant.
Peggy	Dargle Billy						Based at Granton. Apparently not the same vessel as Dargle.
Penhallow, see Century							
Penshurst	Q.7 Manford	1,191 GT	1906	Cargo vessel	2 - 4 inch 2 - 12 pdr 2 - 6 pdr	12.15-25.12.17	Fought eleven actions with U-boats. Sank UB.19 on 30.11.16. and UB.37 on 14.1.17. Sunk by U.110 off Bristol Channel, 25.12.17.
Perim		1,348 GT	1877	Collier			Released as unsuitable.
Perugia	Q.1 Moeraki	4,348 GT	1901	Cargo	1 - 4 inch Mk VII 2 - 13 pdr 4 - 12 pdr	18.4.16-3.12.16	Loaded buoyant cargo. Sunk by U.63 in Gulf of Genoa. 3.12.16.

Name	Tonnage	Year	Type	Armament	Dates	Remarks
Pet LT 560	56 GT	1906	Trawling smack	1 - 3 pdr	2.8.15-9.15	Given up in 1915 because considered unsuitable, subsequently recommissioned. Sunk by U-boat near Gibraltar, 6.11.17.
Peveril Q.36 *Polyanthus Puma Stephenson*	1,459 GT	1904	Cargo	2 - 12 pdr 12cwt	27.2.15-6.4.15 and 17.2.17-6.11.17	Lent to Navy League of Canada as training ship for boys at Toronto.
Pinta	101 GT	1893	American auxiliary schooner	1 - 12 pdr Lance bombs Type G depth charge	4.7.17-22.11.17	
Pladda, see Laggan						
Planudes, see Gunner						
Polyanthus Deverill	1,250 displacement	1917	Flower class convoy sloop *Aubrietia* type	2 - 4 inch 1 - 3 pdr A.A.	10.11.17-11.11.18	Ends war at Dundee.
Polyanthus, see Peveril						
Prevalent BM 337 *Hurter*	42 GT	1913	Trawling smack	1 - 12 pdr 8cwt	30.1.17-4.2.19	Returned to owner.
Prim, see Cullist						
Prince Charlie	373 GT	1905	Collier	2 - 6 pdr 2 - 3 pdr Hotchkiss		Sank *U.36* on 24.7.15. Referred to as *Prince Charlie* ADM/137/1933. Given up as unsuitable.
Prince Ena	1,198 GT	1906	Cross-channel cargo vessel	3 - 12 pdr 18cwt	28.4.15-8.9.15	Built for London and South Western Railway as fruit carrier for Southampton to Channel Islands route. Remained in service as Mercantile Fleet Auxiliary until 1920, classified as fleet messenger.
Princess Louise ex-*Princess Marie José*	222 GT	1913	Steam trawler		26.3.15-1.9.15	*Princess Marie José* is Belgian trawler O.38, renamed in 1915. Partner of submarine *C.26*. A *Princess Louise II*, ex-*Princess Louise* H 140, is listed in Dittmar and Colledge as a minesweeper from 2.15 to 1919.
Princess Marie José H 242 / Armed Trawler 1770	274 GT	1915	Steam trawler	2 - 3 pdr		Served as partner to submarine. Associated with *Princess Louise*, but separate log cards in M.O.D. Historical Library. In April, 1918, was at Invergordon in company with *Oyama*.
Principal PD 520	91 GT	1908	Steam drifter	1 - 6 pdr A.A.		

Name	Alias	Tonnage	When built	Type	Armament	Service	Comments
Privet	*Q.19* *Alcala* *Island Queen* *Swisher*	803 GT	1916	Steel screw steamer	1 - 4 inch 4 - 12 pdr 18cwt	21.12.16-11.11.18	Sank *U.85*, 12.3.17, but severely damaged, towed to Plymouth and beached in Cawsand Bay. Refloated and repaired at Devonport Dockyard. Sank *U.34* in Mediterranean, 9.11.18.

Prize, see *First Prize*

Probus, see *Sailer Thyrza*

Puma, see *Devonport*

Puma, see *Peveril*

Q.1, see *Perugia*

Q.2, see *Intaba*

Q.3, see *Barranca*

Q.4, see *Carrigan Head*

Q.5, see *Farnborough*

Q.6, see *Zylpha*

Q.7, see *Penshurst*

Q.8, see *Vala*

Q.9, see *Mary B. Mitchell*

Q.10, see *Begonia*

Q.11, see *Tamarisk*

Q.12, see *Tulip*

Q.13, see *Aubrietia*

Q.14, see *Viola*

Q.15, see *Salvia*

Q.16, see *Heather*

Q.17, see *Helgoland*

Q.18, see *Lady Olive*

Q.19, see *Privet*

Q.20, see *Bayard*

Q.21, see *First Prize*

Q.22, see *Gaelic*

Q.23, see *Result*

Q.24, see *Laggan*

Q.25, see *Paxton*

Q.26, see *Mavis*

Name	Other names	Tonnage	Year	Type	Armament	Dates	Notes
Quickly ex-*Swift* H 99	*Q.32 Carolina Master Sinton Swift*	242 GT	1897	Steam trawler	2 - 12 pdr 1 - 6 pdr A.A.	7.15-11.18	Owned by Kelsall Bros and Beeching Ltd, Hull.
Ratapiko A 446	Armed Trawler 347 *St George* SN 49	247 GT	1912	Steam trawler	1 - 12 pdr 1 - 6 pdr A.A.	20.4.18-11.11.18	Partner for submarine *C.24*. The trawler *St George* of North Shields, whose identity was assumed by *Ratapiko*, was sunk by gunfire from U-boat on 2.5.15 65 miles from Aberdeen, the crew being made prisoners.
? *Rathmore*							Owned by London and North Western Railway Co.
Ravenstone	*Donlevon*	3,049 GT	1905	Collier		3.5.17-30.9.17	3.5.17 "to be fitted out as S.S. vessel." 21.5.17 torpedoed by U-boat but towed into Queenstown by the rescue tug *Flying Spray*. 22.5.17 commissioned as tender. Paid off at Liverpool, 30.9.17.
Ready, see *Sailer Thyrza*							
Recorder, see *Commissioner*							
Record Reign		200 GT	1897	Auxiliary ketch barge	1 - 4 inch 2 - 12 pdr	25.12.17-12.12.18	25.12.17 "fitting out for S.S."
Redbreast		1,313 GT	1908	Fleet messenger	"not known, locally armed."	S.S. 20.3.16-16.9.16	Served in Eastern Mediterranean. Sunk by *UC.38* in Mediterranean 15.7.17.
Remembrance	*Lammeroo*	3,660 GT	1910	Collier	2 - 4 inch 1 Maxim	10.15-14.8.16	Sunk by *U.38* in Eastern Mediterranean 14.8.16.

Name	Alias	Tonnage	When built	Type	Armament	Service	Comments
Remo GY 1206	*Ameer* GY 397 *Amber*	169 GT	1900	Steam trawler	1 - 6 pdr	1.15-1920	Under command of Rear-Admiral, Stornoway. Owned by G. F. Sleight, Grimsby. *Ameer* was name of trawler owned by E. Sleight, Grimsby, mined off Felixstowe while serving as minesweeper, 18.3.16. *Amber* was name of trawler H 398.
Rentoul, see *Resolute*							
Resolute	*Pamela* *Rentoul*	229 GT	1869	Barquentine	1 - 4 inch 2 - 12 pdr 1 - 3 pdr 1 - 7.5 inch howitzer	27.3.18-14.3.19	
Result	*Q.23* *Capulet* *Dag of Gothenburg* *Ledger No. 928*	122 GT	1893	Three-masted schooner	2 - 12 pdr 18cwt 2 - 14 inch torpedo tubes	11.16-22.12.17	Owned by H. S. G. Clark of Barnstaple. Paid off 24.11.16 and recommissioned as *Capulet* 2.2.17. Fitted out and based at Lowestoft. Now preserved by Ulster Folk Museum.
Revenge, see *Fame*							
Robina, see *Fort George*							
Rolask, see *PC.43*							
Roller, see *Commissioner*							
Rosina Ferrara	*Brig 2* *Emma M.* *Luigi F.* *Mongibello*	227 GT	1876	Brigantine	1 - 4 inch 2 - 12 pdr	8.1.18-11.11.18	
Rosskeen GN 14	*Aldebaran* *Bendigo II* *Ethelwulf II* of North Shields *Hunter* *New Comet* *Roskean*	196 GT	1907	Steam trawler	1 - 12 pdr 1 - 6 pdr 1 - "C" torpedo tube	8.1.18-11.11.18	Assumed names are mainly those of trawlers similar to *Rosskeen*; *Bendigo* GN 2, *Ethelwulf* SN 344, *Hunter* GN 74 and *New Comet* GN 75.
Ruby, see *Pearl*							
Rule, see *Devonport*							
Rupert				Trawling smack		29.3.17-4.4.17	"Sailing temporarily with fishing fleet from Plymouth."
Sailer Thyrza	*Q.30* *Elixir* *Probus*	179 GT	1865	Auxiliary brigantine	2 - 12 pdr 2 - 6 pdr (some on self-	30.8.15-11.11.18	Commissioned as H.M.S. *Ready*. On Granton station.

Name	Alt. names	Tonnage	Year	Type	Armament (on elevating mountings)	Dates	Remarks
Ready *Thirza*							
Sailing vessel 195							Could this be the *Mary B. Mitchell?*
St George, see Ratapiko							
St Gothard, see Auk							
St Laurence, see Taranaki							
Salomea K.	*Brig 5*	225 GT	1914	Brigantine		28.5.18-11.11.18	
Salvia	*Q.15*	1,250 displacement	1916	Flower class convoy sloop *Aubrietia* type	2 - 4 inch 1 - 3 pdr A.A.	29.9.16-30.6.17	Sunk by *U.94* off west coast of Ireland, 30.6.17.
Samuel S. Thorp, see Baron Rose							
Sant' Anna	*Brig 3* *Sant' Anna M.* *Sant' Maria*	155 GT	1914	Brigantine		18.2.18-11.11.18	Commissioned 26.2.18, last log card entry 23.10.18.
Santa Cruz							5.10.15 not taken up on recommendation of Lowry. Possibly the Canadian schooner *Santa Cruz*, 52 GT, built in 1874.
Santee, see Arionian							
Sarah Colebrook	*Bolham* *Meryl*	158 GT	1913	Coasting ketch	2 - 12 pdr	21.12.16-7.10.18	
Sarah Jones, see Margaret Murray							
Saros, see Bradford City							
Sarusan, see Lothbury							
Scatcliff, see Tuberose							
Scavanger				Steam trawler	1 - 13 pdr 1 - 12 pdr		
Seagull, see Breadwinner							
Sea King H 531	*Remexo*	321 GT	1916	Steam trawler	1 - 4 inch 1 - 7.5 inch howitzer	15.7.18-11.11.18	"Taken up for S.S." 15.7.18. Served in Granton Command. Also served until 1919 as minesweeper.
Seetrus, see Heather							
Sequax, see Maresfield							
Sieux, see Baron Rose							
Slingsby, see Loutbye							
Smelt				Motor drifter			Possibly the Cork fishing boat *Smelt C 43*, hired by Queenstown Command in 1915.

Name	Alias	Tonnage	When built	Type	Armament	Service	Comments
Snail, see Pargust							
Spica, see Auk							
Spiraea	Airblast Caleb	1,290 displacement	1917	Flower class convoy sloop Anchusa type	2 - 4 inch 2 - 12 pdr	9.11.17-11.11.18	Ends war in Mediterranean.
Stamford, see Dunclutha							
Stead, see Lothbury							
Steady, see Merops							
Stephenson, see Peveril							
Stock Force	Charyce	732 GT	1917	Steam coaster	2 - 4 inch 2 - 12 pdr 1 - 3 pdr 2 - 14 inch torpedo tubes	4.2.17-30.7.18	"Practically new vessel . . . typical coasting collier . . . speed 9 knots loaded." Crippled by U.98 in Channel and sank in tow, 30.7.18.
Stonecrop, see Glenfoyle							
Stormount	Glenmay Graveney Starmount Tring	2,529 GT	1905	Collier		21.7.17 "completing shortly". 11.6.18 "to revert to trade".	17.10.17 torpedoed but succeeded in entering Plymouth. "Explosion caused fore-rigging to release and clear away as for action, also dummy winches and ventilators at No 2 gun collapsed."
Strathallan GN 76	Sunshine	175 GT	1900	Steam trawler	1 - 12 pdr 1 - 6 pdr	16.5.17-11.11.18	In Granton Command. Sunshine was a trawler very similar to Strathallan.
Strathearn GN 40	Wild Rose	152 GT	1898	Steam trawler	1 - 12 pdr 1 - 6 pdr	16.5.17-11.11.18	"Commissioned under the same regulations as Commissioner and Fort George and leaves for sea today." 1.6.17. Wild Rose SN 325 was steam fishing vessel not unlike Strathearn
Strathendrick, see Imogene							
Strumble M 135		45 GT	1912	Trawling smack	1 - 12 pdr 1 - 6 pdr	1.6.16-11.12.16	Captured by U.65 and sunk by bomb when fishing ten miles N.N.E. from Strumble Head, 4.5.17.
Suffolk Coast		870 GT	1917	Collier	1 - 4 inch 1 - 12 pdr 12cwt	16.8.18-11.11.18	At end of war put "on exhibition in certain ports, charge of 1s. a head to be made, proceeds for naval charities." Post war traded with Coast Lines Ltd.
Suma CF 2		284 GT	1914	Steam trawler	1 - 3 pdr		Owned by Neale & West Ltd., Cardiff.

Name	Other names	Tonnage	Built	Type	Armament	Dates	Notes
Sunshine, see Strathallan							
Superb, see Superior							
Superior ex-*Superb* BM 1	*Superb* *Desmond*	43 GT	1896	Trawling smack	1 - 12 pdr 8cwt	30.1.17-10.2.19	In Portsmouth Command. Returned to owner. Probably renamed to avoid confusion with battleship H.M.S. *Superb*.
Sweetbriar		1,290 displacement	1917	Flower class convoy sloop *Anchusa* type	2 - 4 inch 2 - 12 pdr	9.17-11.11.18	"About to commission" 25.9.17.
Swisher, see Privet							
Syren, see Bayard							
Syringa		1,290 displacement	1917	Flower class convoy sloop *Anchusa* type	2 - 4 inch 2 - 12 pdr	5.11.17-30.10.18	Serves in North Sea Hydrophone Flotilla. Sold to Egypt in 1920.
Tamarisk	*Q.11*	1,250 displacement	1916	Flower class convoy sloop *Aubrietia* type	2 - 4 inch 1 - 3 pdr A.A.	29.7.16-11.11.18	Commissioned to act as decoy ship from Queenstown. Ends war in dock at Dundee.
Taranaki A 445	*Laureate* SN 257 *St Lawrence*	247 GT	1912	Steam trawler	1 - 12 pdr	18.1.15-11.11.18	Partner for submarines *C.24*, *C.26* and *C.27*. *C.24* when partnered by *Taranaki* on 24.6.15 sank *U.40*. Ends war minesweeping off NE Scotland. *St Lawrence* is name of trawler GY 1131 captured and sunk by U-boat in North Sea 22.4.15.
Tay and Tyne	*Cheriton* *Dundreary* Ledger No 928	557 GT	1909	Passenger-cargo coasting liner	1 - 4 inch 2 - 12 pdr 1 - 6 pdr 1 - 3 pdr 1 - 14 inch torpedo tube	28.6.17-11.11.18	A passenger-cargo vessel which traded between Hull and Dundee. Referred to in Muhlhauser: *Small Craft* as Q-ship *Tayne*. Ends war at Murmansk.
Tecaya				Schooner		28.10.16-8.11.16	Requisitioned, then requisition cancelled.
Tees Trader, see Lady Olive							
Telesia LT 1155	*S.4* *CB* *Commodore* *Hobby Hawk*	59 GT	1911	Trawling smack	1 - 3 pdr	20.1.16-17.7.17	23.4.16 With *Cheerio* destroyed *UC.3* in mined nets. Fought a number of other actions. Represented fishing fleets at naval reviews in 1935 and 1937.
Tenby Castle SA 53		256 GT	1908	Steam trawler	1 - 12 pdr 1 - 7.5 inch howitzer	6.15-1917	

199

Name	Alias	Tonnage	When built	Type	Armament	Service	Comments
T. G. Hutton		703 GT	1890	Steam coaster		5.10.15-16.10.15	Not taken up after Lowry had reported she was unsuitable.
Thalia LT 931	Thales	32 GT	1886	Motor drifter	Mined nets ?1 - 6 pdr	30.5.16-24.12.16	"Sailing coble with auxiliary motor." Returned to owners as unsuitable.. Wrecked on Sunk Head when bound from Lowestoft to Plymouth 31.12.18.
Thirza, see Sailer Thyrza							
Thornhill, see Wonganella							
Thornycroft, see Hyderabad							
Toofa, see Merops							
Tosca, see Lady Patricia							
Transvaal GY 953	Armed Trawler No 3307	250 GT	1916	Steam trawler	1 - 6 pdr A.A.		
Trego, see PC.43							
Trica, see Hartside							
Tricord, see Harmonic							
Tring, see Stormount							
Tuberose	Scatcliff	1,290 dis-placement	1917	Flower class convoy sloops Anchusa type	2 - 4 inch 2 - 12 pdr	11.1.18-11.11.18	Ends war on patrol and escort duties in Mediterranean.
Tulip	Q.12	1,250 dis-placement	1916	Flower class convoy sloop Aubrietia type	2 - 4 inch 1 - 3 pdr A.A.	14.8.16-30.4.17	Sunk by U.62 in Atlantic, 30.4.17.
Underwing	Ballantrae Goodwin Moderley	1,928 GT	1917	Cargo	3 - 4 inch Mk VII	23.5.17-2.5.19	"Merchant ship converted". 13.5.18 on convoy duty in Mediterranean and ends war there.
Uniom BF 722	Union II	84 GT	1907	Steam drifter	"Usual trawler armament" plus bombs and Lewis guns.	19.9.18-11.11.18	Disguised as a Dutch trawler. 27.3.18 departs Taranto, Italy. Last log card entry 30.4.18 to go to Taranto for docking.
Vala	Q.8	1,016 GT	1894	Collier	4 - 12 pdr 2 - 6 pdr	7.8.15-21.8.17	"Rather small vessel" considered unsuitable because of low speed. 21.8.17 sunk by UB.54 in Atlantic.
Vassiliki				Schooner		7.12.17-11.11.18	
Vera, see Margaret and Annie							
Vera Elizabeth, see Alma							
Vereker, see Viola							

Name	Alt. names	Tonnage	Year	Type	Armament	Dates	Notes
Victoria		710 GT	1896	Steam coaster	2 - 12 pdr	28.11.14-8.1.15	Was reacquired by Navy in 1918 and used for other purposes under name of *Surf II*. Partner for submarine *C.26*.
Vina				Steam trawler			
Vinetroe, see Willow Branch							
Viola	Q.14 Aubrietia Cranford Damaris	1,250 displacement	1916	Flower class convoy sloop Aubrietia class	2 - 4 inch 1 - 3 pdr A.A.	SS 21.9.16-1.3.18	Ends war in Dundee.
Viola	Vereker Violetta	1,016 GT	1872	Three-masted schooner	2 - 4.7 inch 1 - 4 inch 2 - 12 pdr 2 - 3 pdr 1 - 7.5 inch howitzer	2.2.18-11.11.18	In Granton Command. Tonnage given elsewhere (more probably) as 168; MNL gives *Viola* of Padstow, 141 net reg. tons.
Violet, see Fizzer							
Vittoria, see Pargust							
Volana		616 GT	1913	Store carrier	2 - 12 pdr 2 - 6 pdr		"Not employed, or to be employed, as decoys, although this was originally proposed." 4.8.16.
Volhynia		617 GT	1911	Store carrier	2 - 12 pdr 2 - 6 pdr		As *Volana*.
Volturnus		615 GT	1913	Store carrier	2 - 12 pdr 2 - 6 pdr		As *Volana*.
Waitomo, see Intaba							
Waitoppo, see Intaba							
Walter S. Bailey H 546	May Flower W. S. Bailey	244 GT	1902	Steam trawler	1 - 4 inch 1 - 12 pdr 12cwt 1 - 3.5 inch bomb thrower	10.17-11.18	In Granton Command. Also served as minesweeper.
Warner	Q.27	1,293 GT	1911	Cargo		13.1.17-13.3.17	"To be fitted with underwater turning gear." Sunk by *U.38* west of Ireland, 13.3.17.
Wellholme	Danton	113 GT	1916	Motor ketch	1 - 12 pdr 18cwt	4.9.17-30.1.18	Sunk by U-boat in Channel 20 miles off Portland Bill, 30.1.18.
Wellholme, see Margit							
Werribee, see Margit							
Westphalia, see Cultist							

Name	Alias	Tonnage	When built	Type	Armament	Service	Comments
Wexford Coast		423 GT	1915	Steam coaster	1 - 4 inch 1 - 12 or 6 pdr	Active 29.9.15-13.10.16 and probably outside these dates.	Stock carrier at Queenstown. Requisitioned in 1915 for duties as store carrier and fleet messenger. In Russian waters, 1916.
Wild Rose, see Strathearn							
Willangil, see Lychnis							
Willow Branch	*Bombala* *Britannia* *Juggler* *Vinetroe*	3,314 GT	1892	Collier	"2 - 14 pdr or 2 - 12 pdr 6 or 3 pdr optional"	28.1.17-25.4.18	25.4.18 sunk by U-boat off Cape Verde Islands. "Left Gibraltar 17.00 1st April for Sierra Leone with tug *John of Gaunt* in tow. Reported attacked by two submarines at 12.00 25th April in 20.52 N, 17.36 W. No sign or news of ship. Sierra Leone informed. *John of Gaunt* only found abandoned with rope cut."
Winton, see Aubrietia							
Wirral		308 GT	1890	Store carrier		29.7.18-1.4.19	Sold and renamed *Strymon*.
Woffington, see Acton							
Woganella, see Margit							
Wolsey				Steam trawler			Partner for submarine *C.27*.
Wonganella	*Thornhill*	3,848 GT		Cargo	2 - 4 inch 1 - 12 pdr 1 - 2½ pdr	Active 1.3.16 Paid off 17.7.17	
Wyandra, see Baralong							
X.22		160	1915	Landing craft or X lighter			Built for Dardanelles campaign. Only one of a numerous type to be used as decoy.
Z.1, see Meg							
Zebal, see Aubrietia							
Zedwhale, see Meg							
Zeus, see Mona							
Zinnia		1,200 displacement	1915	Flower class convoy sloop *Azalea* type	2 - 4.7 inch 2 - 3 pdr A.A.	14.9.15-11.11.18	Ends war at Queenstown.
Zylpha	*Q.6*	2,917 GT	1894	Collier	3 - 12 pdr	19.9.15-15.6.17	Buoyant cargo loaded. Sunk by U-boat S.W. of Ireland, 15.6.17.

The Q-Ships in the Second World War

"WILL the mystery ship ever be used again?" Admiral Campbell had asked in the closing chapter of his book *My Mystery Ships*. "Such a question cannot be answered," he concluded, "but . . . if anyone has ideas for such in future wars, he will be wise to keep his mystery to himself until it can be used."

Unfortunately for the success of Q-ships in the Second World War, there was no mystery about them left when that war began. It is just possible that if nothing had been published about them after the First World War they might have been equally effective in the Second. Long before 1939, however, the reading public had been deluged with material about the decoys. Campbell's book had gone into nine editions in two years, and he was merely one of a group of Q-ship authors.

Campbell's adventurous career had attracted attention long before he wrote *My Mystery Ships*. His book appeared amid a blaze of publicity from his many admirers, including Rear-Admiral William Sowden Sims, U.S.N., whose own book *Victory at Sea* had appeared eight years before Campbell's. Sims had been very impressed by Campbell, and said so. Unfortunately Sims' admiration had not remained suppressed until peacetime.

"Shortly after he came here," wrote Rear-Admiral Sir Douglas Brownrigg,[72] "it will be remembered that he went to Queenstown . . . On his return from that visit he was the central figure at a dinner at the Carlton Hotel (at which he lived), and he explained to his party all about our Q boats, which he had seen at Queenstown, how long it took for their sham bulwarks to be dropped and for the guns to be brought into action, and so on, together with every conceivable and extremely interesting detail connected with what was then, and indeed right down to Armistice Day, a very secret branch of our service."

Campbell's books were not published only in English but were translated into foreign languages as well. Among his foreign readers must have been Admiral Doenitz, Hitler's Commander-in-Chief of U-boats, who had been a U-boat commander in the First World War. When war came again, Doenitz warned his commanders to be on their guard against Q-ships, never to approach a vessel except in diving trim, and to be particularly cautious about ships which had lagged behind their convoy. His captains obeyed these orders to the letter.

Campbell's phenomenal success as an author, journalist, and broadcaster had had other results besides alerting the enemy. It had earned him the jealousy of his fellow Admirals. Among those was the Deputy Chief of Naval Staff, Rear-Admiral T. S. V. Phillips, who had served under Campbell as a junior officer and had acquired a lasting dislike for him.

The fact that Q-ships were employed at all in the Second World War was largely due to the presence at the Admiralty of the two men who had been most concerned with them in the first war. Winston Churchill returned to his former post of First Lord of the Admiralty, and it was Churchill, possibly on the suggestion of Vice-Admiral Sir H. W. Richmond, K.C.B., who had inaugurated the Q-ship era during the first war, on 26th November, 1914. In response to the attacks of German submarines off Havre, Churchill had sent a signal to the Commander-in-Chief, Portsmouth, Admiral Hedworth Meux: "It is desired to trap the German submarine which sinks vessels by gunfire off Havre. A small or moderate sized steamer should be taken up and fitted very secretly with two twelve-pounder guns in such a way that they can be concealed with deck cargo or in some way which will not be suspected. She should be sent when ready to run from Havre to England, and should have an intelligent officer and a few seamen and two picked gunlayers who should all be disguised. If the submarine stops her she should endeavour to sink her by gunfire. The greatest secrecy is necessary to prevent spies becoming acquainted with the arrangement."

On Churchill's orders, Campbell, who had been appointed to re-start the Q-ship branch of the navy, began hunting for ships which should be the successors to the Special Service vessels of the First World War. He wanted a fleet of six ships for service on the world trade routes and three ships for use in home waters. It was a very modest opposition force with which to oppose the legions of U-boats that Doenitz had either in being or planned for construction. Perhaps it is only the mistakes in history that are repeated, and certainly it was a great mistake, in both wars, not to create a Q-ship fleet that was an entirely independent entity. This was what Campbell himself had suggested might have crushed the U-boats early in the first war, if it had been organised by someone of outstanding ability such as Bayly.

It is true that Campbell succeeded in obtaining his "navy within a navy," much to the jealousy of some of his fellow officers, but his deployment of his ships was hampered at every turn by the Deputy Chief of Naval Staff. Rear-Admiral Philips cannot be blamed for everything that went wrong with the Q-ship fleet of the second war, however. Incredible as it may seem, Campbell fell into not a few of the errors of the directors of the decoy fleets of the earlier war. His assembly of ships, *Botlea, Cape Howe, Cape Sable, City of Durban, King Gruffyd* and *Williamette Valley* for the overseas trade routes, with three smaller vessels for home waters, were often badly armed, badly engined and badly equipped.

Their guns had been provided from scrapped obsolete warships, and an even more serious defect was that some at least of the new fleet had no anti-aircraft firepower whatsoever. Well might his enemies accuse Campbell of living in the past. A feature which was only too reminiscent of the early Q-ship war was the slow speed of some of the ships; they were just what they pretended to be, tramps. *Botlea* had a top speed of only eight knots, a figure which will be familiar to many readers of these pages, and her engines were constantly breaking down.

Of particular interest to readers of this book was the only British Q-ship to serve in two world wars, the *Chatsgrove*, which had been built as a PC. class patrol boat. PC.s, the same kind of vessels which are referred to as PQ.s on more than one occasion, were submarine hunter and escort craft. They had been designed to look like merchantmen, but the resemblance ended below water. They had a shallow draft (like the famous *Hyderabad*) so that torpedoes, set to hit a merchantman's hull, would pass beneath them.

The guns of the new Q-ships were four-inch or 5.9-inch. *Plus ça change, plus c'est la même chose.*

By an even more surprising oversight, Campbell had cast his overseas Q-ships for a double role. They were to be live bait for U-boats and in addition for the surface raiders. The double-role Q-ship, such as the *Glendevon* and *Chevington*, which had to ply between Avonmouth and France while acting as decoys, had been conspicuously unsuccessful in the first war, and here was the same mistake being made again. The new Q.s would almost certainly have benefited from being equipped solely to hunt U-boats. This might have ensured that they were all fitted with asdic.

Not all the echoes of the first war were mistakes, however, The spirit of 1917 was very much alive in the officers and men who acted as complements of the new decoys. Once again, as in the previous war, their orders demanded that they should let themselves be torpedoed, if that seemed likely to ensure a kill.

Unfortunately the spirit of rivalry between commands was still alive in the Service as well. Philips vetoed Campbell's proposals that his ocean-going Q.s should be deployed in the South Atlantic, Red Sea and Indian Ocean. The idea of a "private navy" still seemed to inflame many high-ranking breasts, and so too, perhaps, did the unorthodox approach which was so much part of the decoy tradition.

Campbell's decoys never encountered a surface raider or a pocket battleship, which was just as well, because, though their Admiral felt they could give a good account of themselves, the superior fire control arrangements and heavier guns of a pocket battleship would have made short work of them.

Nor was their success against the U-boats any better, though one depth-charged and perhaps even damaged a submarine. Two of the Q.s, *Williamette Valley* and *Cape Howe*, were torpedoed and sank with great loss of life. Campbell had decided to repeat the buoyant cargoes experiment of the First World War, and it had considerable success. After being struck by the first torpedo, *Williamette Valley* remained afloat for half an hour, returning almost to an even keel. *U.51* then torpedoed her a second time, and finally sent in a third torpedo before she sank, taking with her sixty-six of her crew of ninety. On 20th June, 1940, *Cape Howe* was torpedoed off Land's End. The panic party went off, for everything was organised as in the previous war. Obedient to his orders, the U-boat commander made no attempt at a surface approach, but fired another torpedo. *Cape Howe* stayed afloat for another four hours, sure proof of the efficacy of a buoyant cargo, and about half the crew were subsequently saved.

After this description of the massive loss of life of the Q-ships of the Second World War, it may seem paradoxical to say that the saddest part of the story is still to come, but it will seem so to many readers. Campbell had stood up well to the goading of Philips as to the deployment of his vessels, until the Deputy Chief of Staff struck at what was the old lion's weak point, his concern for the safety of his men. Philips ordered him to recall two of the high seas decoys and send them to Norway, where they would be at a serious disadvantage because of their lack of defensive firepower against aircraft. Although Campbell pointed this out to Philips, the latter persisted. Campbell refused to obey the order, and when the First Sea Lord, Admiral Pound, took him to task, as he had to do, for this indiscipline, he resigned.

Before long, Churchill came to the conclusion that the Q-ships were not worth their oats. In September, 1940, he sent the signal which brought the Q-ship era to an end. The decoys were turned into armed merchant cruisers. Only the gallant old *Chatsgrove*, which had brought down a Junkers, and a disguised fishing boat, which successfully tackled the shore defences of a Norwegian fjord, stood out in the unrelieved gloom as successes.

MARY B. MITCHELL

General Index

Illustrations in bold type

Crews of Q-ships in fact and fiction. Above are the gunlayers and the carpenter of the
Penshurst, from *Q-Ships and Their Story*, and below is a gun's crew from the film *Q-ships,
Vampires of the Deep*. The film was fiction, but Boatswain Butland, who was gunner aboard
Harold Auten's *Stock Force*, was re-enacting his wartime role.

British Movietone News Film Archive

The concealed torpedo tubes of a large Q-ship. Also standing on the hatch is a Lewis gun mounted on a pedestal.

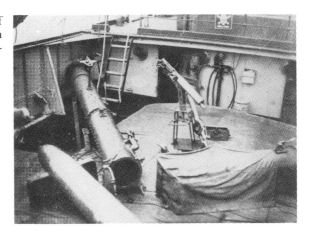

A torpedo tube and a twelve-pounder gun mounted in the forward well deck of a cargo-type Q-ship.

Below: The collier *Suffolk Coast*, which became a Q-ship in 1918 and after the war toured British ports as an example of the "mystery ships" that had so intrigued the public. From *"Q" Boat Adventures*.

Index of Ships

214

See also alphabetical list of Q-ships, pages 174–202.